THE SYSTEM AND THE GOSPEL

THE SYSTEM AND
THE GOSPEL

A Critique of Paul Tillich

KENNETH HAMILTON

WILLIAM B. EERDMANS PUBLISHING COMPANY
GRAND RAPIDS, MICHIGAN

This edition published by arrangement with SCM Press LTD, April 1967.
The material in the Appendix is published by permission of *Interpretation* magazine.

FIRST PUBLISHED 1963
© SCM PRESS LTD 1963
PRINTED IN THE UNITED STATES OF AMERICA

To
Principal C. M. Nicholson
teacher and friend

CONTENTS

PREFACE

PAUL TILLICH's philosophical theology is one of the most spectacular features of the contemporary theological landscape. Its influence is felt everywhere, and it has been much expounded, defended, attacked and pronounced on. Philosophers as well as theologians have been intrigued by it. Yet, although the first volume of the *Systematic Theology* was published almost a dozen years ago, nearly all the critical writing on Tillich to date has been in essay form; and, if ever a theology called out for extended analysis, this one does. Recently, Father Tavard's full-length study of Tillich's Christology, *Paul Tillich and the Christian Message*, has filled a gap—its distinguished Roman Catholic author expressing surprise that no Protestant work has preceded his. There are many other gaps still to be filled. In what follows I have tried to take a part in this ongoing task. My aim is to give a general outline of Tillich's system from one particular angle, the angle of the relation of the system to historic Christianity. Thus, while I have a wide area to cover, what I hope to achieve is less a rounded exposition than a pointed critique.

Consequently, very much will be left unsaid in this study which otherwise would have been said, and said emphatically. Any comprehensive survey of Tillich's thought could not fail to dwell on the massive intellectual drive of his theology and the breadth of its scope, whereas I am occupied chiefly with probing in order to discover inadequacies. So it is not until my final chapter that I refer to the positive contribution which Tillich has made to present-day theology—and even then my emphasis is upon what (in my opinion) we must reject rather than upon what we can gladly accept. Therefore the reader,

9

meeting continual root-and-branch criticism of Tillich's ideas, will perhaps realize that my negative judgments do not tell the whole story. After all, were the ideas not important and relevant in the first place, criticism would be little worth while. Probably no living theologian has more to say concerning the vital issues of faith and the understanding of faith than Tillich has. His example also in the matter of a rigorous and unwearied pursuit of consistency in theological thinking is uniquely inspiring. But it is no compliment to any honest and original thinker simply to repeat his phrases after him; sometimes the necessary result of taking his teaching seriously is to come out in vehement dissent. In the discussion of all fundamental issues William Blake's aphorism holds good: 'Opposition is true friendship.'

Some explanation is required in connection with my making so much use of Kierkegaard in the course of this study. Since Tillich's thought is involved with the modern developments in existential philosophy—his theology being indeed frequently labelled 'existentialist'—no apology should be needed for investigating his relation to the Father of Existentialism. Yet the reason why I should go on from this investigation to measure Tillich continually over against Kierkegaard may not be quite clear. In order to avoid misunderstanding, I wish to stress that I do not suggest that Kierkegaard is an infallible interpreter of the Christian gospel. What seems to be undeniable is that he is a better guide to the area of theology in which Tillich operates than is any other Christian author. I believe that it would be both foolish and ungrateful for us today, when we enter this area, to neglect his special insight.

In order to plough a straight furrow of argument I have kept nearly all engagement with the ideas of other critics out of my text, at the expense of increasing footnotes. Where it seemed useful to consider some debatable issue more fully I have added a Postscript at the end of the chapter in which the issue appears. If the reader wants to concentrate on main themes rather than on details of interpretation these Postscripts can be ignored.

I am indebted to Dr Robert C. Johnson, who read the manuscript in an early draft and made many helpful criticisms and suggestions, and to the Rev. C. Earle Gordon and the Rev.

C. H. Forsyth, who helped me with later revisions. Miss Helen Young relieved me of much of the burden of preparing the typescript.

Chapter VI is an expanded version of an article that appeared in the *Canadian Journal of Theology*, and I am indebted to the editor for permission to reproduce the material which appeared there.

For permission to use copyright material I thank The Westminster Press (from *Instruction in Faith* by John Calvin, tr. Paul T. Fuhrman. Copyright 1949, W. L. Jenkins; from *The Existentialists and God* by Arthur C. Cochrane. Copyright 1956, L. Jenkins; from *The Transcendence of God* by Edward Farley. W. Copyright © 1958, Wm Edward Farley. Copyright © 1960, W. L. Jenkins; from *Authority in Protestant Theology* by Robert Clyde Johnson. Copyright © 1959, W. L. Jenkins; from *Religion and the Christian Faith* by Hendrick Kraemer. Published 1957; from *Language and Religious Language* by Jules Laurence Moreau. Copyright © 1961; *Calvin: Institutes of the Christian Religion* ed. John T. Mcneill, tr. Ford Lewis Battles: Library of the Christian Classics XX/XXI. Copyright © 1960, W. L. Jenkins) and The University of Chicago Press (from books by Paul Tillich: *Biblical Religion and the Search for Ultimate Reality*, Copyright 1955 by The University of Chicago; *The Protestant Era*, Copyright 1948 by The University of Chicago; *Systematic Theology*, Copyright 1951 and 1957 by The University of Chicago).

KENNETH HAMILTON

United College,
Winnipeg

I

SYSTEM AND THEOLOGY

PAUL TILLICH is a controversial figure in present-day theology, and his thought has been very variously estimated. But everyone is agreed on one point: that he is not easy to understand.

So it is perhaps fortunate that the most plain and unambiguous thing about his theology is also the most important thing. This is his use of system. We may find his language abstruse and his ideas elusive, but at least we can hardly fail to see that he is a thinker who has constructed an intellectual universe within which he moves with complete assurance because, as its architect, he knows exactly how it hangs together. More than anything else, it is his skill as a system-builder that has gained him his high standing in his chosen field of philosophical theology. And, if we want to understand his thought, the first step in this direction must be to realize that it is thought organized into a system, planned meticulously to this one end. System is not just a quality of Tillich's theology. We cannot say, 'This theology is of such-and-such a type and it is also systematic.' This theology is not *also* systematic, for it is *thinking in a system*. And the difference between systematic thinking and thinking in a system is as wide as the difference between arguing heatedly and arguing in the heat.

The extent to which his work is dominated by the concept of system Tillich himself explains in the Preface to the first volume of his *Systematic Theology*. There he confesses:

'It has always been impossible for me to think theologically in any other than a systematic way. The smallest problem, if taken seriously and radically, drove me to all other problems and to the anticipation of a whole in which they could find their solution.'[1]

[1] *Op. cit.*, vii. The two volumes of the *Systematic Theology* will from now on

His words are borne out by the extraordinary unity of his works. Indeed his writings in English can be treated as though they were portions of one great treatise—a treatise which has for its core the still uncompleted *Systematic Theology*. However, the revealing item in the above quotation is the phrase 'the anticipation of a whole'. Tillich's thought is close-knit, consistent thought, continually revised to increase its inner coherence. Chiefly, though, it is thought which never halts until it has discovered an overall pattern which can be used to explain all partial patterns, and until it has posited a unity into which all diversity may be gathered. Were he concerned about consistency of statement—and no more than that—he would be a systematic thinker merely. What makes him a thinker-in-a-system is his refusal to be content with anything less than a whole. All problems must be solved by absorbing them within one grand over-arching scheme. If the desired whole is not in sight, nevertheless it must be wooed as though it were. He believes that thought drives on inexorably to uncover final explanations, so that system-building is man's most character-istic achievement so far as his consciousness is concerned. 'The history of human thought,' he writes, 'has been, and still is, identical with the history of the great systems.'[1]

By making such a declaration Tillich puts himself squarely among the traditional metaphysicians. He stands uncompro-misingly in a position which has had few out-and-out supporters (except for the neo-Thomists) since Hegelianism went out of fashion at the beginning of the century. When Dorothy M. Emmet's *The Nature of Metaphysical Thinking* appeared in 1945, it opened with the statement that we are presently 'at the end of a period of metaphysical thinking',[2] going on to remark that both metaphysics and metaphysical theology 'have fallen

be referred to as *ST* I and *ST* II. The third and final volume of the Systematic Theology has not yet appeared.

Page references are to the editions (1951 and 1957) of the Chicago Univ. Press: pp. xi + 300 and xi + 187 respectively. The London editions (1953 and 1957) were published by Nisbet: pp. xiv + 330 and xii + 216 respectively.

[1] *Op. cit.*, p. 59.

[2] *Op. cit.* (London, Macmillan), Preface v.

on evil days'.[1] In contrast with Miss Emmet's doubts about the feasibility of writing systematic metaphysics in the old, spacious style—'the grand style', as she calls it—Tillich has never shown any hesitation in the matter. For him there is no question of metaphysics being superseded, and he takes up his position in the firm belief that it is one for the theologian to support just as much as for the philosopher. If to think means nothing else than to create systems (or to follow those already made), this applies to theological thinking too, the philosopher and the theologian being often the same person.

Here we have, at the outset, an illuminating example of the assumptions underlying Tillich's approach to theology. Having decided that two animals standing in front of him are both horses, he insists that they be buckled into an identical type of harness. There is no philosophy without systems, he reasons; then theologies must come in systems too. Following this line, he proceeds to grade all theological writing into three classes: the essay, the system and the *summa*. Of these three, the system is the standard, showing what the theological task really is. The essay is no more than a fragment of system, while the *summa* is system displayed as comprehensively as possible.[2] In order to prove his point he makes the observation: 'If the title "Systematic Theology" has any justification, the systematic theologian should not be afraid of the system.'[3]

Does the systematic theologian belie his name unless he produces a comprehensive system in which all theological problems find (in principle) their solution? It is hard to believe that he does. It is easier to believe that Tillich, when he makes such a suggestion, is allowing a confusion over words to cloud the issue. For he is saying, in effect, that all systematic theology would logically take the form of a *summa* were it to be worked out in detail; and this does not fit the facts. It may happen, indeed, that a particular theologian shapes his theology in order to make it conform to a particular system of thought. The theologian who expounds a metaphysical theology does this, and for him the *summa* is the natural form in which to present his theology. But many theologians do not aim at the

[1] *Op. cit.*, p. 1.　　[2] *Ibid.*, p. 59.　　[3] *Ibid.*, p. 58.

15

kind of wholeness sought in the elaboration of a metaphysical system. They view theology as the orderly arrangement of material which does not need to be given coherence through being interpreted in terms of a system, since it is self-authenticating and needs only to be displayed in such a manner that it can be readily grasped. The theology of these theologians never approximates to a *summa*, being at all times no more than an expanded confessional statement.

An obvious instance of the second type of theologian is John Calvin. Occasionally people refer to Calvin's *Institutes of the Christian Religion* as a Protestant *Summa Theologica*. Yet the work does not really belong to the same class as the vast masterpiece of St Thomas Aquinas. It does not embody within its structure a 'Christian philosophy', as the latter does. It is no extended system. Its final form of four books in eighty chapters grew by stages out of the first edition, a little book of six chapters structured on the pattern of the Apostles' Creed and the Lord's Prayer. Calvin intended it to be a transcript of the message of the Christian gospel as declared by the Scriptures in the Church, adapted to the limited capacity of finite minds in its orderly arrangement, yet full enough to provide sufficient refutation of heresies which were a present danger to believers. The example of Calvin illustrates pointedly how systematic thinking need not be the same thing at all as thinking in a system, and it would seem reasonable to conclude that a systematic theologian may claim his right to the title if he does the first and has no intention of doing the second. In the same way, we might call a man a systematic gambler, not because he lays his bets according to a system, but because he organizes his time and money to the sole end of gambling in a well-organized fashion.

What has happened is that Tillich has taken his assumption that theology (like philosophy) means thinking within a system and has read that assumption into the word *systematic*. On the face of it, to draw together the words *system* and *systematic* seems the most natural thing in the world, a procedure beyond cavil. And so it might be if words were counters, if they were interchangeable without limit, and if they carried always the same value. But words, far from being mere counters, are vehicles of meaning and, as such, they gain their value from their actual use. The meaning of any particular word cannot be arrived at in any mechanical fashion but has to be inferred from the context in which it is found. Once a word is brought into relation with even one other word its meaning can be altered completely; thus a *shoe tree* is a very different object from a *chestnut tree,* and *to do good* is a world away in meaning from its verbal near-relative *to do well.* So, to a casual inspection, Tillich's conclusion that systematic theologians should accept systems appears to be sound enough. It reveals itself as a piece of special pleading only when care has been taken to compare the meaning which he attaches to the word *system* with the meaning ordinarily attached to the term *systematic theology.*

The most necessary lesson to be learnt by the reader of Tillich's theology is that all his terms must be scrutinized in this fashion. In spite of his highly organized method of writing, his key terms are frequently confused—or, at least, the cause of confusion. This fact probably accounts more than anything else for the widespread impression that he is an unusually 'difficult' writer. Of course, any philosophical theology could hardly be expected to make easy reading for an idle hour, yet the reaction of puzzlement to Tillich's work is so general that a special reason must be looked for; and I believe that it can be found here. Too often his terms conceal rather than reveal because, in deciding how they are to understand any one term, his readers have to be guided less by the term itself (or by anything they are told about it) than by their knowledge of his system. From this knowledge alone can they have insight into the meaning which a term carries in the place where it happens to stand, because the meaning is dictated by the system. During the course of the present study I shall have to return to this point again and again. Indeed the key to reading Tillich with understanding lies in the ability to interpret apparently simple and obvious words in terms of the system, seeing them strictly as technical words the meaning of which is fixed by the system within which they take their place. Although there are other problems in connection with finding one's way through Tillich's works, this one is inescapable.[1]

But, to continue, the interesting question that poses itself is why, if systematic theologians are not all engaged upon constructing systems, Tillich should try to convince us that they ought to be so engaged. The eagerness in the matter raises the issue of his understanding of theology. Here he offers the definition: 'Theology is the methodical interpretation of the contents of the Christian faith.'[2]

Plain and unremarkable as this definition appears to be, it would be wrong to take it at its face value. Indeed (as I have argued) it is never safe to assume that a system-builder means by any statement no more than the average person would mean in making a similar statement. For the system-builder is not an average person, and he does not use words casually. He relates everything he mentions to the 'whole' which his system is constructed to embody, so that his words most likely carry an unsuspected load of meaning. So, in the above definition, the word *methodical* deserves more than a passing glance. The word is not casual but crucial, since it functions as a technical term exactly parallel to the word *systematic* in the phrase 'systematic theology'. It points to Tillich's belief that theology is a branch of what he calls 'methodological knowledge'. Therefore, when speaking about the methodical interpretation of the Christian faith, he does not mean that Christian theology expounds Christian faith piece by piece, considering in succession the doctrines of God, of the Incarnation, of the Holy Spirit, of the Church, and so on. For him theologians are not arrangers but system-builders. He means, then, that the contents of the Christian faith are to be taken in hand and interpreted in such a way that they are turned in the process into methodological knowledge.

If theology is methodological knowledge, this is because it is an activity parallel to the activity of metaphysics. As such, theology is not the concern of Christians alone. Now, there is a

[1] For a more comprehensive statement of the issues involved see the Postscript to this chapter, 'Ambiguity in Tillich's Theology'.

[2] *Op. cit.*, p. 15. Another definition is: 'Theology is the methodical explanation of the contents of the Christian faith' (*ibid.*, p. 28).

sense in which *theology* is a general word, belonging no more to Christianity than to any other faith. We speak quite naturally of Hindu or of Zoroastrian theology. But Tillich would add a universal dimension to the word which goes far beyond this usual general sense. Stating that theology, taken in its broadest aspect, is 'as old as religion',[1] he defines it as the knowledge that interprets 'the religious substance of rites, symbols, and myths'.[2]

When theology is taken in this universal sense and becomes a type of knowledge which interprets religion as such, then the theologies of the various religions are made into sub-types of this knowledge. Christian theology—so Tillich explains—'does the same thing' as does every other theology, even though making for itself the claim that it is *the* theology.[3] Were the claim of Christian theology to be *the* theology substantiated, then one theology would be elevated to a position of special status among the rest; and yet, by the same token, Christian theology would still remain a sub-type neither separated from the rest nor wholly different in itself. It would always retain its function of being one channel of knowledge in a complex of channels. It would give more knowledge than could be obtained elsewhere, but that is all that could be said.

Mostly when Tillich uses the word *theology* he means the universal methodological knowledge which he believes can be drawn from religion anywhere and at any time. So he can make the statement:

'Theology claims that it constitutes a special realm of knowledge, that it deals with a special object and implies a special method.'[4]

Here the sub-types fall away into the background, and it would be irrelevant to ask, 'Do you mean Christian or Islamic or some other theology?' Yet it also appears that when Tillich uses the phrase 'Christian theology' he means this same type of knowledge, only now directed specifically to the methodological

[1] *Op. cit.*, p. 15.
[2] *Ibid.*, p. 16.
[3] *Ibid.* For the meaning of Tillich's description of Christianity as 'final revelation' see below, pp. 25 f., 167 f., 216 ff.
[4] *Ibid.*, p. 18.

interpretation of 'the religious substance' of Christian rites, symbols and myths. That this is the way in which he uses the phrase he never anywhere makes explicit, and yet it is the central issue of his theological system. Thus the reader, who finds in the opening sentence of the Introduction to the first volume of the *Systematic Theology* the declaration that theology is a function of the Christian Church,[1] may well fail to understand that Christian theology is being taken under the umbrella of theology as a universal methodological knowledge. Traditionally, when Christian theologians have spoken about Christian theology they have meant something which was built *upon* the Christian faith and not something which was applied *to* the Christian faith. Whatever method of theologizing they have used, they have subordinated it to the method used by the Church in proclaiming the Gospel, a method well expressed by Charles Gore in these terms:

> 'The method of the Christian Church, then, is not to propound an argument and say, "Is not this a sound argument?" It does not make its appeal primarily to the intellect. It comes into the world proclaiming something which is by its very nature authoritative —a message from God. And as God is to man, the Creator to the creature, the Father to the child, so the message claims to be accepted, not indeed without inquiry, but still at the last resort in faith. The idea is that of "receiving the word of God".'[2]

On Bishop Gore's premise Christian theology can claim that it constitutes a special realm of knowledge on no other ground than that of passing on without distortion the authoritative message from God received by the Christian Church. This does not hinder theology, of course, from using various methods of its own choosing. But it means that theology cannot open up any knowledge more certain than the knowledge of the word of God which the believer receives in faith. In such a view, Christian theology could not possibly be considered to be a sub-type of a universal realm of knowledge, for it is a knowledge

[1] *Op. cit.*, p. 2.
[2] *The New Theology and the Old Religion* (London, John Murray, 1908), pp. 30–1.

built upon the basis of a specific faith and without that faith it has no charter of its own.

The one thing that Tillich never means by 'Christian theology' is an authoritative message to be accepted. He does not wish to defer to the findings of faith but to proceed to the conclusions of knowledge. Where religious believers speak of a message from God, he sees religious rites, symbols and myths; and he asks what is the 'substance' of these manifestations, believing that the special realm of knowledge which is theology will provide the answer. Thus, what is authoritative can be nothing else than the findings of (universal) theology itself. When this theology applies its proper method to its proper object it separates truth from error and displays the essence of religion. By examining the Christian faith, for example, it exposes exactly what the rites, symbols and myths of this type of religion really represent. It carries out a work of methodical interpretation in order to explain to Christian believers the universal significance of their not universally acceptable beliefs, with the result that the obscure is made plain. Because it is a living religion, Christianity must exhibit religious substance and therefore must have truth in it; but only (universal) theology can bring this truth to light by creating the knowledge by means of which the truth can be recognized. Theology as methodological knowledge, then, is one truth-creating realm interpreting all religions. But when the (universal) theologian interprets the contents of the Christian faith he becomes a Christian theologian. He is a Christian theologian in the same sense that an Australian-born anthropologist might be called an African anthropologist because he is engaged in studying tribal life in Africa.

Although Tillich never actually explains the special sense in which he uses the word *theology*, he does enter into a discussion of the relation between 'kerygmatic' and 'apologetic' theology and gives his reasons for believing that theology must always be apologetic.

New Testament scholars, notably C. H. Dodd, have emphasized the part played in first-century Christianity by the apostolic *kerygma* (or preaching-matter) in establishing the faith of the Church. So Tillich's term 'kerygmatic theology' is a useful one for describing a theology which seeks to transmit with fidelity the message of the Church as a message from God. Identifying this type of theology largely with the 'neo-orthodox' movement of the past forty years led by Barth and Brunner, Tillich suggests that such a theology is a helpful reminder of the distinctive character of the Christian religion and, as such, must be indispensable. But, he adds, when the attempt is made to throw the Christian message at men like a stone, then this effort is altogether impossible. Nothing except a union of kerygmatic theology with apologetic theology can survive.[1]

Such a suggestion seems to be a modest one, avoiding extremes. To say that 'kerygmatic theology needs apologetic theology for its completion'[2] appears most reasonable, especially when it is balanced by the warning that apologetic theology cannot stand on its own. Apologetic theology, explains Tillich, takes into account man's cultural and intellectual 'situation' and interprets 'the eternal message' afresh to each generation, answering the questions which the 'situation' poses.[3] Yet what does this mean? Since apologetic theology does a work of interpretation it satisfies Tillich's definition of the theological task. On the other hand, whether kerygmatic theology can be called a theology at all on the same terms—except as a kind of courtesy title—is highly doubtful. Unless it is joined to apologetic theology is becomes, says Tillich, superstitious. Thus a would-be self-sufficient kerygmatic theology (such as Karl Barth's anti-metaphysical dogmatics) 'in the last resort is a self-deception'.[4] While Tillich's explicit objection is to the notion of having the Christian message thrown 'like a stone' (the metaphor is Barth's), yet he apparently leaves no room at all for *any* message except a *methodologically interpreted* message. He never suggests that there may be a message which, to use Bishop

---

[1] *Op. cit.*, pp. 5–6.   [2] *Ibid.*, p. 7.   [3] *Ibid.*, p. 6.
[4] *ST* II, p. 14. Tillich also states that Barth continually departs from that kerygmatic theology which he champions—but without knowing that he has done so (*ST* I, p. 5). In Tillich's eyes Barth achieves greatness through contradicting himself by mistake. This is scarcely a flattering estimate of Barth's critical powers.

Gore's words, is by its very nature authoritative—a message from God.

The section of the *Systematic Theology* where Tillich discusses kerygmatic and apologetic theology carries the heading 'Apologetic Theology and the Kerygma', and this heading shows the proper direction of his thoughts more accurately than anything he says in the text below. For he makes no place in his exposition for two equal types of theology but speaks of theology which is methodological knowledge and of the attempt (ultimately impossible) to found a theology on the Christian *kerygma* alone. Yet he sees that apologetic theology interpreting a non-specific 'eternal message' must interact somehow with the historic message of the Christian Church if there is to be such a thing as Christian theology. It is for this reason that the apologetic theologian needs the *kerygma*. He has need of the Christian *kerygma* just as my imaginary Australian-born anthropologist has need of African tribes. Without African tribal life there can be no African anthropology, and without the *kerygma* proclaimed in the Christian Church there can be no Christian theology.

That Tillich never seriously contemplates the possibility of there being more than one true theology is proved when he comes to the point of debating the question of whether or not Christian theology is *the* theology. I have already argued that the very raising of such a question assumes that Christian theology is no more than a sub-type of a universal theology. Tillich asks whether it is the case that 'the idea of theology is fulfilled in Christian theology in a perfect and final way', adding that this is what Christian theology claims for itself.[1] One would have thought that Christian theology claims rather that the Christian *kerygma* is true, and, being true, leads to a theology which cannot be abandoned for any other theology without having as a result a loss of truth. If the superiority of Christian theology consists in its expressing fully and finally the *idea* of theology, then one must first possess a sure knowledge of that which constitutes the idea of theology apart from all individual embodiments of the idea. Apparently Tillich is quite certain

[1] *ST* I, p. 15.

that such knowledge is available and that it is the task of apologetic theology to demonstrate that Christian theology—and no other—is at the head of the list of the embodiments of the idea:

> 'Apologetic theology must show that trends which are immanent in all religions and cultures move toward the Christian answer. This refers both to doctrines and to the theological interpretation of theology.'[1]

It is because of his own analysis of the idea of theology that Tillich can contemplate the Christian faith and say that Christian theology is *the* theology. Decidedly, he does not mean that any and every reasonably orthodox Christian theology is *the* theology. As I shall have occasion to point out later,[2] he rejects outright the viewpoint most commonly adopted by Christian thought down the ages, complaining that this is a supernaturalism which no enlightened person can accept—which means that he must believe that the greater part of the work of Christian theologians has been *no* theology. He could hardly approve the suggestion, either, that the idea of theology is fulfilled in a perfect and a final way in the (impossible) 'pure' kerygmatic theology that attempts to throw the Christian message like a stone and is guilty of self-deception. Rather he means that Christian doctrine is seen to be the expression of perfect theological truth once an enlightened apologetic theology has done its work of interpretation. And an enlightened apologetic theology will not only interpret Christian doctrine, for it will first demonstrate why it must be chosen to do the work of interpretation by establishing its own credentials. It will show that it alone has grasped the true idea of theology, so that it alone can say *both* what Christian theology ought to be to be truly Christian *and* what it ought to be to be truly theology. Naturally, Tillich advances his own *Systematic Theology* as the best attempt so far to interpret the *kerygma* and to establish the true idea of theology ('the theological interpretation of theology'), an idea in the light of which the *kerygma* finds its adequate affirmation. There is, of course, nothing in the least

[1] *ST* I, p. 15.   [2] See below, Chapter IV and pp. 176 ff.

egotistical in his judgment. He regards his own system as just one moment in the ongoing work of philosophy and theology, a work which never fails and never wholly succeeds, a work which is unending and ever-enduring but which continues to mark the path of the history of human thought in sober triumph and in humble achievement.

Nevertheless, this vision of the pursuit of the idea of truth—however lofty and however disinterested—is difficult to reconcile with the belief that what lies at the heart of Christianity is an authoritative message from God and that the principal task of Christian theology is to concern itself with the adequate publication of this message. The Christian may be happy to learn that Christianity has been nominated *the* revelation and that Christian theology has been proven to be *the* theology. Yet he may well wonder by what mechanism Christian theology has been thus elevated and whose voice it is that has cried, 'Friend, go up higher!' And, when he finds that the invitation is based on a theory concerning the idea of theology in general and that the means of elevation is a particular apologetic system, he is likely to ask the question, 'By what authority?'

The problem of authority is indeed—as in all theologies—the crucial problem in this one. Tillich has asked himself what theology is, and has answered his own question by saying that it is the methodical interpretation of the Christian faith. But, if he has gone on to ask himself what it is that ought to interpret the Christian faith and upon what authority, he has not given his readers a chance to overhear his answer. All the same, he has answered this question silently, and the answer is written out all through the *Systematic Theology* and the rest of his published works. He has answered, in effect, 'My idea of theology shall interpret the Christian faith. And the authority by which it will act shall be the appeal of the idea itself, backed by the coherence of my system which will show the implications of the idea and how it can be used to give an intelligible picture of human life and the Universe within which life is lived.' Had he made an explicit statement of this sort, he would have been a much easier author to read. However, he did not, and many of the explanations he has given concerning the principles which have guided him have been clouded by the absence of direction concerning this key principle. In the rest of the present study I shall try to show in detail how his principle works out in practice. In particular, what happens to the *kerygma* when it comes to be interpreted by means of his idea of theology and in terms of his system—this is my main concern.

The proof of the pudding is in the eating. The value of Tillich's idea of theology can be assessed from a Christian point of view only when the declarations he has to make about God, man and the world are examined. Yet, before serving a pudding, one may learn something about it by tasting a morsel on a spoon; so, in similar fashion, I should like to pick out a couple of sample declarations:

> '. . . if we speak of the actuality of God, we first assert that he is not God if he is not being-itself. Other assertions about God can be made theologically only on this basis.[1]

> 'Without an understanding of "being" and "the power of being" it is impossible to speak meaningfully of grace.'[2]

Both declarations show how one must expect the *kerygma* to be handled when the authority by means of which it is 'interpreted' and 'explained' is a particular idea of theology. The idea takes its place within a system of ideas consistent with it, and the system develops its own technical vocabulary. Interpretation of elements found in the *kerygma* therefore becomes a process of taking words from there (e.g. *God* and *grace*) and of translating them into the technical terms of the system, after which the system can absorb them without trouble and nothing characteristic of the *kerygma* remains. Thus it is not considered possible to speak 'meaningfully' of grace until grace has been defined in terms of being and the power of being. Why? Because otherwise the term *grace* would not fit into the system or carry the meaning which the system recognizes; it might threaten to disrupt the system by raising ideas incompatible with the assumptions making possible the system's existence. It is not considered possible to make theological assertions about

[1] *ST* I, pp. 238–9.   [2] *ST* II, p. 125.

God except on the foundation of one technical term. Why? Because otherwise some other idea of theology might emerge to challenge the idea of theology which gives support to the system and is supported by it. Perhaps some notion of the actuality of God might be imported from the *kerygma*, a notion proving impossible to digest within the body of the system. Were this to come about, then the work of proving Christian theology to be the perfect fulfilment of the idea of theology would come to nothing, since the Christian message would be seen not to measure up to the system's requirements and thus Christian theology could not be brought under the cloak of the idea of theology in general.

Of course, there is no means of deducing *a priori* that the *kerygma* cannot be translated without loss into the language of the system. At the same time, because he has set up his idea of theology quite independently of the *kerygma*, Tillich has put himself in the position of having to show that his translation really translated and does not merely substitute his own gospel in place of the Christian one. Recognizing this, he has characterized his system as one using 'the method of correlation'. In a later chapter (VI) I shall be looking at Tillich's concept of correlation and assessing the use he makes of it, so that for the present the question of whether correlation does all that he claims for it can be postponed. But, even without going into the matter of what exactly constitutes 'the method of correlation' (which for convenience I shall call *the Method*), one thing can be said at once. It is completely certain that the Method is not just a way of handling the system but is itself one of the elements found within the system. Tillich himself confesses as much when he writes that the Method is 'derived from a prior knowledge of the system which is to be built by the method'.[1] Unfortunately, he does not draw out the implications of the confession. Did he do so, it would become obvious that the method he uses in working out his theological system is very much wider than the Method. The latter is the final stage in a process which begins with the choice of a particular idea of theology. This idea controls everything else.

[1] *ST* I, p. 60.

From it issues the system, and in turn the system is related to the Christian *kerygma* by means of the Method (correlation). Consequently, whatever the Method may turn out to be, it cannot possibly be used to show that Tillich's translation of the *kerygma* is a legitimate translation. It cannot be used in this direction because it is an integral part of the process of translation. Falling within the totality of the system, it is useless as a guarantee of the validity of the system.

The reason why Tillich is at pains to identify systematic theology with the construction of a speculative system should now be sufficiently clear. Authority resides in his idea of theology. This demands the development of a 'whole' in which all the parts shall find their place in accordance with the idea. Then, since his idea of theology includes the belief that it is a special kind of knowledge, he goes on to include within this whole an account of how knowledge is possible, following that up with a description of all (in principle) there is to know. This means that his system must embrace the area of philosophy as well as that of theology.[1] Once the universal nature of the system is recognized it should be very little of a puzzle to guess how it is possible for him to say that he uses a Method derived from a prior knowledge of the system which is to be built by the Method. His system can be known before it is actually constructed, for the simple reason that the principles undergirding it have been laid down in advance. His speculative picture of the Universe stands logically before and above his interpretation of the Christian faith as the latter is set forth in his *Systematic Theology*. One can compare the relation between his prior knowledge of the system (call it *system-known*) and the system as it comes to be written (call it *system-built*) to the relation between a Latin Grammar and a schoolboy's Latin composition. The schoolboy can be sure of getting his exercise right so long as he keeps to the rules laid down in the Grammar. Just so, Tillich composes his system-built by following the outlines of system-known. But, of course, Tillich is the author of his own Grammar, so he does not have to hold any book in his hand before he begins his exercise. He is certain that he

[1] See below, pp. 59 ff.

can produce the correct interpretation of such words as *God* and *grace*. Knowing the accidence and syntax of theology as these are implicitly present in his idea of theology, he can readily apply his knowledge to the completion of his allotted task.

Once we come to see that Tillich conceives his task to be one of converting the raw material of religious faith into a 'theological' knowledge surveying the whole world of religion and determining the amount of truth and error in all religions, we shall find no great trouble in understanding him. Our chief difficulty arises from the fact that we are shown system-built but we have to piece together system-known as we go along. For this reason, even his definitions need to be them-selves defined—the words of which they are composed being already orientated to the requirements of system-known. There is nothing surprising about this, since he has told us that theology for him means bringing all problems into a whole. Because his system is a structured one intended to exhibit internal coherence, it is built to a plan, like a piece of architec-ture. And every student of architecture knows that it is necessary to look at more than the façade of a building in order to discover why it looks as it does. Taken broadly, understanding Tillich means being able to relate the façade of his building to its ground-plan, i.e. discerning the outlines of system-known visible behind each of his statements in system-built.

There is another aspect to the system, however, that so far I have not considered. The system is not just meant to be an inclusive structure embodying the true idea of theology. It is also intended to provide an adequate apologetic for Christian faith and to exhibit the character of a Christian philosophical theology. Up to now I have argued (and shall argue further through the chapters that follow) that Tillich's starting-point in an idea of (universal) theology by-passes the starting-point of Christian theology in an authoritative *kerygma*, and for that reason has cut loose from the specific ground of faith out of which all Christian thinking grows. It is true that Tillich claims that, on the strength of his Method, he can establish a link with the *kerygma* which does not appear from his starting-point. Until this particular claim is examined in detail the question must remain open. Yet, as I have indicated, there is a *prima facie* case against the Method being able to bridge the gap that has to be crossed if his system is to make contact with the Christian gospel, a case resting on the evident fact that the Method itself is a product of the system and inevitably shares the presuppositions underlying the system. If the Method accepts the assumptions of (universal) theology-as-methodological-knowledge how is it to join itself to Christian theology based on an authoritative *kerygma*? However, granting for the moment that Tillich *may* have a satisfactory solution for that problem, there is one other consideration which Tillich brings forward in connection with the relation of his system to Christianity. This is what he calls 'the theological circle'.

The theological circle is first introduced in order to define the distinction between a philosopher of religion and a theologian: it is described as 'the circle within which the theologian works'.[1] Since we are at once told that it is the narrowness of the theologian's circle that distinguishes it from the circle occupied by the philosopher of religion, it is reasonable to suppose that Tillich is talking about the commitment of the Christian theologian to his faith; and this impression is strengthened when we learn that, while philosophers of religion assume the reality of the 'mystical *a priori*', theologians in addition accept 'the criterion of the Christian message'. Afterwards, coming across such a phrase as 'those who stand within the circle of the Christian life',[2] we are likely to have no more doubts about the matter. It seems as though standing within the theological circle is altogether equivalent to confessing belief in the Christian gospel.

Nevertheless, a closer inspection will renew our doubts. It is far too simple a view that imagines Tillich to be ready to receive gladly believing commitment to an authoritative *kerygma* within the boundaries of his (universal) theology. He states quite openly his conviction that no one can say of himself that he is 'in the situation of faith', adding that every theologian is both committed *and* alienated, inside *and* outside the theological circle.[3] This clarification reveals that Tillich has not

[1] *Op. cit.*, p. 9.   [2] *ST* II, p. 5.   [3] *ST* I, p. 10.

modified his starting-point. He sees the theologian as a person who holds fast to his idea of theology even while he seeks to encounter the meaning of the Christian faith 'from the inside'. The Australian anthropologist must *become an African* as he shares the African life—yet he also carries with him the wider experience which is his precisely because he is not altogether an African. Of course, the parallel is not wholly exact; and it is misleading if for 'African' we read 'Christian' without qualification. But it is near enough if for 'African' we read 'Christian who accepts an authoritative *kerygma*'. For Tillich never asks the question, 'What does it mean to be a Christian?' without assuming that the answer can be given solely in terms of the answer dictated by his idea of theology.

So in the present instance he does not talk of standing inside the Christian circle, but of standing inside the theological circle—a very different thing. When he says that the theologian accepts as his charter the criterion of the Christian message, he does not mean that the theologian accepts the *kerygma* itself, for he means that the theologian accepts that interpretation of the *kerygma* which his system produces. The theologian he has in mind has accepted as authoritative the idea of theology found in the system, and on this authoritative basis he judges the 'substance' of the religious reality to be found in the Christian religion. Having found what this 'substance' really is, he then uses his knowledge to produce a 'criterion' of the Christian message in line with the requirements of the system. This is why Tillich decides that the theologian goes beyond the philosopher of religion to the extent of accepting the criterion—the system's criterion—of the Christian message. Just as the Method is drawn from system-known, so the theological circle is a concept having its origin in the same source.[1]

Through the rest of the present study I shall be investigating how the details of Tillich's theology gain their meaning from their place within his system. But, since my theme is the relation of Tillich's system to the Christian gospel, something

[1] The particular criterion which Tillich chooses he calls 'the Norm of systematic theology': see below, pp. 141 ff. He also produces two 'formal criteria of every theology': see below, pp. 42 ff.

more needs to be said in a general way concerning the belief that Christianity can be explained by bringing it within a system. So the next chapter, while opening up some basic theological formulae used by Tillich, is mainly an attempt to examine the adequacy of the systematic way in theology. This will involve a short excursus into theological history and a glance at Tillich's own opinions concerning the historical setting of his system.

Postscript: Ambiguity in Tillich's Theology

Whenever there is discussion over interpreting Tillich's writings the ambiguity of the language he uses is almost always mentioned. In the first place, some critics are troubled by the fact that his theology seems to lend itself to contradictory interpretations. They find a radical ambiguity in it that is destructive of meaning. Thus William Hordern objects:

'. . . his work has proved to be of such a nature that different readers or listeners come away with radically different views of what he has said. Naturalistic humanists and quite orthodox Christians are prepared to call Tillich their own. In view of the emphasis that Tillich has given to the importance of communication, it is ironical that there is no agreement upon what he has in fact said.'[1]

Some would blame the obscurity of Tillich's style for this failure of communication. Yet it may well be that our perplexities come less from the style than from the subject-matter displayed through the style. At least one critic has given Tillich high praise for his stylistic brilliance,[2] and, for what it is worth, I should like to add my own testimony here. It seems to me that the organization of Tillich's sentences reflects the

[1] 'Recent Trends in Systematic Theology', in the *Canadian Journal of Theology* VII 2 (April 1961), p. 89.
[2] Gustave Weigel in 'The Multidimensional World of Paul Tillich', a review of Tillich's book of essays, *Theology and Culture*, in the *Christian Scholar* XLIII 1 (Jan. 1960), pp. 67 ff.

organization of his thinking, and that there is a directness and absence of ostentation in all he writes that is truly admirable. He is not easy to read (why should he be?); but he is a pleasure to read. If his style has a fault it is over-terseness, although what is obscure by reason of brevity in one place is usually explained more fully in another. In short, Tillich is an artist in words—a fact commonly admitted in connection with his sermons but overlooked in connection with his work as a philosophical theologian. When complaint is raised over the problem of understanding him, then, there is little cause for blaming his style as such.

A more plausible reason given for finding Tillich radically ambiguous is that his language is opaque and incomprehensible in itself. G. E. Moore, the Cambridge philosopher, is reported to have said after hearing Tillich read a paper: 'Now really, Mr Tillich, I don't think I have been able to understand a single sentence of your paper. Won't you please try to state one sentence, or even one word, that I can understand?'[1] In this anecdote Moore takes Hordern's objection one stage farther, for, while the latter thinks Tillich's words so thoroughly ambiguous that diverse meanings are read into them, Moore simply states that no conclusions of any kind are warranted until the ambiguity in the words has been removed, i.e. until Tillich produces some clearly understandable statement.

Yet is Tillich's thinking really so obscure that those who think they understand it are deluded and the wise will not try to make sense of it? The answer to this question is implicitly present in the comment supplied by John Herman Randall, Jr, who recounts the Moore incident. Randall says dryly, 'Tillich is clearly not a Cambridge analyst.' In other words, Moore was unwilling to believe that he had understood even one word of Tillich's paper because the paper had been written from a philosophical standpoint very much at variance with his own. While the individual words were obviously not unfamiliar to him, the whole background of thought which they assumed was an alien one. Yet, even then, the problem was

[1] *The Theology of Paul Tillich*, edited by Charles W. Kegley and Robert W. Bretall (New York, Macmillan, 1952), p. 133.

actually one of less than radical ambiguity. And readers today, who can turn for guidance (as Moore could not) to a sizeable body of Tillichian literature, need not ask for additional explanation in order to know what is being said. Those who try to interpret Tillich without taking his words in the context of the system that shapes them, of course, are likely to produce conflicting results. But Tillich can hardly be blamed for that.

At the same time, complaints that Tillich often fails to communicate his meaning plainly, even when vital issues are at stake, are not merely captious. Granted that there is not radical ambiguity in Tillich's theology making it totally incomprehensible; granted also that his theology is written with considerable deftness and stylistic skill; yet it remains true that Tillich does not always set out his arguments with clarity and that he sometimes establishes conclusions by means of what looks very like verbal legerdemain. In an article entitled 'Some Notes on the Theology of Paul Tillich' J. Heywood Thomas has drawn attention to Tillich's assumption that the meaning of words can be lifted out of dictionaries and established apart from the passages in which the words are actually used.[1] Thomas argues that this assumption results frequently in vagueness covered over by an appearance of consistency. He notes also a 'tendency to exploit the ambiguity of language in order to make some point'. As I see it, the two phenomena remarked by Thomas are closely connected and together form the greatest obstacle of all to an intelligent understanding of Tillich's thought. Here the barrier to communication is a genuine one because it represents a failure on Tillich's part to share candidly with his readers either the presuppositions underlying his arguments or the conclusions to which he is arguing.

This particular barrier to communication is one which has come to the fore already. My contention that Tillich uses the term 'systematic theology' in a special sense—i.e. as meaning theology organized within a system—links up with Thomas's observation about exploiting the ambiguity of language. It

[1] *Hibbert Journal* LVII 3 (April 1959), pp. 253 ff.

links up too with all that Thomas says about Tillich's preoccupation with 'the inanimate language of the dictionary' and neglect of the use of language in 'living speech'. In fact, ambiguity arises over such a word as *systematic* precisely because the reader assumes that it carries the 'living' meaning provided by the context within which it is set, while Tillich assumes that the word carries a rigid meaning irrespective of context. Tillich's use of the word *theology* gives us a good example of the same cause of confusion. Using a 'dictionary' definition of the word, Tillich takes it to mean the *logos* (reasoning) concerned with *theos* (God or divine things),[1] thereby changing drastically the usual meaning of the term 'Christian theology'.

In all this, it should be noted, there is no complete and final ambiguity. The definitions are given, and, so long as they are carefully attended to, the sense of what they say is not in doubt. Nevertheless, uncertainty haunts the path of the reader, who may very easily read the words before him and yet fail to see the full implication of what he reads. This is the explanation underlying Hordern's complaint that different readers or listeners come away with radically different views of what Tillich has said. It is not possible, unless one has a fairly intimate acquaintance with the system, to be sure of the technical meaning being attached to seemingly ordinary words; and therefore each person tends to read the system in terms of his own presuppositions instead of in terms of the presuppositions proper to the system itself. Thus, even such an acute theologian as George H. Tavard confesses that he had one opinion about the implications of Tillich's theology up to the time of the publication of the second volume of the *Systematic Theology*, and a totally different opinion afterwards.[2] It is true that Tavard changed his mind on account of Tillich's Christology, and that this part of the system was not developed in detail earlier. Yet it is also true that the first volume gives us the decisive orientation of Tillich's Christology—as well as showing us the shape of his 'universe' (i.e. his systematic vision), which Tavard now

[1] *ST* I, p. 15.
[2] *Paul Tillich and the Christian Message* (New York, Scribner's and London, Burns & Oates, 1962), Foreword vii and p. 132.

rejects as strongly as he formerly was prepared to support it.

Why does Tillich allow ambiguity to cloud his exposition to the extent of misleading experts? It is hardly sufficient to plead that there must be 'even in a well organized work such as my *Systematic Theology* a certain inconsistency and indefiniteness of terminology'.[1] For, though details might perplex, the main tendency of the system should still be evident enough. The suspicion inevitably arises that, if Tillich does not expose unequivocally the fundamental characteristics of his system, it is because he himself draws back from the logic inherent in the system. In *Religion and the Christian Faith* Hendrik Kraemer, making a short examination of the Tillichian system, has put this suspicion into words. He writes:

'. . . he lives in the incompatible situation of wanting to be *wholeheartedly an ontological philosopher and as wholeheartedly a Christian thinker or theologian*. This is impossible . . . Tillich has in his definitions avoided a single-minded decision, and has to pay for this omission by imprisonment in opaqueness.'[2]

While I believe that Kraemer has underestimated the overall consistency of Tillich's definitions,[3] his observation that their author is being pulled in two directions at once seems to me to be altogether sound. The desire to prove his system the necessary apologetic basis for the Christian message may well be the hidden force which has caused Tillich to blur the exposition of the system. Ambiguity of language can apparently reconcile the irreconcilable and make incompatibles agree.

The present study brings forward ample evidence to support this hypothesis. Tillich's system, when examined, shows itself to be a coherent structure, overwhelmingly consistent in its own terms, and quite comprehensible. Ambiguity arises precisely at those times when the attempt is made to relate it to Christian faith and to demonstrate it as having not merely systematic cogency but also religious adequacy.

[1] *The Theology of Paul Tillich* ('Autobiographical Reflections'), p. 15.

[2] *Op. cit.*, (London, Lutterworth Press, 1956), p. 428. The italics are in the original.

[3] See below, pp. 74 ff.

II

ANTI-KIERKEGAARD

IN THE previous chapter I mentioned that Tillich's defence of the metaphysical system is notable because it represents a point of view rare since Hegelianism ceased to be a dominant influence in philosophy. Now, the first total opponent of Hegel's standpoint was Søren Kierkegaard, father of modern existentialism. Hegel had many critics in his lifetime, but they were mostly those who attacked his system because they believed that they could construct a better one themselves. But his Danish critic attacked him for being the most consistent system-builder among system-builders. In the name of Christian faith Kierkegaard rejected not this or that element in Hegelianism but the whole, referring to it in mockery as 'the System'. So it happens that the issue of system *versus* the Christian faith has been debated more than a hundred years ago. And that encounter between system and anti-system is very relevant to any examination of philosophical theology to-day.

Certainly Tillich, who is often critical of Hegel, nearly always speaks in praise of Kierkegaard, and he gives such an important place in his own thinking to the category of existence that he seems at times to be travelling in the Danish thinker's footsteps. Thus he explains that in making use of the word *existential* he is borrowing from Kierkegaard.[1] At the same time, by defending the system as needful for theology, Tillich is confessing himself to be a nay-sayer of the other's message—an anti- Kierkegaard.

Making a comparison and a contrast between these two men is more than just a beguiling detour, for, in trying to show why Tillich stands over against and not beside the thinker he so frequently praises, I shall be led into the quite vital matter of his perspective on philosophy.

[1] *The Protestant Era* (London, Nisbet, 1951), p. 98.

Tillich regards the existentialist way of thought, reaching through Kierkegaard, Marx and Nietzsche in the nineteenth century to Heidegger and Sartre in the twentieth, as one of the great formative influences in the evolution of his own thinking.[1] He traces the roots of the movement to the revolt against Hegel's philosophy which was seen first in the Positive Philosophy of Friedrich Wilhelm von Schelling. Yet he also includes Hegel himself as one of the true begetters of Existentialism, making this comment:

'The revolt against Hegel's Essentialist philosophy was accomplished with the help of Existentialist elements present, though subdued, in Hegel himself.'[2]

The comment is most illuminating, because it opens up plainly Tillich's whole approach to existentialist philosophy. Tillich is very widely supposed to be a Christian existentialist, but such a title can be bestowed on him only when it is hedged about with so many reservations that it becomes virtually meaningless. For he has never believed that an existentialist outlook can be a self-sustaining vision of life. On the contrary, he has consistently maintained that existentialist elements must be brought into relation with their opposites (essentialist elements) within a rounded philosophy, since on their own they can provide nothing but a negative contribution to knowledge.[3] His position—which has never altered basically—is set out unequivocally in an article contributed to the *Christian Century* in a series 'How my Mind has Changed'. Remarking first that during the previous ten years his mind has changed but little, Tillich continues:

'I have never been an existentialist in the sense that Kierkegaard or Heidegger is an existentialist. In regard to every meaningful proposition, the existentialist lives from his opposite, the essentialist. In the past few years this insight has gained in strength; it could not be otherwise if one tries to build a theological

---

[1] *The Theology of Paul Tillich*, pp. 11, 14.
[2] *The Courage To Be* (London, Nisbet, 1952), p. 128.
[3] See *ST* I, p. 154; *ST* II, pp. 24–6.

system. . . . For this reason my present inquiries are predominantly essentialist.'[1]

These words set the stage admirably for a confrontation of his views with those of Søren Kierkegaard.

Tillich dates the beginnings of existentialism from the later teachings of Schelling. In November 1842 Kierkegaard visited Germany and stayed five months in Berlin to hear Schelling lecture, having hopes that in Schelling's declared opposition to Hegel he would find an acceptable alternative to Hegel's system. He went away disappointed. Walter Lowrie, Kierkegaard's biographer, describes what happened thus:

'He was especially eager to hear Schelling demolish the Hegelian system. . . . His enthusiasm for Schelling was short-lived. His first lectures inspired the hope that he had something real to say about "reality", but that hope was deluded, and on February 27, S.K. wrote to Boesen, "Schelling drivels on inordinately . . . I am leaving Berlin and hastening to Copenhagen . . . not to bind myself to new ties . . . but to complete *Either/Or*".'[2]

Kierkegaard's disillusionment over Schelling came about when he realized that this philosopher had not really broken out of the circle of ideas within which Hegel moved. He looked in vain in the lectures for a recognition of the 'existential relation' which was to be the focus of all his own writings. Lowrie picks out of *Either/Or* a barbed quotation which sums up its author's decisive revulsion from Schelling as well as from Hegel:

'The fact that philosophers talk about reality is often just as deceptive as when a man reads on a sign-board in front of a shop, "Ironing done here". If he should come with his linen to get it ironed, he would be making a fool of himself, for the sign-board was there only for sale.'[3]

[1] 'On the Boundary Line', Article XX in the series (*Christian Century*, 7 December 1960, p. 1437). Some of the implications of this statement are presented in the Postscript to this chapter: 'Tillich and the Existentialists'.

[2] *A Short Life of Kierkegaard* (Princeton, Princeton University Press, 1942), p. 93. For the view that Schelling helped Kierkegaard to clarify his own thinking see J. Heywood Thomas, *Subjectivity and Paradox* (Oxford, Blackwell, 1957), pp. 51–4.

[3] *Kierkegaard* (London, Oxford University Press, 1938), p. 234.

In Kierkegaard's eyes, Hegel remained *the* philosopher; and so he directed his polemic against him. But he set his face against every philosophical system, even if it bore the label *anti-Hegelian*. Whoever was not against Hegel in respect of the system-ideal was for him, being a thinker who had by-passed existence.

Kierkegaard's whole teaching stresses the impossibility of uniting Christianity and speculative thought. What he termed his first authentic literature, the book *Either/Or*, was written on the surge of his rejection of Schelling, and its title epitomizes his practical programme. His demand is for decision, action and the leap of faith. He tells the individual that he must judge for himself, it being foolish to imagine that one can justify existential choice by an appeal to the laws of the intellect or to the nature of the Universe objectively considered. In existence it is irrational to wish reason to do what faith must do, so that believing 'for three reasons' is merely comic. By way of contrast, Tillich has never doubted either the desirability or the possibility of joining religious faith and speculative thought: his watchword is *synthesis*. Deploring the 'breakdown of the great synthesis between Christianity and the modern mind as attempted by Schleiermacher, Hegel, and nineteenth-century liberalism', he exclaims, 'But there is no choice for us. We must try again.'[1] And he writes of his early discovery of the tension between humanistic culture and religion:

'. . . the way of synthesis, was my own way. It follows the classical German philosophers from Kant to Hegel, and remained a driving force in all my theological work. It has found its final form in my *Systematic Theology*.'[2]

In short, Kierkegaard believes that man's relation to his

[1] *Biblical Religion and the Search for Ultimate Reality* (Chicago, Univ. of Chicago Press, 1955; London, Nisbet, 1956), p. 57. Elsewhere he seems to deny that the nineteenth-century synthesis ever really failed, for he speaks of 'the so-called breakdown of Classical German philosophy, especially of Hegel's system . . .' (*Love, Power, and Justice*, London, Oxford University Press, 1954, p. 73). One synthesis that Tillich questions is the synthesis of philosophy and theology—but that is a different question; see below pp. 59 ff.

[2] *The Theology of Paul Tillich*, p. 10.

existence demands that he recognize the authority of faith above and beyond the guidance of reason. Tillich believes that a philosophy of an essentialist character can include existence within its horizons and therefore can find a place for faith there as well.

For the most part, Tillich avoids entering into any detailed discussion of Kierkegaard's teaching, and when he refers to a Kierkegaardian term or idea he does not explain why he interprets it in one way rather than in another. Yet whenever he avails himself of some piece of Kierkegaardian lore he always does so assuming that the authority of his system (like the editor's decision in a newspaper competition) is final, even though he has to contradict Kierkegaard in the process. For example, he states:

> 'Kierkegaard's stages of the aesthetical and the ethical and the religious are not stages but qualities which appear in structural interdependence.'[1]

Now it so happens that Kierkegaard discusses what he means by his three stages (illustrated in *Stages On Life's Way*) in the work where he explains most fully his opposition to Hegel's System, the *Concluding Unscientific Postscript To the Philosophical Fragments*. There he points out that the three stages can be abstractly represented as three standpoints, but in the life of an existing individual always present an either-or, a choice between two decisions. From the abstract point of view there is no 'decisive conflict' between the standpoints. In actuality the notion that the standpoints can be reconciled, or that one can pass without a break from one to another, is 'a chimera, an illusion'. The sole passage is by way of a leap, and the only 'category of transition' is a breach.[2] While Kierkegaard's immediate protest is against having the three stages read in terms of Hegelian logic, Tillich's suggestion that they be taken as qualities in structural interdependence is equally an assertion of what Kierkegaard calls 'the immanent transition of speculative philosophy'. Where an existentialist sees a call to

[1] *Love, Power, and Justice*, p. 31.
[2] *Op. cit.* (Princeton, Princeton University Press, 1941; London, Oxford, 1942), pp. 261–2.

decision, there an essentialist sees parts finding their unity within a whole.

A head-on collision of this sort is impossible to overlook, at least when the reader is alive to the possibility of something of the kind. But there are other instances of Tillich's habit of reversing Kierkegaard's opinions in the course of interpreting him that are less obvious and much more important in the long run. These are found in places where parts of his system are developed from a starting-point suggested by a prominent element in Kierkegaard's thinking. Sometimes key phrases in the system are involved. So, from this angle, the study of Tillich's relation of opposition to Kierkegaard has not simply historical interest but becomes important for an understanding of the theology of the *Systematic Theology*.

Probably the most striking of the instances where Tillich borrows from Kierkegaard and almost at once utterly transforms what he has borrowed into its opposite is one occurring near the beginning of the *Systematic Theology*. Here Tillich is setting out his two 'formal criteria' of theology. The first criterion is stated thus:

> '*The object of theology is what concerns us ultimately. Only those propositions are theological which deal with their object in so far as it can become a matter of ultimate concern for us.*'[1]

Tillich connects his category of 'ultimate concern' with Kierkegaard's notion of 'infinite passion and interest'. He is no doubt referring to Kierkegaard's description in the *Concluding Unscientific Postscript*, where Christianity is said to be 'in its maximum an infinite, personal, passionate interest in one's eternal happiness'.[2] And this reference opens up aspects of his category which otherwise might be difficult to notice.

'Ultimate concern' and 'infinite interest' are nearly enough alike to make it seem possible to use them as synonyms in some contexts. At any rate, there is no plain contradiction between them. Yet the context in which they are used is, in each case, very different. Tillich's statement is a general one, establishing a universal class, that of the theological proposition.

[1] *ST* I, p. 12. The italics are in the original.   [2] *Op. cit.*, p. 33.

Kierkegaard's is particular, or at least more particular. It also seeks to define, but it defines a particular religion—Christianity—and it draws no universal conclusions out of itself.

Perhaps the reader may notice in passing that Tillich has left out the word *personal* from the phrase he has taken from Kierkegaard. This fact has some significance, as will later appear.

Next, Tillich adds his 'second criterion'. This, he says, answers the question concerning the content of our ultimate concern. It runs as follows:

> *'Our ultimate concern is that which determines our being or not-being. Only those statements are theological which deal with their object in so far as it can become a matter of being or not-being for us.'*[1]

The second proposition, we are told, is derived from an analysis of the concept 'ultimate concern'. If so, it must be asked what are the principles on which the analysis has been made, for nothing has been said about these. It is true that Tillich mentions that his formal criteria are both 'derived from the whole of the Christian message',[2] but he gives us no further information, and a great deal is needed before it becomes clear where *being* and *not-being* have sprung from. For instance, how is 'whole of the Christian message' identified? What constitutes its wholeness? Again, supposing that the message is identified, what method has been used to distil these two abstract propositions from the total *kerygma*? Can we be sure that the very quintessence of Christianity lies in these brief and abstract sentences which, in any case, claim to describe not Christianity in itself but theology in general? Decidedly, the second proposition raises many questions and answers none. Why should our ultimate concern be identified with our being and not-being? What hinders the claims of other possible contents? In short, why this analysis rather than another?

The answer appears to be that Tillich is operating with an 'idea' of what an ultimate concern must be, just as he builds his system upon the 'idea' of theology that he has espoused. I will be considering the nature of this idea in another

---

[1] *Op. cit.*, p. 14. The italics are in the original. [2] *Ibid.*, p. 11.

place when I come to discuss how Tillich builds his system.[1] For the moment my concern is with the way in which the second criterion has left behind everything which Kierkegaard stands for. This analysis of ultimate concern which has been brought in so silently shares no common ground with an 'infinite, personal, passionate interest in one's eternal happiness'. For Kierkegaard an infinite interest arises because the individual stands confronted with the claims of Christianity and has to make his personal decision in the face of this claim. Why one discovers an infinite interest in one's eternal happiness is for the simple reason that the Christian gospel promises this particular promise. Christianity, says Kierkegaard:

> '. . . proposes to bestow an eternal happiness upon the individual man, thus presuming an infinite interest in his eternal happiness as *conditio sine qua non*; an interest by virtue of which the individual hates father and mother, and thus doubtless also snaps his fingers at speculative systems and outlines of universal history.'[2]

Christianity's proposal is made to the individual man, and he must respond to the proposal—this particular proposal and no other. In such a context it is meaningless to speak about someone's infinite interest in the abstract and in connection with a universal concept called *being*. Nor is being-in-general made one whit less abstract by being called 'our' being. It is that kind of being still which universally characterizes the entity Man (an entity which nobody has ever anywhere encountered), and it is defined as 'the whole of human reality, the structure, the meaning, and the aim of existence'[3]—a definition requiring for its elucidation one of those speculative systems at which the individual man snaps his fingers. Instead of the individual personally concentrated upon his eternal happiness, Tillich introduces humanity at large making speculative statements about the meaning of existence as such.

The example of the two Criteria of theology is only one out of many instances where Tillich handles material taken from Kierkegaard, and through the rest of the present study I shall be uncovering a consistent pattern of the same sort. First, the

[1] See below, Chapter IV.   [2] *Op. cit.*, p. 19.   [3] *Op. cit.*, p. 14.

Kierkegaardian, 'existentialist' material is introduced by Tillich, and then it is promptly transformed by being related to his system and 'placed' there. But it happens that the case of the two Criteria is a more than usually revealing one, because the two propositions setting forth the Criteria make visible the two stages involved in the work of turning Kierkegaard into anti-Kierkegaard. By formalizing Kierkegaard's thesis that the individual can be infinitely concerned about his eternal happiness, Tillich gets rid of the individual and his happiness. In place of these he sets up a contentless 'ultimate concern'. He then is in a position to introduce an entirely different object of concern than Kierkegaard's happiness-promised-by-Christianity, namely *being or not-being*. And, when he follows this second step immediately by general pronouncements concerning the nature of man, his 'true being', his relation to the infinite, his meaning, and his destiny,[1] he has arrived at his resting-place—the system.

In claiming for his two Criteria that they are valid for every theology whatsoever, Tillich has in fact argued that they are based upon the true idea of theology. After all, that is the sole basis on which they could be claimed to be valid. And, if *being* is the true content of the concept of ultimate concern, it represents the true idea of that concept, thus helping to define the nature of theology-in-general. The second criterion, indeed, is like the first in being a formal one. It does not prescribe any concrete content for any particular theology, but, as Tillich points out, it 'excludes contents' not having the right to enter 'the theological realm'.[2] This veto power is easily seen to be the means whereby Tillich's system exercises its authority over all individual religions. No content which does not meet the approval of the system of ideas that constitutes theology-in-general is allowed to appear. It is promptly denied to be worthy of a place within the theological realm. Therefore, if it should happen to be noticed at all, it will be dismissed out of hand as meaningless. The speculative system at which Kierkegaard's Christian believer snaps his fingers is given authority

[1] *Ibid.* The passage is quoted in full below, pp. 90–1.
[2] *Ibid.*, pp. 14–15.

45

here to examine the contents of the Christian faith (and of all other faiths as well) and declare what is or is not logically permissible, what has or has not the power required to make it a genuine ultimate concern.

Once theology has been identified with a regulative idea— i.e. ultimate concern for our being or not-being—then the way is open for it to be fused with a constitutive idea, with a special metaphysic of being, a specific ontology. One speculative theory will decide henceforth what is true and what is false in the utterances of religious faith. Without fear of contradiction it will proceed to examine the words spoken by religious believers (or by kerygmatic theologians) and declare what these words 'really' mean. Religious faith must then bow down and worship the system. Now, when Tillich proceeds to make an analysis of a concept such as *ultimate concern* without explaining on what principles the analysis is being carried out, the reader can be certain that he is making use of a consistent system-known. In the course of the *Systematic Theology* and his other writings the outlines of this system are methodically set out. No one could possibly miss the fact of the system being there. What even the careful reader may not realize is the extent to which the system, purely by virtue of being a speculative system of comprehensive scope, has been given authority over the realm of faith.

Although it has been constructed so as to take into account the so-called existentialist revolt against Hegel, Tillich's system still stands firmly in the Hegelian succession. Nothing else is at all possible, since its author and builder follows the way of synthesis in the steps of the classical German philosophers. How little Tillich has parted from Hegelianism can be discovered in the surprising aptness of Kierkegaard's criticisms of the System, when these are applied to the system that shapes the *Systematic Theology*. In the matter of whether system shall have authority over faith, or whether faith must assert its authority in spite of system, Kierkegaard's insight into the issues involved remains completely relevant to the present day. Very much to the point are his remarks concerning the claim of system to support and establish Christian truth:

46

'Speculative philosophy does not by any means say that Christianity is false; on the contrary it says that speculative philosophy grasps the truth of Christianity. Surely one could not demand anything more; has Christianity ever claimed to be more than the truth? And when speculative philosophy apprehends its truth, everything is in order. And yet . . . it is not Christianity which is and was and remains the truth, and what the speculative philosopher understands is not that Christianity is the truth; no, it is the philosopher's understanding of Christianity which constitutes the truth of Christianity.'

His conclusion is that the system-builder is bound to think that truth is given in the system, so that 'it is not the case that speculative philosophy has arrived at a true understanding, but that the truth which it understands has come into being'.[1]

The claim which Tillich makes for theology according to his idea (i.e. theology-in-general) is exactly along these lines. If theology is methodological knowledge, then it follows—as I have already argued[2]—that the knowledge which it communicates must be knowledge that it itself has brought into being. Here Kierkegaard, after snapping his fingers at speculation as such, lays a deliberate hand on the weak point of the speculative programme to link itself with religious faith: the question of authority. It is impossible for the system-builder to adjust himself to the authority of faith as the source of truth. He renders his system superfluous the moment he attempts to do anything of the kind. The most he can do is to agree that faith is an indispensable element in the business of arriving at truth. But he must always stand by the authority of his system to demonstrate *where truth is and where it is not*. As he views the world, all religion contains some truth, some error. And system is the threshing machine which separates (for the first time) chaff from grain. With characteristically bitter wit, Kierkegaard puts this point strongly by allowing the speculative philosopher to congratulate himself on his achievements in these terms:

'. . . I have not only believed, but I have even explained Christianity, and shown that as it was expounded by the Apostles

1 *Op. cit.*, p. 200.   2 See above, p. 21.

and appropriated in the early centuries it was only to a certain degree true; but that now, through the interpretation of speculative philosophy it has become the true truth, whence I must ask for a suitable reward on account of my services to Christianity.'[1]

To a certain degree true . . . Nothing perhaps that Kierkegaard says has so much relevance to Tillich's view of religious faith. However, this is to anticipate another aspect of the attempt to make a synthesis of speculation and faith. The first and fundamental problem that besets the road of synthesis is the question of authority arising in the form of the question, 'Faith or knowledge?' And the synthesist, who wants to answer, 'Both!' finds himself compelled to murmur also *sotto voce*, 'But, nevertheless,—in the last resort and if absolutely necessary——knowledge first!' The would-be philosophical theologian, to use Kierkegaard's vivid image, sets his hand to the plough and looks about for something to know. And, either he must be willing to subject his faith to the limits of his methodological knowledge, or else he must be prepared to find his knowledge sometimes giving way to faith. To the extent that Tillich suggests that his own systematic theology has found a means of avoiding this dilemma through the use of a special theological method he has failed, in fact, to disclose this method in full. There can be no doubt that he stands upon the basis of a knowledge which is *prior* knowledge, a knowledge which is answerable only to itself and which abides no question from the side of faith but is free in and for itself.[2]

This knowledge is where the idea of theology (as Tillich understands theology) has its source. In the light of this knowledge his system (the *Systematic Theology*) is built. Such a system at once displays what is conceived to be the genuine nature of theology-in-general and also demonstrates how the *true truth* concerning Christianity must be arrived at by the system's interpretative activity. But the system can be built solely because the system-builder has trustworthy *prior* knowledge

[1] *Op. cit.*, pp. 207–8.
[2] Therefore Tillich's theological Method (the method of correlation) rests upon and is explicable only in terms of his idea of theology. See above, pp. 27 ff., and below, Chapter VI.

of what he must build. His system-built rests upon system-known. Everything hangs together, like a chain suspended from a hook, when once the all-important idea of theology is not questioned. This idea is what the philosophical theologian, with his hand resting upon the kerygmatic plough, has to look about him in order to discover. This is what he has to know; and, once he knows it, then the chosen theological method of the system can go into operation, interpreting Christianity and showing how Christian theology (properly understood) is *the* theology. Only on the basis of a completely authoritative knowledge can the system offer its services to the Christian faith.

Tillich makes faith the servant of knowledge because he has started out from the assumption that truth comes nowhere else but in the whole that a system gives. It is this assumption above all that casts him in the rôle of anti-Kierkegaard, making the contrast between the two outlooks so absolute. For, while Tillich believes that thinking and system are inseparable, Kierkegaard denies that any individual can ever live in time and space and, without ceasing to exist, sum up the whole of reality in a system. The title of the volume containing Kierkegaard's most sustained assault upon the System was not casually chosen, for the *Concluding Unscientific Postscript to the Philosophical Fragments* indicates, in its mock-grandiloquent repudiation of the philosophical ideal of knowledge of the whole, a good deal about its author's convictions concerning the limits of human thought. And the following confession given within the book helps to explain the title further:

> 'When it is impossible to think existence, and the existing individual nevertheless thinks, what does this signify? It signifies that he thinks intermittently, that he thinks before and after. His thought cannot attain to absolute continuity. It is only in a fantastic sense that an existing individual can be constantly *sub specie aeterni*.'[1]

[1] *Op. cit.*, p. 293. The phrase *sub specie aeterni* is Kierkegaard's own version of Spinoza's well-known *sub specie aeternitatis*, and it rings like a bell through his writings. For him the attempt to view life 'under the aspect of the Eternal' is the fundamental error of the System because it ignores the fact that we are not God Almighty but men living under the conditions of existence. Hence all his attacks upon the System are based on this either-or: admit individual existence or else fantastic knowledge *sub specie aeterni*—but not both.

Because Kierkegaard does not think it possible for living men to attain to the wisdom of eternal truth, so he teaches that it is needful for each of us to live by the authority of a faith not objectively certified but trusted 'in subjectivity'—i.e. in the individual's response. Therefore he looks for no higher justification for his faith in the Christian message than that of 'infinite passion'. He certainly could not contemplate looking for it in a concept of being equivalent to 'the whole of human reality'—which is Tillich's basic theological standard. To take one's place inside existence and from this position to speak about something involving the whole of human reality seems to him to be fantastic and also comical, because it is trying to be inside and outside at the same time—something like a man trying to meet himself unexpectedly coming round a corner.

In his rôle of anti-Kierkegaard, Tillich takes for granted that man must endeavour to see himself *sub specie aeterni*, since this is the philosophical quest. He takes for granted that there can be—and must be—a true continuity in man's thinking, since the evidence for such a continuity is shown by the existence of a 'classical' philosophical tradition. It is from this essentialist viewpoint that he surveys existentialist statements, seeking to incorporate them (after suitable modification) within the totality of his vision. Kierkegaard turns away from the System because he finds that the individual and his relation to his existence is lost there. Tillich builds his system because he thinks that embedded in the nature of every man is the urge to know the ultimate truth about himself and his world, to ask essential and not merely existential questions, and to press on until indubitable knowledge is gained.

In order to discover the kind of confidence which Tillich feels as the root of his conviction about man's ability to see life steadily and see it whole, I shall now turn to look at his theory of the place of reason in man. This will open up the system to view, displaying how it comes about that the authoritative idea becomes enthroned in the midst.

Postscript: Tillich and the Existentialists

While most critics and commentators have proclaimed Tillich an existentialist theologian, there have been a few dissentients. In *An Analytical Philosophy of Religion* Willem F. Zuurdeeg links him with Hegel and the Greek metaphysical tradition, remarking: 'There is a modern element in the problems which he discusses, but the way in which these problems are treated appears to be far from modern.'[1] Zuurdeeg notes that existentialism can be fitted into the system only by ignoring the existentialist denunciation of ontology, and that Tillich, when describing existentialism, suppresses whatever he finds inconvenient to admit.[2] A condensed but stimulating analysis of Tillich's theology set out in a chapter of Robert C. Johnson's *Authority in Protestant Theology*[3] also finds the inspiration of his system in nineteenth-century German sources (Schleiermacher and Hegel). According to Johnson the existentialist label applied to Tillich 'is misleading if it is used to associate him directly with any particular type or tradition of philosophical existentialism'. The system can be called 'existentialist theology' solely on account of having its own theory about the meaning of existence.[4] Tavard too agrees that Tillich's relationship with existentialism is far from being one of actual identification with the movement. He writes: 'Though Tillich's thought is clearly existential, it cannot be identified with Existentialism itself: Tillich is not a disciple of Heidegger or Sartre, Jaspers or Camus.'[5]

If it is a little puzzling to hear that the system is 'clearly existential' and yet not the same as Existentialism, the clue to Tavard's distinction is to be found in Zuurdeeg's parallel distinction between a 'modern element' in the problems posed by the system and the far from modern way in which the

[1] Nashville, Abingdon Press, 1958 (London, Allen & Unwin, 1959), p. 152.
[2] *Ibid.*, p. 165.
[3] Philadelphia, Westminster Press, 1959; Chapter V, 'The Contextual Approach', pp. 111–43.
[4] *Ibid.*, p. 114.
[5] *Op. cit.*, p. 11 footnote 32. Tillich's various comments on existentialism are discussed on pp. 10–11.

problems are treated. This seems to indicate that what is existential or modern about the system is more of a veneer upon the surface that anything integral to it. And such a conclusion is confirmed by Tillich's own witness. He has recorded how, in Marburg in 1925, he began work on his *Systematic Theology* and at the same time encountered existentialism in the philosophy of Heidegger, who was then teaching in the same university. His record continues: 'I resisted, I tried to learn, I accepted the new way of thinking more than the answers it gave.'[1] So it would appear that existentialism has indeed influenced his system, but externally and without disturbing his basic essentialist vision. It is not really surprising that Zuurdeeg should find that he presents a partial and one-sided picture of existentialism, for the account he gives is an essentialist's view of the movement—which is something like an agnostic's view of religious faith, or a Marxist's view of private enterprise.

Thus the system can be approached in two directions. Attending to its 'modern aspects', readers may look at what it has in common with Heidegger and his brethren. Or, considering the way in which it solves its problems, they may interpret it in terms of traditional metaphysics. Arthur C. Cochrane begins his analysis of the system in *The Existentialists and God* by saying that Tillich's philosophy and theology 'can be evaluated properly only in the light of religious and atheistic existentialism.'[2] Yet the conclusions he reaches are very close indeed to those of Kraemer, who pays no attention to existentialism but sees in the system 'pure Greek rationalism' and calls Tillich crypto-Hegelian and crypto-Neo-Platonic.[3] A judicious summing-up of the situation is provided by Randall, who writes:

'The immediate background of Tillich's philosophy is certain of the more ontological and historical strains of nineteenth-century German speculation. . . . To express his own insights, Tillich employs the language of the existential philosophy. Whether this is the best possible language in which to put what he has to say is immaterial.'[4]

[1] *The Theology of Paul Tillich* ('Autobiographical Reflections'), p. 14.
[2] Philadelphia, Westminster Press, 1956, p. 77.
[3] *Op. cit.*, pp. 439, 434.   [4] *The Theology of Paul Tillich*, p. 132.

Randall evidently believes that existentialist words do not necessarily mean existentialist thoughts.

Nevertheless, we should not conclude that the connection between Tillich and twentieth-century existentialism is purely a matter of verbal borrowings. Although the system need not be evaluated *only* in the light shed by this school, it can be so evaluated. There are many close resemblances between the best-known modern existentialist thinkers and Tillich, and whole areas of their thought have a common basis. Here Heidegger is the most obvious influence, but there is also a surprising overall likeness between the thought of Jaspers and Tillich's system.[1] The reason for this affinity is to be found in the fact that twentieth-century existentialism in general, having been inspired by Husserl even more than by Kierkegaard, contains strong essentialist elements which tend to neutralize its genuine existentialist foundation. Hence most of the school, following Heidegger, value existential analysis solely as a starting-point for the construction of a metaphysic; and it is interesting to note that there has been a revulsion even from the name of *existentialism*—Heidegger again leading. Tillich's sympathy with this direction in thought, as a self-confessed essentialist, is obvious.

Looking at the situation broadly, then, I would agree with Tavard when he says that Tillich's thought is 'clearly existential', if by this is meant that it shares some common ground with modern existentialists' theories. But this is a very different thing from being related to the anti-metaphysical existentialism of Kierkegaard (and of Dostoyevski and Nietzsche too, incidentally). Just as Henry Ford of the Model 'T' days allowed his customers to choose any colour provided it was black, Tillich will join forces with all existentialists provided they support essentialism.

[1] Surprising in view of Jaspers's declared opposition to biblical religion. Cochrane draws some striking parallels between the thought of Jaspers and Tillich. See also my article: 'The Language of Transcendence and the Language of Biblical Faith', *Theology and Life* III 4 (November 1960).

III

DIVINE REASON

THE EARLIEST of all Tillich's writings specially written for the English-speaking world was the first part of *The Interpretation of History*. There, under the general title of 'On the Boundary: An Autobiographical Sketch', he makes the most illuminating comment:

> 'I nurtured [*sic*] German Idealism, and I do not believe that I can ever unlearn what I learned there . . . I am an idealist if idealism means the assertion of the identity of thinking and being as the principle of truth.'[1]

Although Tillich does not always express himself in his later works exactly as he does in this relatively early one, these sentences take us into the heart of his system and reveal the tap-root of his *Systematic Theology*. In them is the direct expression of the nature of the idea of theology-in-general, which is the hook supporting the full weight of his system and the source of all his judgments concerning the truth of Christianity and every other religious faith.

First of all, Tillich uncovers what for him is 'the principle of truth'. The identity of thinking and being is the axiom with which he begins, and so he rules out from the start all ideas which are not founded upon his chosen principle. On this score he can ignore any criticism of the ideas of the system as the necessary form of all human thought. That thinking and being are identical means that anything in the history of human thought worth considering at all must play a part in reproducing the structure of reality. Therefore, all thinking must be

[1] *Op. cit.* (London/New York, Charles Scribner's Sons, 1936. Part One translated by N. A. Rasetzki; Parts Two, Three and Four by Elsa L. Talmey), pp. 60–1.

structural thinking, i.e. thinking in a system. As an argument this one recalls the reasoning parodied in Dr Samuel Johnson's line:

'Who drives fat horses must himself be fat.'

But then Dr Johnson's common-sense principles are a far cry from the principles of idealism. The good Doctor trusted his senses, while the idealist starts by positing the unity of all reality. For the latter there is no possible way for truth to be formed in the mind unless the order of thought mirrors the order of being—and indeed contributes to that order.

Secondly, if truth is bound to the system, the creation of systems is characteristic of man in his capacity of contemplator of truth. Thus to the idea of the system is added the idea of man as the thinker-in-systems. Since thought and being are one, so man and being must share a conspicuous identity. In so far as he is a thinker-in-systems man cannot be separated from the true and the real. To Tillich's idealistic reasoning man's status in the Universe as part of the very stuff of reality is involved in the principle of truth. He concludes his explanation of that principle by saying:

'Finally, it cannot be denied that a correspondence exists between the human spirit and reality, which is probably best expressed in the concept of "Meaning" and which led Hegel to talk of the unity of the objective with the subjective in an absolute spirit.'[1]

One further element must be added, however, before Tillich's principle leads directly to his idea of theology. This element is the *logos*, the rational *word* of human speech. For idealism demands that man's reason shall not be considered primarily as man's way of assessing his environment. His reason is in no sense his own possession, being rather ultimate reality unfolding itself in man's spirit. Tillich explains how truth is called in Greek *alethia*, or that which is not hidden. He goes on to say:

'In the word—the logos—being ceases to be hidden; in the rational form being becomes meaningful and understandable.

[1] *Ibid.*, p. 61.

Being and the word in which it is conceived cannot be separated. Therefore, wherever beings are, there is logos of being, a form and structure in which its meaning is manifest. But, although logos is in every being, it is outspoken only in that being which has the word, the rational word, the word of truth and light—that is, in man.'[1]

Having the gift of language, man is linked with a realm transcending all the kingdoms of the world. The rational word functions as his passport to the kingdom of being. In his *Systematic Theology* Tillich assigns the interpretation of reason as *logos* to a 'classical' tradition reaching from Parmenides to Hegel. (Note that this appeal to a single line of philosophy makes Greek thought find its genuine succession in German idealism.) He defines reason as 'the structure of the mind which enables the mind to grasp and to transform reality'. And he adds, 'the denial of reason in the classical sense is antihuman because it is antidivine'.[2]

At this point Tillich's principle of truth makes contact with his idea of theology. The true and the real (thinking and being) are one. And in the *logos* (the rational word of man the thinker-in-systems) truth and reality find a voice to speak with. In the *logos* alone the divine and the human meet. It follows that the principle of truth, made vocal in the *logos* under the rational form of the thinker's system, can sound forth in its divine aspect. There is no need, then, for theology to wait until some religion or other supplies material so that true thinking about the divine may begin. Instead, man as the thinker-in-systems already knows the truth about the divine. By virtue of the presence within him of divine reason, man already possesses a true idea of theology. All that remains now to be explained is just why reason is divine as well as human.

An explanation is readily available. The *logos* is inseparable

---

[1] *The Protestant Era* ('Philosophy and Theology'), p. 101.

[2] *ST* I, p. 72. Dorothy M. Emmet points out that Tillich does not argue the case for a *logos* philosophy but assumes it. She asks how we are to know that we can accept the Hegelian view of the coincidence of subjective and objective reason to the exclusion of other views, since it is not enough to appeal to the view we favour (in this case, idealism) and name it the 'classical' one (*The Theology of Paul Tillich*, pp. 207–8).

from the concept of being, and the *logos* declares the concept of being to be identical with the concept of deity. Thus, following the terminology of medieval metaphysical theology, Tillich says that God is to be thought of as being-itself (*esse ipsum*). Exactly what it is that Tillich understands by this designation —how much and how little he asserts when he uses it—is something of crucial importance and something that will be clarified, I hope, as my argument is set out in later chapters. For the moment, however, my concern is not what Tillich means when he says that 'God is being-itself or the absolute';[1] it is what use he puts the definition to—whatever it may mean —once he has introduced it. Obviously requiring explanation is the way in which Tillich uses the concept of being-itself in order to show how reason brings forward this concept as the authoritative one and the one alone making theology possible.

In this connection I should like to pick up again the statement examined briefly in my first chapter[2] concerning the authority exercised by Tillich's philosophical theology, a statement voicing the sentiment that:

'. . . if we speak of the actuality of God, we first assert that he is not God if he is not being-itself. Other assertions about God can be made theologically only on this basis.'[3]

I have already pointed out how final these words are. No appeal is allowed against the theological assertion here asserted. This is *the* foundation of theology, and other foundation can no man lay! Moreover, Tillich's philosophical theology confi- dently claims to be universally and completely adequate as a foundation for all religious thinking whatsoever—'the founda- tion is implicit in every religious thought concerning God'.[4] Because he possesses the true idea of theology, Tillich is sure that he can tell all theologians what they must do in order to earn their title. ('Theologians must make explicit what is implicit in religious thought and expression.')[5] In addition, because he possesses the ultimate principle of truth, he is sure

[1] *Ibid.*, p. 239.   [2] See above, p. 26.   [3] *Ibid.*, pp. 238–9.
[4] *Ibid.*, p. 239.
[5] *Ibid.* For a comment on Tillich's use of the words *implicit* and *implies* see below pp. 100 ff.

that he can tell all the theologians what they must do in order to make meaningful statements and to keep in touch with reality. ('They must begin with the most abstract and completely unsymbolic statement which is possible, namely, that God is being-itself or the absolute.')[1]

Other assertions about God can be made theologically only on this basis . . .; the consequences of this categorical proclamation are far-reaching. Tillich is ruling out entirely the possibility that there can be any theology anywhere except the system of philosophical theology which he presents, or, at least, one built upon an identical basis. His idea of theology judges and is not judged. But, in excluding the false, what is the nature of the true that he proposes instead? How far does the principle of truth extend? These are the necessary questions which present themselves. And the answers are to be found in his presentation of the *logos*.

In the rational word being ceases to be hidden. In the rational word being becomes meaningful and understandable. Granted then that being-itself is God, in man who—as man—has the rational word God is not hidden but becomes meaningful and understandable. At one point in man, at any rate, the biblical description of God, 'Truly, thou art a God who hidest thyself' (Isa. 45.15), is not accurate. Tillich insists that the one point where man finds God to be entirely unhidden is where he can say that God is being-itself—and there is no other point where the same conditions prevail:

> 'The statement that God is being-itself is a nonsymbolic statement. It does not point beyond itself. It means what it says directly and properly.'[2]

The interesting thing in this connection is that Tillich does not make the remark that he might be expected to make. He does not refer to the word that uncovers the true Deity as the word

---

[1] *ST* I, p. 239. Note the assumption that theologians normally deal with symbolic terms.

[2] *Ibid.*, p. 238. Tillich has qualified this opinion and now states that the statement is 'the boundary line at which both the symbolic and the nonsymbolic coincide' (*ST* II, p. 10). See also *The Theology of Paul Tillich*, p. 335. All the same, this qualification does not affect the claim that saying God is being-itself is a direct and proper statement.

of revelation. And yet, following the most proper use of that term, revelation is exactly what takes place when the *logos* is outspoken in man. The rational word in man points directly and says, '*This* is God. God is *here*.' And it speaks properly and nonsymbolically in order to declare the true nature of God, making explicit what is implicit in religious revelation. Since God alone can reveal God, the *logos* by definition is well fitted for its revelatory task. It makes manifest the meaning of being-itself because it is one with being.

Once Tillich's idea of theology has been brought into relation with his principle of truth, one of the most elusive facets of his system is in full view: his description of the relationship between philosophy and theology. Probably the best approach to this subject is through the definition of theology given in *The Interpretation of History*. There he calls theology *theonomous metaphysics*, a title that might be paraphrased loosely as 'thought controlled by the divine'. Although he uses this definition no longer, it is a useful one and has the great merit of stating without equivocation that theology-in-general (the theology derived from his idea of theology) is merely one kind of metaphysical speculation and is not dependent upon any of the religions of mankind. For him knowledge as such is pregnant with the divine, or, as he states it in *The Interpretation of History*:

> '. . . thinking is rooted in the absolute as the foundation and abyss of meaning . . . theology and philosophy, religion and knowledge embrace each other.'[1]

In the *Systematic Theology*, however, he has dropped the phrase *theonomous metaphysics* (though he uses prominently the words *theonomy* and *theonomous*) and, instead of speaking about theology and philosophy embracing, he speaks about the two converging and diverging. He emphasizes that the two never meet: 'Neither is a conflict between theology and philosophy necessary, nor is a synthesis between them possible.'[2] Yet the reader would be wrong to imagine that there is any real change of mind involved in this change of presentation—getting rid of an odd

[1] *Op. cit.*, p. 39.
[2] *ST* I, p. 26. Much the same explanation is given in the essay 'Philosophy and Theology' in *The Protestant Era*, pp. 93 ff.

59

piece of furniture or two does not add up to refurnishing completely. Theology and philosophy have not been taken out of their mutual embrace. If the two are said never to meet, it is for the same reason that a smile and a frown could be said never to meet, because, being formed by the same set of muscles, the one 'converges' or 'diverges' in relation to the other so that when the one appears the other disappears. Just so, Tillich conceives the rôles of the philosopher and the theologian. The theologian is sometimes a philosopher. The philosopher is sometimes a theologian. Both are sometimes themselves. But the philosopher cannot avoid being sometimes a theologian-in-spite-of-himself and *vice versa*. And, Tillich warns us, the theologian must always be *also* a philosopher, for part of his work must be strictly non-theological, carried on solely by his philosophical alter-ego while his theological ego lies inactive. Should the 'hidden theologian' in the philosophical alter-ego of the theologian intrude while he is engaged in philosophical analysis, his philosophic conscience ought to protest and intervene.[1]

In so far as his principle of truth established his idea of theology Tillich has actually caused theology and philosophy to embrace. Man, informed of the true nature of deity through the indwelling of the *logos*, is philosopher and theologian at one and the same time. Yet, Tillich is very conscious of the fact that, although the idea of theology is detachable from any and all religions, yet in practice theologians work out their theologies in connection with some religion or other. Theology, aiming to establish a knowledge that is universally true (i.e. one operating with the genuine theological idea), nevertheless works upon definite religious material, material which belongs

[1] *ST* I, pp. 18 ff., 63. In the course of a television interview, Tillich was asked what he would have been had he not been a theologian. His answer was: 'My first answer is that I would be what I am anyhow, a philosopher; and my second answer would be that the dream of my earlier years was to become an architect: and since I did not become an architect I have become an architect of a theological system. So I am not too far away from my two desires' (*The Listener*, 14 December, 1961, p. 1026). In this statement is expressed both the conviction that the theologian must be, as a matter of course, a philosopher and the assumption that a theology is constructed as a building is, or as a metaphysical system is. An architect brings a new structure into being just as Kierkegaard said that the speculative thinker brings his speculative 'truth' into being.

to particular faiths and which is bound often to exclusive beliefs. No philosopher would think of dealing with the peculiar world that the theologian makes his own. Myths, dogmas, sacred rites—all the symbolic paraphernalia of religious cults— seem to have nothing in common with the rational word in man. Religion appears remote from the intellectual wisdom which the philosopher seeks to possess. By bringing theology into relation with specific religions (for example, when he speaks of *Christian* theology) Tillich has surely caused philosophy and theology to diverge . . . or so one might be led to imagine.

At the same time, no apparent divergence can ever lead to a total break in the mutual embrace of philosophy and theology. For, written into the system is the belief that knowledge-of-being and religious cults are both alike concerned with the divine. Theology, when it is least philosophical, is a partner of philosophy still. As Tillich has expressed it in *The Interpretation of History*, thinking is rooted in the absolute; or, as he says in the *Systematic Theology*, all thinking involves the presence of an unconditional element.[1] God can be called 'the absolute'[2] and also 'the unconditional'.[3] He is the One whom the philosopher seeks to know, and he is also the object of the religious believer's quest. Theologians, since they are concerned to *know* (i.e. to possess methodological knowledge) are partly philosophers. But equally they are partly believers—or at any rate they belong to the 'theological circle'. They are prepared to take seriously the claim of the religious believers to the extent of agreeing that the faith of the latter group is a genuine way of reaching the divine.[4]

[1] *Ibid.*, pp. 206–8.

[2] *Ibid.*, p. 239. In *The Theology of Paul Tillich* ('Reply to Interpretation and Criticism'), Tillich says that he now speaks no longer of the 'the absolute' or 'the unconditioned'. Instead he uses the terms 'unconditional' or 'ultimate' or 'infinite concern'. His wish is to make his concepts *existential* 'in the very beginning' (p. 340). But it may be doubted whether changing from noun to adjective really accomplishes much so long as these adjectives continue to derive their force from the substantive being-itself which is also 'the absolute'.

[3] *ST* II, p. 10.

[4] On the question of the theologian's faith and of the theological circle, see above pp. 30 ff; and below, pp. 218 ff.

61

That theology and philosophy cannot be parted is confirmed by Tillich's description of theology as mediation:

> '. . . the term "theo-logy" implies, as such, a mediation, namely, between the mystery, which is *theos*, and the understanding, which is *logos*.'[1]

Theology always preserves its *logos* character. It has the rational word upon which philosophy is built. And yet, unlike philosophy, it deals with mystery or *theos*. Now, if *theos* is taken to mean God, no mediation can be required, since God as being-itself is altogether at one with *logos*. But the concern of mediating-theology is not the divine as known (what I have called the revelation of the *logos*) but the divine as mystery. And the divine as mystery is not God as such but God as the religions of mankind know him. This understanding of *theos* is indicated in the definition of theology-in-general:

> '. . . "theo-logy", *logos* of *theos*, a rational interpretation of the religious substance of rites, symbols, and myths.'[2]

The mystery of *theos* lies in the fact that God is not directly, properly and non-symbolically indicated in human religions. Instead, he is indirectly known through the various ways in which the different faiths know him, viz., through rites, symbols and myths. The religious approach to him is symbolically undertaken, all religious statements having a symbolic character. Theology, therefore, mediates between the philosophical way of knowledge (reaching its peak in the non-symbolic statement that God is being-itself) and the symbols of religious faith (remaining opaque to knowledge until they have been explained, interpreted and exhibited in the form of methodological knowledge through theology's mediating work).

The fact that religion and religious beliefs have been brought into the realm of theology does not mean, of course, that they have authority there. The mediation of theology that brings knowledge (and so truth) into being is all-important, and

[1] *The Protestant Era*, Author's Preface, xxvii–xxviii.
[2] *ST* I, p. 16. This is the theology which is 'as old as religion'. See above, p. 19.

religion becomes just what the voice of theology-in-general declares it to be. Suppose, for example, that a rationalist were to adopt Tillich's definition of theology. For him rational interpretation would mean so analysing the religious substance of religious practices that this substance would be discovered to consist of an imaginative presentation symbolizing human possibilities.[1] As against the rationalist and anti-theistic humanism Tillich raises an idea of theology based on the idealistic principle of the identity of thinking and being. Divinity (identified with being) is therefore discovered directly by thinking. But the divine that is 'properly' approached by reason is indirectly discovered elsewhere, and this indirect, non-immediate approach to the divine is through the symbols accumulated in the religions of mankind. God is reached in two ways: philosophically and through faith.

I have argued that Tillich's conception of the discovery of God through the *logos* is a conception actually involving the idea of revelation. Since Tillich, in fact, recognizes two means whereby God ceases to be hidden, I shall call the revelation of God as being-itself 'primary revelation'. It deserves to be called primary because it comes straight to man through the divine indwelling of the *logos*. Then there follows a 'secondary revelation', the distinctive feature of this being that it is mediated and symbolic. Secondary revelation comes by way of the *logos* too, in its own way. How Tillich relates the symbolic message about the divine to the *logos* is a leading feature of the system, and I shall examine it shortly. What is immediately relevant, however, is to note how this symbolic message—which Tillich simply refers to as 'revelation'—must of necessity function through the *logos* in order to give any information at all about the divine. Did it not do so it could not be true, for it would not partake of the rational form which the *logos* brings

---

[1] This has actually been the method of rationalists from Ludwig Feuerbach's *The Essence of Christianity* to John Dewey's *A Common Faith*. When Dewey speaks of 'religion against the religious' he makes much the same distinction as Tillich does when he sets religious faith over against the idea of theology—only Dewey's idea of what constitutes 'the religious' (i.e. the real meaning of religious symbols) is different from Tillich's. See also below, p. 181.

to light. Instead, it would remain sunk in darkness, without meaning and opaque to the understanding. Yet this 'secondary revelation' (as I have called it) is not full of light either. It is not wholly understandable or meaningful. Were it so it would at once proceed to grasp and to transform reality—being in itself inseparable from reality—and banish the hiddenness of mystery.[1] As it is, it is secondary, incomplete, and partially divorced from reality, meaning what it says only indirectly, improperly and through the use of symbols. It cannot banish the darkness of mystery because it does not possess the rational word in its fulness and brightness. The mystery of *theos* is the subject-matter of secondary revelation. And this subject-matter the theologian takes in hand as it reaches him through holy books and sacred lore and mystic rites. He renders it at least partly intelligible, using the good offices of the *logos* as these are available in primary revelation.

In the economy of the system the distinction between primary and secondary revelation is far more vital than the distinction which Tillich labours to make between philosophy and theology. The latter distinction really breaks down, because as Tillich himself admits, in the last resort the system must hold that the two are the same. Every theologian worth his salt, Tillich insists, must be a philosopher as well. And the philosophers who turn out to be theologians in disguise, he says, are the creative ones.[2] But what sets some types of thinking apart from others, he also remarks, is that some (the philosophic) turn 'toward pure reality' in the power of the 'universal *logos*', while others (the theological) turn to find meaning in the 'particular *logos*'.[3] In the terminology which I have suggested

[1] Tillich remarks that the word *mystery* is derived from *muein*, 'closing the eyes' or 'closing the mouth' (*ST* I, p. 108). This makes *mystery* an anti-word to *truth*. The closing of eyes and mouth shows that all genuine mystery 'is experienced in an attitude which contradicts the attitude of ordinary cognition' (*ibid.*).

[2] *Ibid.*, p. 25. Compare the explanation of the 'theological impulse' in philosophers driving them to 'a statement about the concrete situation in which the logos of being can appear' which Tillich gives in *The Protestant Era* ('Philosophy and Theology'), pp. 101 ff.

[3] *Ibid.* Both the particular *logos* and the universal *logos* must certainly be taken to be revelatory.

this same thought can be put quite simply by saying that philosophers and theologians tend to follow the same course; but, while neither can escape making use of both primary and secondary revelation, philosophers tend to avoid secondary revelation in their conscious philosophizing, while theologians must use secondary revelation prominently always, though not (of course) exclusively every step of the way.

Once again, Tillich's manner of presentation does not give the reader a view of the essential outlines of his system. The issue is not philosophy *or* theology, since this problem is resolved in the concept of the final unity of all knowledge. The issue is why secondary revelation should have claims as well as primary revelation. Why is it not enough to turn towards 'pure reality'? Why should there be a particular *logos* as well as a universal *logos*? Why should there be *theos* as well as *logos*? And how is mystery related to reason? The answers to these questions can be found in the *Systematic Theology*. But they have to be dug out of it. They do not lie on the surface.

The problem opens out when it is realized that primary and secondary revelations are two distinct channels of communication with the divine. They cannot be combined any more than a radio operator can tune into two different wave-lengths at once. Yet they are both revelations (that is why knowledge and religion 'embrace'); both can be heard on the same radio-set; both are rooted in divine reason. At this point the query arises why anyone should trouble his head over secondary revelation, with its uncertain results, when primary revelation is available. Why tune in on a wave-length that gives nothing but cryptic and to some extent misleading signals when you can dial to another which broadcasts thoroughly reliable news in plain English? The reason, we learn, is that primary revelation is not sufficiently available to meet our needs. Secondary revelation has—somehow—to fill at least part of the gap between what we have and what we undoubtedly require. For the idealism that gives the system its orientation believes that we cannot remain content to accept existence as we find it, since this would be to accept shadow instead of substance. The identity of thinking and being is to be discerned only with difficulty here and now, where what is most visible is 'a split in reality between potentiality and actuality'.[1] In this world we inhabit:

> 'Being is finite, existence is self-contradictory, and life is ambiguous.'[2]

Therefore the *logos*, instead of reigning in the world and over it, does not appear to us in its fulness but merely potentially. Tillich explains how philosophers, although following the way of true devotion to right reason ('ontological reason'), never encounter reason in its essential perfection but always as it is involved in the 'predicament' presented by the conditions of earthly life. The universal *logos* itself appears to human eyes, like everything in the terrestial sphere, split and spoiled. Here the split results in the *logos* being parted from its own 'depths'. The depths of reason disappear under the conditions of existence to reappear in the guise of mystery. But mystery, fortunately, can be revealed (i.e. experienced in secondary revelation) and, when revealed, discloses 'the ground and abyss of reason' (i.e. reason's power, positively and negatively experienced). In encountering the revelation of mystery man knows something because he really has experienced something. But he knows in an extraordinary way, because he cannot put his knowledge into conceptual terms. What he knows is experienced in a state where the mind acts outside its normal conceptual processes, a state commonly called *ecstasy*. Since the experience of ecstasy is a real experience it is not irrational, or without the *logos*, but rather extra-rational, or not coming specifically within the purview of 'ontological reason'. It is an

---

[1] *ST* II, p. 21. The reason for this split is the division between being and existence, which is the subject of the next chapter. The 'reality' referred to in the quotation is 'the whole of being as it is encountered', which Tillich contrasts with 'being as a whole' or that being which is identical with thinking. Both Randall and Emmet point out that this distinction makes sense only within the presuppositions of idealism (*The Theology of Paul Tillich*, pp. 137, 203–7).

[2] *ST* I, p. 81. 'But, although every man has the word of truth potentially, not every man has it actually and no man has it perfectly. Therefore, philosophy asks for the way in which man can find the revealing word, the *logos* of being' (*The Protestant Era*, p. 101). Because of the ambiguity of life the philosopher must ask for revelation; he does not possess it actually.

experience of 'ecstatic reason'. And in this experience the hidden depths of the *logos* are revealed, though they are not indeed made known in the same way as primary revelation makes the truth known. Human reason—*split* reason—is lifted beyond itself into the realm of pure, ultimate reality which is outside its earth-bound limits. As Tillich explains the event:

> 'Ecstasy unites the experience of the abyss to which reason in all its functions is driven with the experience of the ground in which reason is grasped by the mystery of its own depth and of the depth of being generally.'[1]

Such a view assumes that, in the experience of ecstasy, man's reason goes beyond itself only to come back to its true self. Ecstatic reason is reason still, belonging to the *logos* and hence divine. Secondary revelation is as truly revelation as is primary revelation, although necessarily indirect because not transmitting the rational word.

Inferior in 'meaningfulness' to primary revelation, secondary revelation brings to our consciousness the effective power of the divine. Revelation of mystery means bringing part of the resplendent reality of the *logos* into our darkened world—a light which otherwise would not shine there. Without understanding the ecstatic experience as a rational word bearing knowledge concerning his being and all being, man can feel the genuine experience of the *power of being* borne in upon his existence. After all, the *logos*—in whatever shape it comes—is the *logos* of being, the bearer of truth and the guarantor of reality. So man knows that, where he experiences *theos*, there he experiences the power of the real; even though he has received no unambiguous revelation of the true God being-itself. But in terms of religious faith this means that every religious believer can trust his faith—and must trust it—knowing that there is some revelation of the true God in it. Yet he can never be quite sure how much actual

---

[1] *ST* I, p. 113. Randall points out that Tillich's metaphor of *depth* follows Boehme and Schelling (whose later philosophy was greatly influenced by Boehme). Here the Platonic tradition uses the metaphor of *above*. But both metaphors refer to that which lies 'one step beyond intellect' (*The Theology of Paul Tillich*, p. 143).

revelation he receives through his religious beliefs and practices, since he does not know how much is there of the divine and how much of the irrational, the misleading, the fanciful and the unreal. For the characteristic of secondary revelation is that it can point to the truth yet never to the truth solely. It cannot express being-itself properly, directly or non-symbolically. Being is encountered in secondary revelation always in a disguised form, appearing there as the mystery which is *theos*— truth hidden still in the revelation that illuminates but does not banish mystery. Secondary revelation inevitably lacks the full disclosure of the divine reality abiding in the rational word and appearing with it.

Because of these limiting characteristics inseparable from secondary revelation, the need for the mediating work of theology is evident. The apologetic theologian is one who mediates between mystery and understanding, and religious believers require the services of theologians who are also philosophers in order to prevent their religion from becoming 'narrow and superstitious' from lack of a synthesis between the faith which they profess and the cultural situation in which they stand and through which they interpret their existence.[1] The apologetic theologian, busying himself with the task of setting out a philosophical theology, is indeed an indispensable figure since he is the one who holds in one synoptic view the universal and the particular *logos*, forgetting neither primary nor secondary revelation in his concern for the true and the real.

At this point it may be useful to raise the question as to why Tillich does not use the word *revelation* in connection with the universal *logos* but reserves it solely for the truth conveyed through the particular *logos*. Of course, this way of speaking follows the normal restriction of the word to the area of religion. Tillich may find it easier to fall in with the ordinary usage (shown in the common antithesis: *human reason* or *divine revelation*) rather than stop to point out that in his system reason itself is divine. But, if so, then we have here another example of his failure to make explicit that the customary forms of speech will not reproduce his thinking.

[1] *ST* I, pp. 5–7.

One of the remarkable features of Tillich's exposition is the emphasis he lays on the need for keeping philosophy and theology separate—and this after admitting that they cannot be separated. Seizing on this issue, some critics accuse him of serious inconsistency.[1] While these critics have located correctly the place where his system gets into difficulties, I prefer to think that there is less actual inconsistency involved than a lack of candid disclosure of the constituent elements of the system. I have already stated my conviction that, since the unity of all knowledge under the *logos* is the main prop of the system, the philosophy-theology question can be no more than a subordinate one. At the same time, a confusing use of the word *theology* is the first major problem we meet in the *Systematic Theology*. The philosophy-theology question grows out of the same root and provides a like impediment to a right understanding of the system. It also, when resolved, sheds light on the question of why the word *revelation* is avoided when the universal *logos* is discussed.

Why Tillich wishes to draw a definite line between philosophy and theology is not hard to discover. He is writing as a theologian justifying the theological task. Yet, because he will not base theology upon the authoritative message of any single religion, he bases it upon the authority of a comprehensive insight into the true and the real—the system. Therefore he has to show that philosophy cannot undermine the authority of his system, and this demands that the theologian shall be a philosopher and that his theology be philosophical theology. In this way attack from philosophy is neutralized. His system is safe, provided he can find a true synthesis of the philosophical and the theological view of reality; and such he believes he has found in the *logos* philosophy. But, having succeeded in his task to his own satisfaction, he has still to satisfy both parties with whom he engages. The philosophers are likely to object, 'Your scheme is suspect, for you have become a theologian while pretending to be engaged in philosophical analysis.' And the theologians may well retort, 'You are no theologian, but a philosopher substituting reason for revelation.' So his

[1] See the Postscript to this chapter: 'The Issue of Synthesis'.

defence has to be a declaration that the true philosophy is open to genuine revelation of the divine, where reason is not contradicted but extended. Then, having convinced the philosophers that a synthesis between the philosophical quest and the theological attitude is possible, he can go on to urge theologians to accept an interpretation or revelation which makes room for the *logos* philosophy.

It is this practical apologetic purpose which compels Tillich to argue, on the one hand, that the two disciplines have a 'basic unity' and yet to maintain, on the other hand, that there must be a 'qualitative difference' between them and that they do not 'lie on the same level'.[1] Unless philosophy and theology are essentially one, philosophical theology cannot be considered to be a live option. Yet, if these are offered in the form of a complete synthesis, both philosophers and theologians will turn away and refuse the offering. It is small wonder, therefore, that Tillich ceased to speak of 'theonomous metaphysics' and began to speak instead of 'the method of correlation'.[2] The motive behind this tactical move is evident enough; yet there is no indication that the overall strategy has been changed. Even within the *Systematic Theology* itself there are indications of a desire to close the door to any objection that philosophy in the system is being made too theological or *vice versa*.[3] Nevertheless, there is no alternative to continuing to skate over exceedingly thin ice. Any meeting-ground for philosopher and theologian vanishes if the *logos* philosophy is found unacceptable, for any

[1] *The Theology of Paul Tillich* ('Reply to Interpretation and Criticism'), pp. 336–8.

[2] *The Protestant Era* ('Author's Preface'), xlii.

[3] For example, where in the first volume the philosophical discovery of being-itself is said to result in a non-symbolic statement of God being being-itself, in the second volume this statement is said to be the line where symbolic and non-symbolic statements meet (see above, p. 58n). The former statement makes philosophy declare a theological truth, announcing the nature of *God*. The amended statement merely suggests that a necessary philosophical discovery becomes the basis for the theologian to use when he utters an essential theological truth.

On the matter of suspicions being raised by Tillich's procedure, note the criticism of Randall that being-itself is not a philosophical truth but a theological symbol—and Tillich's answer (*The Theology of Paul Tillich*, pp. 160, 335).

reason, to either party. Because Tillich has to walk so warily, he is compelled to stress the distinction between the universal and the particular *logos* rather than the all-embracing character of the *logos* as such. In these circumstances, to speak of revelation in connection with the universal *logos* would be to invite the very opposition which he seeks to avoid.

Without speaking of revelation outright, Tillich uses the word *theonomy* to indicate the essential unity of the philosophical and the theological outlooks. Since reason's sad 'predicament' in the world of time and space prevents a perfect theonomy being known here and now, he can plausibly argue that what is most important for us to note is the distinction between them. This he describes as a difference between 'levels'. (My metaphor of the wave-lengths has already indicated this aspect of his thinking, using a not dissimilar image.) But, while laying down the difference as a qualitative one, he does not pretend that it absolutely divides what it distinguishes, and he even makes the statement that 'there is an interpenetration of levels between theology and philosophy'.[1] Now, if the distinguishing mark of 'levels' ceases to distinguish, surely difference fades into identity.

The notion of levels, of course, follows from the description of revelation as the depth of reason, and the possibility of the interpenetration of levels arises out of the revelatory work of the *logos* driving all thinking in the direction of theonomy. This is why the creative philosopher must always be partly a theologian-in-spite-of-himself. Experiencing the power of the depths of reason, he becomes a theologian 'in the degree to which his intuition of the universal *logos* of the structure of reality as a whole is formed by a particular *logos* which appears to him on his particular place and reveals to him the meaning of the whole'.[2] What is noteworthy here is that the creative philosopher is not a theologian in the sense that he wishes to engage in a methodical interpretation of any religious faith as such. He becomes involved with the depths of reason in terms of Tillich's two formal criteria of every theology, i.e. because he has an ultimate concern.

This point is important because it pinpoints one of the

[1] *ST* II, p. 30.   [2] *ST* I, p. 25.

confusions arising over Tillich's handling of terms. This same confusion is seen where Tillich denies that the philosophy which employs the concept of being-itself can be called a theological discipline, saying that it must be called instead a *theonomous philosophy*.[1] Yet the debatable question is whether a theonomous philosophy deserves to be called a philosophy. In view of the admitted interpenetration of philosophical and theological levels, it cannot readily be considered either one thing or another without weighty objections being raised against the proposed title. Nor can the matter be decided by appealing to the content of theonomous philosophy. Is being-itself a philosophical concept? Is it 'a concept at which ontological analysis can never arrive'?[2] Arguments for and against fail to reach a common agreement concerning the principles which regulate analysis and concerning the scope of ontology, so that no progress can be made by taking this route. In addition, those denying that being-itself is a psuedo-concept, created merely to serve as a jumping-off place for religious apologetic, cannot easily counter the suggestion that only those persons who, in fact, go on to erect an apologetic system support their denial. It is only philosophical theologians who require being-itself to be counted a philosophical concept.

The whole problem presents itself in the first place because theonomous philosophy is said not to involve a theological reference. Yet the very notion of thinking having a theonomous aspect presupposes the admission of the theological within the framework of the philosophical. What is denied admission through the front door has been slipped in previously through the back.

Therefore, although Tillich talks of philosophers not intending to be theologians, he has already assumed that—intentionally or not—they must become theologians in their essential attitude to the whole of reality which is their object of study, or else they doom themselves to uncreative thinking. Their investigations into the meaning of the whole arise out of their acceptance of revelation. Theonomous philosophy is not a theological discipline in the sense that it seeks to interpret the

---

[1] *The Theology of Paul Tillich*, p. 337.
[2] The phrase is Randall's. See *The Theology of Paul Tillich*, p. 161.

religious substance of rites, symbols and myths (Tillich's first definition of theology). It is none the less theologically based, since it is formed by the particular *logos* and thus takes shape under the control of an ultimate concern (Tillich's description of the nature of the theological as set forth in his two formal criteria for every theology).[1] Under my suggested headings of primary and secondary revelation, the confusion of the philosophy-theology question would not have darkened counsel. It would have been clear enough that both disciplines, as Tillich presents them, use a different emphasis while remaining open to both sources of revelation.

Tillich's way of presenting his case hardly helps the reader to see how the *logos* doctrine sets up an absolute standard, making everything else relative to this absolute. One means of ensuring that religion and knowledge shall agree is to assert that reason is divine (as well as human) and then proceed to define God by defining reason. Undoubtedly it is a tidy method of procedure, but it has the disadvantage of restricting the divine within narrowly marked-out limits. This particular 'theological' stand results in a 'theology' of a very special type. In the event, it is hardly surprising that wherever the words *theology* and *theological* occur within such a theology there should be difficulty in discovering exactly what meaning is to be attached to them; for this usage is peculiar. And, equally, *philosophy* and *philosophical* are words causing similar trouble because they are caught up in the web of the *logos* philosophy and become involved in the revelatory power of the divine.

The system based upon Tillich's chosen principle of truth is a system that has built a fence and refuses to admit that anything of value can exist outside that fence. It claims to be the place from which an inclusive and panoramic view is obtained, for it assumes that within the fence is all that there is to see. Having

---

[1] Tillich remarks that his second formal criterion 'does not point to any special content, symbol, or doctrine' (*ST* I, p. 14). It remains 'open for contents' expressing 'that which determines our being or nonbeing'. This is why Tillich is able to arrive at a theological standpoint which he can separate from theology proper. In a similar fashion—although with far greater clarity—Dewey distinguishes between 'religion' and 'the religious' (see below, p. 177).

erected the fence, Tillich has to argue that it is not a restriction. From this situation comes the confusion of terms which I have been investigating in the present chapter, since the *logos* philosophy pays a price for the synthesis of faith and knowledge that it effects. For it reconciles philosophy and theology at the cost of denying to either an independent existence. It is this loss of independence that Tillich seems to be attempting to minimize at all costs; and the result is that the mists of ambiguity have been allowed to settle down upon the landscape within the fenced-off area, concealing the true state of affairs that obtains when the *logos* philosophy dictates conditions.

Every part of a theological system, says Tillich, is dependent upon every other part: 'The arrangement is only a matter of expediency.'[1] That is true if logical consistency is all that is being considered. But no theology can be merely—or mainly— a logically consistent whole. Theology rests upon a claim to be authoritative, and the claim rests upon an assertion that revelation is found in a particular place. Thus there is an end to every theological ball of twine, however firmly the twine is wound up, and, when you find the end, you can unravel the ball. 'Reason and Revelation' is the heading given to the first part of the *Systematic Theology*. I believe that this first section of the work is indeed the proper place to begin, but perhaps the presuppositions of the system would have been more openly displayed had the title been 'Primary and Secondary Revelation, or the Universal and the Particular *Logos*'.

The next step in understanding the system in its relation to the Christian gospel is to find out how the revelation which comes by the *logos* reaches man in his 'predicament' of imperfect rationality. Afterwards, the message brought by the *logos* will begin to unfold.

Postscript: The Issue of Synthesis

Under the title of 'A Criticism of Paul Tillich's "Reconciliation" ' Hendrik Kraemer has made a forceful attack upon

[1] *ST* I, p. 11.

the argument in the *Systematic Theology* denying the possibility of a synthesis between philosophy and theology. He writes:

> 'According to his contention that the ontological, that is to say the philosophical question as he conceives it, is implied, is immanent in Biblical religion, he should, for the sake of consistency and clarity, unhesitatingly say that a synthesis is not only possible but even required, and that a conflict is not only unnecessary but in principle excluded. He does not do so, but remains constantly wavering.'[1]

In this passage the reference to the ontological question being immanent in biblical religion refers to the thesis of the book *Biblical Religion and the Search for Ultimate Reality*—which I shall consider in a later chapter.[2] But, in general, Kraemer's argument is clear enough. He rightly protests that Tillich's belief about ontology being immanent in biblical religion depends for its force upon his ability to effect a synthesis of the Christian *kerygma* and his ontology. On these grounds he is quite justified in saying about Tillich, 'what he does is synthesizing pure and simple'.[3] However, he misses entirely Tillich's reasons for saying that philosophy and theology can and must be distinguished from each other within the system.

Here we have illustrated admirably the confusion resulting from the word *theology* as used in the system. The theology which Tillich believes he must distinguish from philosophy is not the same theology which Kraemer would have Tillich join to philosophy. The first is apologetic theology-in-general erected on the foundation of the *logos* philosophy, while the second is kerygmatic theology conceived as an authoritative message. Kraemer understandably, but unwisely, identifies Tillich's 'theological circle' with Christian belief in an authoritative revelation.[4] He naturally finds it hard to understand how this authoritative revelation can be equated with an

---

[1] *Op. cit.*, p. 427.　　[2] See below, p. 109 ff.　　[3] *Op. cit.*, p. 433.

[4] 'He maintains at the same time what he calls the theological circle, which means the unsurpassable, decisive, final revelation of God in "Jesus as Christ", *the* sole criterion for all truth' (*ibid.*, p. 427). Apparently Kraemer has not noticed that the criterion of 'Jesus as the Christ' is a criterion set up in terms of the system, not in terms of an authoritative message.

ontological system, but he understands that it must be, if Tillich's proposals are to be carried out. He is apparently unaware of Tillich's explicit statement in *The Theology of Paul Tillich* concerning the basic identity and actual divergence of philosophy and theology.[1] And he takes no notice of the less explicit but very similar declaration in the first volume of the *Systematic Theology* where philosophy and theology are said to be both concerned with the question of being, but from different perspectives.[2]

Coming later into the field, Robert C. Johnson makes a more careful analysis of all the relevant statements relating to the issue of synthesis.[3] He finds the way the issue is presented 'enigmatic and questionable' from the start, and he concludes that nothing is done to banish the suspicion of 'an unavoidable contradiction at this point'. Thus he is inclined to agree with Kraemer that, if he is to be consistent, Tillich must come out in favour of a synthesis—'that he must simply because he must'. At the same time, he sees better than Kraemer the extent to which Tillich's understanding of theology is shaped by his system, so he realizes that the issue is not simply one of harmonizing Christianity and philosophy but rather one of defining two different parts of the territory fenced in by the *logos* philosophy. At least, his thought is tending in that direction. For instance, after remarking that the relationship established between philosophy and theology is actually more coalescent than correlative, he proceeds:

> 'If theology can or must be pursued on the basis of the assumption that philosophy inherently infolds a theological element, and theology has an intrinsic philosophical element, it is, to say the least, very difficult to avoid the impression that the two have in reality, in some way, been united.'[4]

In thus arguing that the system assumes a basic unity prior to the division between the disciplines, Johnson seems to be joining those critics whom he describes as labouring to convict Tillich of holding opinions to which he gladly subscribes. Yet

[1] *Op. cit.*, p. 336.   [2] *Op. cit.*, p. 22.
[3] *Op. cit.*, pp. 125–9.   [4] *Ibid.*, p. 127.

Johnson's main point is that Tillich has been betrayed into an inconsistency, since his argument that philosophy and theology cannot meet is contradicted by his assumption that each can contain elements of the other. This point—which is essentially the same one that I have made about the breakdown of the distinction based on 'levels'—cannot be brought out too strongly. For the entire confusion over the philosophy-theology relation has come about as a result of Tillich's failure to make open admission of the fact that his system, assuming a synthesis from the start, subsequently puts forward distinguishing definitions wholly on the basis of this synthesis. 'Unity does not exclude definitory distinction,' Tillich writes, 'And this distinction between the two becomes important even if the unity is real only in a fragmentary way.'[1] But the reverse is equally true. Unity is important even if distinctions are not excluded, and wherever Tillich appeals to the distinctions a prior unity is presupposed. Tillich's presentation of the issue is so little helpful in exposing his actual assumptions that it is very necessary to underline the truth that Tillich's way is indeed, as he has admitted, 'the way of synthesis'.[2] Once this fundamental truth is no longer in doubt, it may readily be granted that theology (in Tillich's sense) is ordinarily distinguishable from philosophy because the particular *logos* is not the same as the universal *logos*. Yet, at all times, the frame of the *logos* philosophy holds the two together and will not allow either to be sundered from the other. This is something which becomes crucial when the method of correlation enters the picture.

---

[1] *The Theology of Paul Tillich*, p. 337.

[2] See above, p. 40. Johnson finds evidence of a reluctance on Tillich's part to use the word *synthesis* in places where it would seem to be natural to introduce it. He writes ' . . . it would be refreshing if he would revert to his earlier habit of simply speaking as though we may assume that such a synthesis is intended and presupposed' (*op. cit.*, p. 129).

IV

BEING AND EXISTENCE

IN THE previous chapter I argued that Tillich, in taking his stand upon the *logos* doctrine, assumes two grades of revelation. What I have called his 'primary' and his 'secondary' revelation cannot properly be given any other title than that of *revelation*, for both flow—though through diverse channels—from divine reason. The problem which arises next is why reason should manifest itself in two different ways, and the answer to the problem lies in Tillich's understanding of the conditions of man's existence in time and space. A system based on the self-asserting truth of divine reason starts from the given certainty of primary revelation. Since the same system claims to tell the truth also about man's 'predicament', it can go on to explain the necessity for a secondary revelation (the revelation given in human religions), showing why the symbols of *theos* are as needful as the knowledge of *logos*.

According to Tillich the prime characteristic of the world of time and space is an absence of wholeness. Ours is a 'split' world where human existence is by no means at one with being. This fact is hardly surprising, of course, when we bear in mind that primary revelation tells us that only being is at one with being. Being-itself, the sole true God, *is* being, and God is God because nothing else *is* in the same way—i.e. in perfection of being. Thus Tillich places his picture of our world in the setting of a relative dualism between the divine, which is a state of wholeness in perfection, and the human, which is a state neither whole nor perfect. He supports his picture by appealing to the example of Plato, who, as he points out, contrasted the *essential* and the *existential* levels of being. And he maintains that, in respect to this contrast, 'the Platonic and the Christian evaluations of existence coincide'.[1]

[1] *ST* II, p. 23.

Characteristically, Tillich presents this far-reaching claim as though it were a self-evident fact. He does not pause for an instant to consider what is involved in the claim. Yet, granted that Platonism and Christianity both distinguish between the divine and the human, it does not follow in the least that the distinction they each make is the same one or that it is made in the same way. Tillich allows no such disturbing thought to interrupt his explanation of how the two outlooks agree, however. He is anxious to establish the Platonic world-view as the accepted norm because Platonic dualism is the essential foundation for the theory of existence which he is advocating. For him human existence can only be understood if Plato was right and terrestial life is to be imagined as a shadow of the really real and the truly divine. Therefore he jumps immediately from the starting-point of a highly general similarity between Platonism and Christianity to the desired conclusion that they agree on a most specific matter. The question of how two evaluations of existence can coincide when they spring from totally diverse explanations of the origin of existence is passed over in silence.

At a later point in the present study I shall show how Tillich, when faced with the divergence between the Christian and the Platonic views of existence as this is made evident by the Christian doctrine of Creation and the Fall, tries to disguise the fact that he has to choose between two incompatible views by arguing that in Platonism alone we are given the clue to a proper understanding of the biblical message.[1] But the most striking indication of the way in which Tillich's allegiance to the 'classical' philosophical tradition controls his approach to existence is not to be found in any one argument of his. It is written into the total pattern of his *Systematic Theology*. Although second in the order of presentation, Part II 'Being and God' is described as standing first in importance;[2] and only when this exposition is completed can the problem of existence be discussed as a topic in its own right. Tillich believes not merely that ontology has been the necessary preoccupation of all philosophers from Parmenides to Hegel (and beyond Hegel to

[1] See below pp. 153 ff. [2] *ST* I, p. 163.

the true philosophers of today) but that no theology can stand which is ontologically uninformed.

Undoubtedly the whole of the *Systematic Theology* is dominated by the analysis of 'the structure of being' which opens Part II. Without this extended analysis the rest of the work would not be intelligible. Yet Tillich insists that systematic theology 'cannot and should not' attempt to enter into ontological discussion. This is, of course, in line with his belief that the theologian and the philosopher have separate tasks to perform, even if their work cannot be separated. He adds at once, nevertheless, that systematic theology 'can and must consider' the ontological concepts of the philosopher 'from the point of view of their theological significance'.[1] Here the reader should note that the theologian is free to consider what the philosopher has done after he has done it, but at the same time he is bound to accept it. The philosopher's concepts are not to be called in question, for to attempt any such thing would be to trespass on to the philosopher's territory. This situation should not be overlooked, because it points directly to the method which the *Systematic Theology* actually employs, as distinct from the explanations offered purporting to give a sufficient description of method. In working out his system, Tillich, in his rôle of philosopher, outlines what can be known about reality. Then, in his rôle of theologian, he accepts gratefully from his philosophical *alter ego* information about the nature of the Universe which enables him to say (knowing now what theology is all about) what Christian faith can and cannot mean. The philosopher, by means of ontological analysis, describes the whole. The theologian, following after, sees where his activity fits into the whole and what meaning it has there.

It is in the light of the knowledge of the whole that the systematic theologian can come to realize why the symbols of *theos* are as necessary for man as is the knowledge of *logos*. Tillich's assumption that this is so springs from his belief in the two levels of reason and their essential unity. Because of his belief in the whole which is pictured in his system he does not consider looking beyond the fence he has erected. Within this

[1] *ST* I, p. 164.

fence he sees, on one side, the identity of thinking and being—that state of perfect theonomy toward which man aspires in his quest for the truth-itself and the good-itself—and, on the other side, ontological reason in its existential predicament where it is parted from its own depths. The panoramic view of essence over against existence makes him confident that, when he proffers his ontological analysis to the theologian, the latter cannot do other than accept it; for it is a 'theologically' grounded analysis, i.e. it has grown out of a theonomous vision.

As always, the basic question is one of authority. Although Tillich says that his system, being theological, is not wholly demonstrable but made with risk and passion, yet he never seriously considers the possibility that another idea of theology could supplant his own. To doubt the entire adequacy of his panoramic view would be to relinquish his idealistic principle of truth, and such a sacrifice he never contemplates. Risk and passion are the marks of existential thinking in Kierkegaard's presentation of what it means to be a believer. Tillich always starts from an essentialist's vision in which existential elements can play no more than a subordinate rôle. Therefore risk and passion are less significant than speculative certainty, and religious belief must yield to the authoritative voice of the system. The *Systematic Theology* contains no kind of admission that the drive toward theonomous thinking may not, after all, be the basic truth about human self-consciousness or that the *logos* philosophy may prove to be less than a final and all-sufficient explanation of the scope of human knowledge. Once, perhaps, Tillich comes very near to an admission of this sort when, early in the Introduction, he suggests that his work will have fulfilled its function if only it has helped people to find the Christian message relevant to the questions they are asking in their own generation.[1] Yet even here he makes the claim that the questions for which his system provides the answers are the truly human questions raised by the fact of existence itself in every generation. And, because of this claim, he shows that he has never ceased to assume the complete validity of the panoramic view. Certainly his position is 'theological'. But the

[1] *Ibid.*, p. 8.

theology it recognizes is not one grounded in trust in any religious *kerygma*; it is trust in the possibility of resolving the dilemma of cognitive reason sufficiently to be able to proceed with the construction of a system to embrace reality as a whole. Reason which simply tries to argue from within the contradictions of existence can have no still centre of certainty about which to revolve, but reason which rests upon the self-revelation of total reality has risen above the fragmentary to anticipate the whole.

The lesson to be learnt from all this is that Tillich does not expect Christian theologians to dispute the adequacy of his ontology or its authority to interpret the Christian faith. My concern with the system being its relation to the Christian gospel, there is no need for me to consider the details of his ontological analysis or to review his ontological concepts for their own sake. At the same time, the background out of which they have emerged (i.e. Tillich's relative dualism with its two stages of being) makes his ontological concepts interesting for what they reveal, for these concepts illustrate in specific ways the presuppositions which brought them to birth. For this reason I shall now look at a single one of these concepts, considering it—as Tillich suggests, though not quite in the perspective he has in mind—from the point of view of its 'theological significance'. In other words, I shall try to lay bare the message about the divine inherent in this particular concept.

Prominent among the ontological concepts is 'the subject-object structure of reason'. On the human level of being (finite being), our reason finds everything split into subjects and objects. For example, in the domain of knowledge the knower is distinguished from the known. But we must understand that on the divine level of being the subject-object structure of reason is transcended. Divine omniscience, indeed, embodies within itself all truth because it is not dependent upon this 'structure' but is its source.[1] Tillich regards this contrast as one aspect of 'the basic ontological structure' which, once accepted, allows us to comprehend the make-up of reality. Inadequate philo-

[1] *ST* I, pp. 171–4, 278–9.

sophies try to explain the Universe in terms of either subject or object divorced from each other. A philosophy recognizing that the divine holds together what humanity experiences as polar opposites is safe from all such errors: it rests on the self-revelation of being.

The reader is soon introduced to the theological implications of the concept, for he is told that, if God is brought into the subject-object structure of being, he 'ceases to be the God who is really God'. On that account theology 'must always remember that in speaking of God it makes an object of that which precedes the subject-object structure. . . .'[1] Now the first reaction of a Christian believer to this explanation may well be to say, Amen. Certainly an opinion which will not tolerate the thought of God becoming 'one being among others' appears to be a reverent one. Only, unfortunately for the believer, this opinion is dogmatic as well as reverent. It denies with great emphasis that God can be known in the same manner that we know anything temporal and spacial. The same denial is present in the biblical witness to the reality of God, as in the prophet's cry: 'To whom then will ye liken me that I should be equal to him? saith the Holy One' (Isa. 40.25). But it is one thing to deny that God can be defined in terms of our human experience and quite another to affirm that he can be properly defined in other terms available to us. Tillich offers a description of the divine by means of which genuine deity may be tested: the God who is really God is *that which precedes* the subject-object structure of being. Such a description is hardly one which can be applied to the God of Christian revelation. The God of scripture is indeed prior to all beings. He is prior because he is the Creator of all things in heaven and in earth: 'I am the Lord, and there is none else' (Isa. 45.6). Yet what makes God prior is the truth that Lordship belongs to him. He is not called Lord because he is known to be the necessary precondition for that grade of being which things in heaven and in earth demonstrably possess.

The distinction here is far more than a quibble over terminology. It is one which strikes to the root of Tillich's

[1] *Ibid.*, p. 172.

systematic method. On a superficial view, Tillich's warning to theology concerning the things that 'it must always remember' is nothing except a wholesome reminder that any statement about God is not equivalent to a statement about a stone or a snow-storm. But such a superficial view overlooks the main point. Tillich is not saying that God is beyond human understanding, for he is saying instead that God is quite adequately represented in the picture of the Universe given by relative dualism. God has been identified authoritatively by means of ontological analysis. Let theology mark well what has been done and adjust its statements accordingly!

The philosopher, casting the net of ontology, believes that he has caught God in his net. What kind of a God is it who makes himself available to this technique? The answer must be found by taking up again the meaning of 'being-itself' in Tillich's system, an investigation which I dropped temporarily in a previous chapter and which now calls for attention.[1]

Tillich explains the term 'being-itself' by the phrase 'the creative and abysmal ground of being'.[2] This phrase (which he more usually gives in a simplified form as 'the ground and abyss of being') he admits to be symbolic. Its usefulness is that it indicates how being-itself has a twofold relation to all things that have being (i.e. that are beings). Being-itself transcends all things both positively and negatively. Positively speaking, all things have what being they possess because they participate in being, so that being-itself upholds them. Negatively speaking, all things lack the full being of being-itself, so that the absoluteness of the latter seems to blot out the merely relative being of everything except itself. This twofold relation of being-itself to beings means, according to Tillich, that we can come to know certain things about the ontological God. And, while God's 'abysmal' nature is never to be forgotten, his positive nature as 'ground' is naturally the chief source of enlightenment. So Tillich spells out how we are enlightened:

'Since God is the ground of being, he is the ground of the structure of being. He is not subject to this structure; the

[1] See above, pp. 57–8.   [2] *Op. cit.*, p. 238.

84

structure is grounded in him. He *is* this structure, and it is impossible to speak about him except in terms of this structure. God must be approached cognitively through the structural elements of being-itself.'[1]

Here God seems to be tied so closely to the Universe by being identified with the structure of being that the query arises as to whether the God revealed in Tillich's primary revelation is not a God of pantheism. Tillich denies this, giving precise reasons. As the 'ground' of being, he argues, God is more than the unity and totality of all that the Universe can be, and a pantheistic God is that unity and totality merely.[2] Now this point may be admitted without banishing the query; for, when Tillich explains why God can be known as being-itself, he does so by stressing that being-itself cannot be denied to be the ultimate reality because thought is driven to posit a Universe.[3] Thus the question at issue is chiefly one of how pantheism ought to be defined. Strictly speaking, Tillich's system is not pantheistic in that it does not identify the Universe and God. All the same, because God is identified with the reality *of* the Universe, it must be classified as a monistic system standing in very close relation to pantheism, differing from the latter in the detail of its ontological analysis but sharing with it a common vision.

How nearly allied it is to pantheism can be seen when Tillich, deploring the fact that the word *pantheist* has become a 'heresy label', seeks to show that a pantheistic element is necessary if we are to arrive at a satisfactory conception of God.[4] Of more than casual interest also is Tillich's admission that, since being-itself and the structure of being are not identical, he ought perhaps to have distinguished between the two more carefully.[5] Manifestly, a God who can be spoken of only in terms of the Universe cannot be so very different from a God conceived to be one with the Universe. Of each God it can be said alike—though not exactly in the same sense— 'He *is* the structure of being.'

But, if pantheism and Tillich's system do not hold that God *is*

---

[1] *Loc. cit.*   [2] *Ibid.*, p. 236.   [3] *The Theology of Paul Tillich*, p. 335.
[4] *ST* I, pp. 233-4.   [5] *The Theology of Paul Tillich*, p. 335.

in just the same way, precisely how do they differ? To this question no clear answer can be given for the very good reason that the difference lies principally in Tillich's use of the word *ground*, and the meaning of this word cannot be tied down too closely. Tillich himself has declared the word to be a symbolic one. So, by definition, the word is incapable of conveying any direct and proper meaning. The consequence appears to be serious for the analytical side of his system, because it becomes very certain that he is crossing over the line which he has drawn so carefully between philosophy and theology, and introducing theological symbols where theological concepts ought to reign. We have already seen how unsatisfactory is his defence of the strictly philosophical status of being-itself,[1] and later his use of symbols in presenting his whole apologetic standpoint will be considered.[2] Clearly, it is not enough to stand by the conviction that being-itself is a true, unsymbolic, philosophical absolute, for the criticism is directed not simply at the starting-point of the analysis but also—and more particularly—at its development. Having stated that thought must start with *being*, Tillich goes on to explain how being-itself must be understood in terms of words such as 'ground' and its companion 'power'. But if being-itself is philosophically acceptable, being-itself as interpreted through the phrases 'the ground of being' or 'the power of being' is quite another matter. Its intended conceptual clarity has become blurred and uncertain, its meaning no longer univocal but vanishing with muffled echoes into the clouds of mystery.

I started my scrutiny of Tillich's concept of being-itself with the motive of discovering what kind of God it could be that could be caught in the net of ontological analysis. The result of my short inquiry appears to be that in Tillich's system philosophical demonstration is subordinated to 'theological' conviction, with the result that the philosopher who wields the net turns out to be a metaphysical theologian. That is why the Christian theologian (or the theologian of any religious faith) is told so forcibly what he must or must not say. The God who appears in the system has his nature laid down in advance by

[1] See above, pp. 80 ff.   [2] See below, p. 221.

the requirements of a theology resting upon the belief that mankind is conscious of a 'power' and rests upon a 'ground' which reveals itself so directly that it cannot be denied.

The God of the system—the God caught in the net of the metaphysical theologian—is not primarily a philosopher's God, and for this reason he is not purely and simply a God of pantheism. But he conforms more closely to the pattern of pantheism than to any other. And, very conspicuously, he makes contact with his worshippers through that dimension which is as closely linked to pantheism as is laughter to comedy: the dimension of mystical union. So Tillich writes:

'The pantheistic element in the classical doctrine that God is *ipsum esse*, being-itself, is as necessary for a Christian doctrine of God as the mystical element of the divine presence.'[1]

As always, his view of what is 'necessary' for Christian doctrine is decided by the requirements of the net of his metaphysical theology, for many Christian theologians would judge both elements to be equally alien to the historic Christian doctrines. Tillich's trust in the mystical relation is revealed in an illuminating footnote where he challenges Harnack's belief that Greek rationalism perverted Christian theology. Tillich objects that Greek thinking, far from being rationalistic, was basically mystical—seeing knowledge as 'union with the unchangeable' and the 'really real'.[2] Undoubtedly, he diagnoses the nature of Greek thinking accurately, and Harnack's thesis, in the way he presented it, is vulnerable. Yet, other things being equal, Greek mysticism would appear to be much more likely to clash with Christianity than Greek rationalism would be, for mysticism makes claims within the territory of religious faith which rationalism does not necessarily make. And Tillich has not only countered Harnack's thesis, declaring that the Christian message need not suffer when it is translated into Greek terms. His demand for a 'reorientation' of our understanding of the history of Christian doctrine goes much further, for it rests on the judgment that the Christian message can be identified with a message concerning man's union with the unchangeable. Say

[1] *ST* I, p. 234.   [2] *Ibid.*, p. 157 a(9).

nothing about Greek thought intellectualizing Christianity (so he reasons), say rather that Greek mysticism keeps Christianity true to itself!

If Harnack's hypothesis is questionable, Tillich's is even more so. The point is, however, that Tillich does not in the least regard the axioms of his metaphysical theology (or theological metaphysics, if you will) as hypotheses to be verified one by one. His system can remain a system only when it is accepted as a whole. Therefore, he never raises the question of whether it is appropriate for a Christian believer to adopt a theology where God is conceived in pantheistic and mystical terms. Instead, taking for granted that a right understanding of *being* entails recognition of a God conceived in these terms and in no other ones, he proceeds to point out what Christian theology must or must not say. Whenever he says that theology 'must' say this or that he is, in fact, silently supplying the comment, *if my system is to call the tune*. At no time can he afford to allow the content of the Christian *kerygma* to have any weight in deciding issues within the system. The system must always be true to itself, and whether it can at the same time be true to Christianity must depend upon Christianity happening to agree with the system and not the other way round. The procedure is inexorably laid down, as I pointed out in my first chapter,[1] in the methodological rule that system-built must follow the pattern set out in system-known.

The problem confronting the reader of the *Systematic Theology* is that of grasping firmly all that is comprised in system-known, the metaphysical theology upon which everything else depends. There would be no problem if Tillich were to set out in an orderly fashion the axioms he employs instead of leaving his readers to discover these for themselves. On the other hand, all the revelant material is supplied, and Tillich makes no secret of the philosophical tradition which he follows, so that the outlines of system-known are visible to anyone who is prepared to look for them behind system-built. But it means looking. In the present chapter I have been examining Tillich's belief concerning being and the nature of God as these emerge

[1] See above pp. 28–9.

against the background of the relative dualism of essential and existential being which he has adopted from Plato. It is now time to consider these beliefs with specific reference to the background; and in particular to discover how Tillich's monistic thinking, as revealed in his concept of God-the-ground-of-being, is related to the relative dualism of his two levels of being.

Tillich's relative dualism is no more than relative because the distinction between the divine and the human can never amount to a separation. The human level can have its being solely because it stands within the divine 'ground'. So the fact of human existence does not disrupt the monistic scheme required by ontological thinking. But the problem immediately arises as to whether the system (which so frequently has been called *existential*) can have any place in it at all for an existence that is really real or for individuals who truly exist.

Here Kierkegaard's opinions are instructive. The Danish father of existentialism maintains that any system whatsoever and belief in the existing individual are totally imcompatible, arguing in his *Concluding Unscientific Postscript* that an 'existential system' is a contradiction in terms. For him the logical end of every attempt to understand being as a whole results in a deification of the concept of totality, so that there is no alternative open to the system-maker other than unconditional surrender to some type of pantheistic thinking. He explains:

'. . . every such system fantastically dissipates the concept *existence*. But we ought to say this not merely of pantheistic systems; it would be more to the point to show that every system must be pantheistic precisely on account of its finality. Existence must be revoked in the eternal before the system can round itself out; there must be no existing remainder, not even such a little minikin as the Herr Professor who writes the system.'[1]

Behind the wish of speculative philosophy to bring existence under the sheltering wing of being, Kierkegaard senses an intention to replace Christian faith by another religious outlook. It is for this reason that he speaks of pantheism being a

[1] *Op. cit.*, p. 111.

wider term than it is usually taken to be, considering it a label applicable to monistic thinking of different types. He sees the issue as an either/or where Christianity is faced by a rival, its authority challenged:

> 'For the only consistent position outside Christianity is that of pantheism, the taking of oneself out of existence by way of recollection of the eternal, whereby all existential decisions become a mere shadow-play beside what is eternally decided from behind. . . . The pantheist is eternally set at rest from behind; the moment of existence, the seventy years, is a vanishing entity. The speculative philosopher, however, desires to be an existing individual who is not subjective, who is not in passion, aye, who exists *sub specie aeterni* . . .'[1]

Kierkegaard realizes that the system-builder is someone who cannot help making theological claims, whether he wishes to do so or not. For he is bound to make pronouncements as though he shared the knowledge of the Eternal, reaching beyond the human to discover the divine and leaving behind his own individual existence to unveil the secrets of reality as a whole.

The speculative 'idea' that Kierkegaard identifies with pantheism finds its expression in Tillich's key-phrase 'ultimate concern'. I have already indicated how the phrase has its roots in Kierkegaard's 'infinite interest' and how it is changed in his hands from a description of the individual's recognition of the authority of the Christian gospel to an assertion about man-as-such.[2] Tillich cannot admit that an ultimate concern can really be ultimate unless it is that specific concern which it 'must' be in order to satisfy the terms of his system. Having set out man's 'true' concern in the second formal criterion of every theology, he expands on the theme as follows:

> 'Man is ultimately concerned about his being and meaning. "To be or not to be" in *this* sense is a matter of ultimate, unconditional, total and infinite concern. Man is ultimately concerned about the infinity to which he belongs, from which he is separated, and for which he is longing. Man is totally concerned about the totality

---

[1] *Op. cit.*, p. 203. [2] See above, pp. 43 ff.

which is his true being and which is disrupted in time and space. Man is unconditionally concerned about that which conditions his being beyond all the conditions in him and around him. Man is ultimately concerned about that which determines his ultimate destiny beyond all preliminary necessities and accidents.'[1]

Now a Kierkegaardian response to this pronouncement would be along some such lines as these: 'If the speculative philosopher were to address his advice to its proper object, mankind, and under suitable circumstances somewhere beyond existence with all its preliminary necessities and accidents, no doubt both parties would be duly edified. But as for me, a poor single existent occupied with the continual striving which existence demands, I confess that I lack the time to consider a matter which can concern me only in a fantastic sense—for it is fantastic for a man to imagine that he can here and now take wings and fly off into the eternal. Existence in time and space makes me an individual; and to deny the conditions in me and around me would be to undertake an essay in the comic, like someone jumping a few inches off the ground and insisting that he is flying. Christianity, however, tells me that through faith I may become an eternal spirit. Christianity meets me as an existing individual, and in my relationship with Christianity I discover an infinite interest.' It needs only the slightest variation of phrase to adapt Kierkegaard's criticism of speculative philosophy so that it applied directly to Tillich's theology. And in this connection the relevance of Kierkegaard's opposition to 'pantheistic' systems is easily grasped.

Tillich, in fact, separates the divine and the human at one level of being, but that level is no more than a preliminary one. So, when man seeks the ultimately real (God) beyond everything preliminary, he must say that it is his own being and meaning that he seeks. Man's true being is divine. Man's total meaning unfolds within the totality of divine meaning in the Universe. Very differently, Kierkegaard refuses to contemplate the Ultimate mystically and pantheistically. Instead of merging the human and the divine, he asserts the possibility (promised in the Christian message) of a relation between the two. He is

[1] *Op. cit.*, p. 14.

91

able to prevent his existential dualism from being drawn into a mystical monism because he stands firmly by his belief that, so far as the individual is concerned, existence must be an ultimate. We cannot grasp existence by means of thought, and neither can we think it away. Above temporal existence lies the eternal being of God. No concept available to us will unite the two. How God can meet with us is beyond our understanding. In the presence of God each individual, like Job, must lay his hand upon his mouth and proceed no further (Job 40.4, 5)—the speculative philosopher as much as the next man. Yet we can know the reality of the encounter between God and man. Objectively, certainly, the relationship is not knowable, since it breaks through the boundary of human possibilities and leaves thought twisted in contradictions. It can be known in one way alone: subjectively (i.e. through faith) and as a result of trust in the reality of the promises of Christianity.

For a system to be complete, said Kierkegaard, existence must be 'revoked into the eternal'. And the method used to take the existing individual out of 'the moment of existence, the seventy years' was to proceed 'by way of recollection'. Here Kierkegaard was referring, of course, to the Platonic theory of recollection, according to which all our knowledge arises out of our halting memory of truths which in eternity we once knew perfectly but forgot when we entered the shadows of the temporal. Tillich, who so readily suggests that Plato's estimate of existence can be our guide, produces his own version of the theory (which I shall consider later in another connection).[1] He also introduces two concepts which stand in front of the theory, so to speak, like two pillars of a porch in front of a building. These are the concepts that he has called 'ontic anxiety' and 'ontological shock'.

Anxiety is another technical term adopted by Tillich in the first place from Kierkegaard. In Kierkegaard's *The Concept of Dread,* dread or anxiety (in Danish and German *angst*) is a menacing, omnipresent element in the individual's life. It is bound up with the guilt-feelings connected with original sin, and so it can neither be explained adequately nor dealt with

---

[1] See below, pp. 122–7.

adequately except by Christian faith. Tillich—partly following Heidegger—takes over the psychological description of *angst* from Kierkegaard, but transforms it into a general theory of man's universal condition inseparable from his 'predicament' in existence. Thus the cutting-edge of Kierkegaard's meaning has been completely blunted. Instead of pointing to the individual as a sinner and as one who can win eternity through the inwardness of faith, *angst* has been generalized and made to point to that speculative conception of man-in-relation-to-the-Universe which Kierkegaard believed to be one of 'a hundred ways of escape' from taking immortality seriously discovered by *angst* itself.[1] Tillich's explanation of ontic anxiety is that man is longing for the infinity to which he belongs and from which existence separates him: 'Anxiety is the self-awareness of the finite self as finite.'[2] The finitude of existence is what marks out the human level of being from the divine. On the level of existence, non-being is mixed with being, causing the 'split' in being which makes the world of time and space the kind of world it is. Because man lives in a split world, he finds the unhappy consequences of the division of being and non-being and their opposition in every area of experience. The causal aspect of the world, for instance, illustrates the tensions of existence. Every cause reveals the presence of being, but the fact that anything can be acted upon by a cause outside itself indicates the presence of non-being in that thing. From this evidence Tillich draws the conclusion that man's experience of causality initiates ontic anxiety:

> 'The anxiety in which causality is experienced is that of not being in, of, and by one's self, of not having the "aseity" which theology traditionally attributes to God.'[3]

This is a statement strongly recalling Nietzsche's famous argument that, did God exist, we could not endure not being

[1] *Op. cit.*, (London, Oxford, 1946) p. 137. It is interesting that Kierkegaard mentions Schelling as one whose understanding of dread has nothing in common with his own (*ibid.*, p. 53 and note). For an analysis of the handling of Kierkegaard's concept in modern existentialist philosophies see my article, 'Life in the House that "*Angst*" Built' (*Hibbert Journal*, Vol. LVII, 1, Oct. 1958).

[2] *Op. cit.*, p. 192. [3] *Ibid.*, p. 196.

God—therefore there is no God. Tillich starts by agreeing that we cannot bear not to be God, and, the evidence of existence suggesting that we lack what God enjoys, the result is to plunge us into perpetual torment of spirit.

There is more to be said, all the same, because a diagnosis of anxiety includes the knowledge of how it can be countered. In Kierkegaard's eyes the person who is educated by dread can 'repose only in atonement', as he learns that Christianity promises him deliverance from his guilt.[1] But for Tillich the antidote to anxiety is man's knowledge that he belongs 'to that which is beyond non-being, namely, to being-itself'.[2] In other words, man can turn away from the level of the human to the level of the divine. Although we cannot endure not being God, our torment is not an ultimate one or such as might force us to a denial of God's being; for we belong to the infinite and to the totality of the divine, and we cannot deny God without denying ourselves. Ultimately, we are one with God, and his being is our's. Anxiety can be no longer a final threat once we realize the truth about the structure of the Universe and understand man's cosmic dignity.

Surely Kierkegaard was right when he believed that every pantheistic system asks man to turn away from the seventy years of human existence in order to 'recollect' his membership of the eternal world, a world not received as a gift but entered into as the only real world and the one to which he eternally 'belongs'. The actual act of recollection is brought about, in Tillich's system, by means of 'ontological shock'. This shock, which brings consciousness of the real condition of man and why he lives under the burden of ontic anxiety, is nothing else than revelation. In fact, it is God speaking by allowing man to experience the Ground of being in its negative or abysmal character.[3] Confronted by a realization of the finitude of everything in time and space, man is overwhelmed—he has no aseity, he is not God! After receiving revelation in its negative form, he is able to turn equally to the positive face of the same message when he will 'recollect' his essential unity with the Ground of being. Tillich does not use the Platonic term

[1] *Op. cit.*, p. 145.   [2] *Op. cit.*, p. 191.   [3] *Ibid.*, p. 113.

'recollect' because he does not employ Plato's myth of the soul drinking the waters of Lethe before being joined to its body, but his term 'awareness' carries the same basic meaning of passing from ignorance to knowledge. In both Plato and Tillich reality is made manifest through the divine element in human consciousness coming to self-knowledge and learning to cast aside the illusions of existence.

Tillich's ontological shock apparently operates at two levels. It is effective on the level of conceptual thinking and also at the level of religious experience.[1] Thus, operating as primary revelation it acts through ontological reason, and operating through secondary revelation it shows itself through what Tillich has called 'ecstasy'. The first level gives the impetus to philosophy, while the second begins and ends among the phenomena of religious faith.

Since human religions belong to existence they illustrate the beliefs of existing individuals and groups. But do they do more? By making religion a specific area where ontological shock is effective, Tillich claims to relate religious beliefs to reality, demonstrating authoritatively how much or how little truth they contain. And, in claiming thus to possess the true 'idea' of what all religions stand for, he is also claiming (according to Kierkegaard) to take them out of existence into the eternal. At the same time, Tillich himself says that his system is not merely idealistic but includes the existential. In turning now to examine his teaching about religious faith, I hope to be able to prepare the way for more direct approach to his theory of existence than has been possible so far. Does it actually happen that, so far as the system is concerned, *all existential decisions become a mere shadow-play beside what is decided from behind*?

[1] *Loc. cit.*; see also *ibid.*, p. 163.

V

EROS-FAITH

IN SOME of his later writings Tillich suggests that the word *metaphysics* ought to be dropped altogether and the word *ontology* substituted for it. That *ontology* is the best word to use in connection with a *logos* philosophy will hardly be questioned, indicating as it does the 'word of being' which exhibits the truth concerning being. But the objection raised against *metaphysics* is less obvious. Tillich avers that the word encourages misunderstandings:

> 'This name was and is unfortunate, because it conveys the misconception that ontology deals with transempirical realities, with a world behind the world, existing only in speculative imagination.'[1]

Understandably enough, the author of a speculative system does not wish his system to be called by a name encouraging the idea that the system is imaginary rather than real. At the same time, it is not certain that the issue of 'transempirical realities' hangs on the use of one particular word rather than another. The issue may well spring out of the nature of system as such.

This initial suspicion is confirmed by a second look at the evidence. Although Tillich complains of the misconception introduced by thinking that ontology deals with a 'world behind the world', he freely talks about the very same thing. For he says that the depth of reason is 'the expression of something that is not reason but which precedes reason and is manifest through it'. He says that this depth is 'hidden under the conditions of existence'. And he says that reason, though essentially 'transparent toward its depths', is 'opaque' in the world of time

[1] *Biblical Religion and the Search for Ultimate Reality*, pp. 6–7. Compare *ST* I, p. 163.

96

and space.[1] The metaphors of space—'manifest through', 'hidden under', and 'transparent towards'—all tell in these three statements the same story. Each presents a picture of two worlds, one of which lies behind the other and may be (or sometimes may not be) glimpsed through it.

The second world produced through Tillich's system is, however, not separate from the first in so far as it appears in proportion as the other disappears. In this sense alone it is not another world, because it is the only true world. It precedes the realm of the empirical and is manifest through it whenever the empirical does not intrude itself as though it were something determinate. We look down through the shifting water to the solid bottom of the sea, and if we fail to see the pebbles there it is not because the water has grown solid but because its surface is ruffled by some transient agitation. Or we look across the valley and we cannot see the mountains because a mist destroys our vision, so we must just wait until the obscuring mist lifts. Tillich varies his metaphor of the obstructing medium—the opaque which can be, and ought to be, transparent—with another metaphor of a more active kind. The rational word 'grasps being' and—as though coming to the end of a game of hide-and-seek—'drives it out of its hiddenness into the light of knowledge'.[2]

Neither metaphor suggests that there is much to be said for opacity or darkness (i.e. the world of existence).

Therefore, whether Tillich's analysis of being is called *ontological* or *metaphysical* is hardly of moment. What matters is what his system does, not how it is named. One of the reasons for his wishing to avoid the word *metaphysics* is connected with the fact that 'metaphysical speculation', thanks to the influence of Kierkegaard, has become a term of disparagement among theologians. He writes:

'*Speculari*, the root of the word "speculation", means "looking at something". It has nothing to do with the creation of imaginary worlds. . . .'[3]

[1] *ST* I, pp. 79–80.
[2] *Biblical Religion and the Search for Ultimate Reality*, p. 6.
[3] *Ibid.*, p. 7.

The information is relevant but does nothing to advance his argument, because the question to be answered is, 'What does speculation look at?' And his answer in the system seems to be that it looks only at the light of knowledge, at what is driven out of hiddenness. Although the ontologist professes to look at 'things as they are given', he is seeking to know only 'the constitutive principles of being'.[1] Consequently he cannot help prejudging the nature of what is given and finding that what seems to be given is merely 'preliminary' and 'really' something else.

In this connection it is instructive to find how Tillich looks at 'things as they are given' in the matter of defining the concept of faith, a matter which has occupied him a good deal and has been made the subject of one of his most recent books, *Dyamics of Faith*.[2] From the point of view of the present study, his approach to the concept is important because here is a place where his system engages with the Christian message and traditional Christian theology. And, moreover, the definition of faith becomes something of a test of the accuracy of Kierkegaard's contention that, in a system, all existential decisions become a mere shadow-play beside what is decided from behind. For faith is so closely bound up with the individual that any theory dealing with faith inevitably discloses its basic assumptions about human existence.

Sociologically speaking, faith appears to be a group phenomenon. People associate together on the basis of common beliefs and in consequence claim to belong to 'the Christian faith', 'the Buddhist faith', or perhaps even 'the faith of humanity'. Yet, although faith may be mainly the result of being born into a particular community and may often seem to be as involuntary as measles, it is experienced as individually as toothache. And it does not have to be endured as toothache has to be. In the end, every individual decides what faith he will adopt. So it happens that, while a group of believers meeting together finds great psychological satisfaction in singing:

[1] *Biblical Religion and the Search for Ultimate Reality*, p. 8.
[2] New York, Harper & Bros; London, Allen & Unwin; 1957.

'Faith of our fathers, holy faith,
We will be true to thee till death!'

or the equivalent, the most aggressively orthodox church can never rid itself of the heretic reared within the fold; and, equally, the most rigorously secularist society finds itself confronted with 'superstition' in its midst. Faith is uncompromisingly existential. As Luther said, every one must do his own believing just as every one must do his own dying.

By means of his concept of 'ultimate concern' Tillich has found a way to by-pass the existential basis of religious belief. His system demands that a subjective approach (what Tom or Harry thinks he believes) must give place to an objective one (what the system says is the truth). Accordingly, he assumes that the ultimate concern of an individual cannot be anything other, in the last analysis, than the concern which 'really' is ultimate for man-as-much. Existence then drops out of the picture and the system finds itself unopposed. So much I have already discussed. But, although the system has reduced the existential act of believing to the generalized formula of acknowledging the content of the theological circle as one's ultimate concern, yet the inescapable fact that belief is always belief in a determinate some*thing* by a determinate some*one* has not been entirely suppressed. This is a fact which looms up very conspicuously when there is mention of the word 'faith'.

In the Introductory Remarks to his book, *Dynamics of Faith*, Tillich says that his aim is to convince at least some of his readers of 'the hidden power of faith within themselves'. Yet he also emphasizes his disappointment that 'there is as yet no substitute expressing the reality to which the term "faith" points'.[1] The explanation of this combination of guarded hope with positive disappointment can only be that Tillich will not admit anything to be real that is closely tied to existence. That which has reality is beyond time and space, and under the conditions of existence the real remains hidden. Faith points to a reality not itself—it is not itself real. The power inherent in this reality remains hidden in so far as the opaque face of existence obscures its true nature—it needs to be grasped by the

[1] *Op. cit.*, vii.

99

rational word and driven out of its hiddenness into the light of knowledge. But, so long as faith is simply believed to be faith as the term is commonly accepted, the reality will not be grasped and the power will not be acknowledged. Faith must step down from its throne whenever the real king can be found—which, alas, is not yet. In the meantime everyone must be made aware that the royal crown is on the brows of a mere pretender.

As a matter of fact, although Tillich believes that the term 'faith' must be retained for convenience, he does find a related concept which expresses much more directly the 'reality' he believes to lie behind the concept of faith. This concept is love. But it is love interpreted in one special sense. He writes:

> '. . . faith as the state of being ultimately concerned implies love, namely, the desire and urge toward the reunion of the separated.'[1]

Note that Tillich does not say in so many words that he proposes to identify faith with love. His procedure is to define faith in terms of ultimate concern and then, without more ado, remark that faith implies love. This is a transparent tactical move. Let it be assumed, for example, that the basis of capitalism is greed, so that greed is what capitalism 'really' stands for. It follows logically that capitalism implies greed. All the same, before anyone proceeds to state categorically that capitalism implies greed, he should be prepared to give reasons why capitalism cannot be defined without making greed an essential element in the definition. It is not enough for him to say, 'Capitalism as the economic system built on acquisitiveness implies greed, namely, the instinct to amass wealth,' since the reasoning is obviously circular.

That a similar circularity appears in the above definition of faith can be seen when we remember Tillich's explanation of what it means to have an ultimate concern. The second formal criterion of every theology stated that man is infinitely concerned about nothing else except his being and non-being. There it was said that man's true concern is about the infinity to

[1] *Op. cit.*, pp. 113–14.

which he belongs, from which he is separated, and for which he is longing.[1] The one piece of information not supplied in that particular passage was that the longing for reunion constituted love. Now Tillich hastens to make good the omission. The ultimate concern which is faith, so he makes plain,

> '. . . presupposes the reunion of the separated; the drive toward the reunion of the separated is love. The concern of faith is identical with the desire of love: reunion with that to which one belongs and from which one is estranged.'[2]

The reality toward which the term 'faith' points has at last been driven out of its hiddenness into the light of knowledge, standing revealed as love-faith or the urge toward the reunion of the separated. Just as the term 'ultimate concern' was necessarily vague until it was given precision by being connected with being and not-being, so there is no doubt about what 'the hidden power of faith' signifies after faith has been linked with love in the context of the desire to overcome separation. Nor is this all. The various terms used in Tillich's system can be seen coming together, so that the system begins to show its outlines—like a bulky package when someone is tying it up and tightening the string around it.

That the system should reject faith in the sense of personal belief and commitment is natural enough. Such an approach to the concept leaves it on the level of existence and hidden in the darkness that, according to the systematic viewpoint, belongs to everything sharing the conditions of existence. The system demands that we look 'behind' faith in order to discover the reality which faith partly obscures. It is not enough for the individual to decide what he ought to believe, for the system is at hand to explain what there is to be known and to help all men adjust their beliefs so that these conform to reality. By substituting love-faith for faith, Tillich confirms Kierkegaard's belief that every system turns existential decisions into shadow-play. His system rejects 'I believe' in favour of 'Theology must always assert.'

In turning away from existence towards love as the desire to

[1] See above, p. 90.   [2] *Op. cit.*, p. 112.

overcome separation, Tillich follows the path taken by Plato. And he remains in it after obtaining some guidance from Hegel. His definition of love follows very closely Plato's description of *eros* in the *Symposium*, a love in itself a blending of the human and the divine whose function it is to carry the human soul beyond the world of sense to the eternal realm of perfection. Yet he does not admit that his concept of love is that of *eros*. Instead, he urges that love is one and that the *eros* quality is one quality of love amongst others. He sets out his argument most fully in his study, *Love, Power, and Justice*, where love is defined as 'being in actuality' and 'the moving power of life' as well as 'the reunion of the separated.'[1] There he explains why he believes the *eros* quality to be essentially part of love. Theology, he says, is inspired by the *eros* toward truth, ritual by the *eros* toward the beautiful, while 'without the desire of man to be united with his origin, the love towards God becomes a meaningless word.'[2] These arguments not only show that Tillich takes *eros* to be an essential element in love, for they also suggest that all other elements in love must be subordinate to this one. And his definition of love actually excludes any other conclusion; love as the urge towards reunion is *eros* and nothing but *eros*.[3] In addition, there is the telling evidence of his monistic worldview. Anyone agreeing with Plato about the status of existence can hardly disagree with him over the true nature of love.

Eros ('the moving power of life'—'being in actuality') moves in man-as-such and proves that the relative dualism of the divine and the human is relative only. The divine in man reaches out in *eros* in order to escape from the predicament of

[1] *Op. cit.*, p. 25.   [2] *Ibid.*, p. 31.

[3] In an essay on 'The Life and Mind of Paul Tillich' which opens the volume *Religion and Culture, Essays in Honor of Paul Tillich* (New York, Harper & Bros; London, SCM Press, 1959) the editor, Walter Leibrecht, asks: '. . . does Tillich not inadvertently elevate the *eros* concept over the others?' (p. 26). The question is an odd one, for anything so central to the system could hardly be there by chance oversight. More cogently, E. La B. Cherbonnier argues in the article 'Biblical Metaphysics and Christian Philosophy' (*Theology Today* IX 3, October 1952, pp. 360–75) that Tillich's 'ontological approach' has as its very heart the aspiration for union between knower and known which is *eros*. He points out that love as *eros* contradicts the biblical view of love as *agape*, a view assuming a relation between persons instead of a drive toward unity.

existence and find reunion with eternal, infinite being. Such is the creed which Tillich shares with Plato, and, so long as this creed is not questioned, any view of love toward God other than the view set forth by Socrates in the *Symposium* is automatically excluded. Once the real meaning of a word is known, all efforts to attach some different meaning to it are seen by the enlightened person to be futile and confessions of invincible ignorance: hence love means reunion or nothing! Tillich is confirmed in his understanding of love by Hegel's concept of estrangement, concerning which he writes:

'The profundity of the term "estrangement" lies in the implication that one belongs essentially to that from which one is estranged.'[1]

The point is perhaps less that the term is profound than that it is altogether congenial to the viewpoint which, in Kierkegaard's words, revokes existence into the eternal. The concept of estrangement allows man to belong to a split universe and at the same time straddle the split. It allows him to be parted from the whole and yet to belong essentially to it, so that he is not 'really' apart from it. Against this background Tillich's plea for 'an ontological interpretation of love' and for 'starting with an understanding of love as one'[2] stands out as a declaration of the essential divinity of mankind as knowing love and the power which is effective in love. Love to God means that the good in us feels itself driven toward the good-itself, from which it is derived—'estrangement presupposes original oneness'[3]— in order that it may truly become again a part of that whole which includes all, the *summum bonum*.[4] And the *eros* for the good is itself part of the more inclusive *eros* for being-itself. Love is one because being is one, the sole Ground of the Universe. It is being-in-actuality, so that, although felt as an urge by men, it is ultimately the power of being-itself manifest in all that is.

Platonism, with a little support from Hegel, supplies Tillich with the setting for his concept of love. When he turns to apply this setting to love as it appears in the Christian gospel he at

---

[1] *ST* II, p. 45.   [2] *Love, Power, and Justice*, p. 28.   [3] *Ibid.*, p. 25.
[4] 'Basically, however, one's love to God is in the nature of *eros*. It involves elevation from the lower to the higher, from lower goods to the *summum bonum*' (*ST* I, p. 281).

once runs into difficulties. He is compelled to deny that there is any basic difference between *agape*, the New Testament word for love, and the philosophic (Platonic) *eros*, and to contradict sharply those theologians who would drive a wedge between them.[1] Arguing from the premiss that love must be one, even though it may—and does—have expression in different types, he defines the *agape* type of love as that which 'seeks the other because of the ultimate unity of being with being within the divine ground'.[2] But this definition illustrates exactly what those theologians who separate *agape* from *eros* say will always come about unless the separation is strictly observed. For they maintain that where there is *eros* there can never be love for the other that is freely offered as is God's *agape* which comes freely in Jesus Christ to sinners like ourselves.[3] Love that seeks the other because of an ultimate unity does not, after all, seek the other. It seeks unity. If *agape* seeks the unity of being with being, then God's love of man is not free and unmerited. It cannot be free when it rests on the condition of man having an ultimate unity with God, and it cannot be unmerited when God loves man precisely on account of this ultimate unity. Certainly God's love comes to man in spite of his existential estrangement, but this says nothing about the quality of love involved. Man in existence is loved, not as existing, but as being. He is loved for what he potentially is, and for what he actually is to the extent to which he has not left the divine Ground. In short, God loves himself—for what else is there to love or be loved except being-itself and the structure of being which God *is*? It is also noteworthy that Tillich should regard it to be a manifestation of *agape* when man loves himself 'as the eternal image in the divine life'.[4] Here again God loves himself because of his eternal divinity. God's love is restricted to that

---

[1] *Love, Power, and Justice*, pp. 27 ff.; *Biblical Religion and the Search for Ultimate Reality*, pp. 50–1, 71–2.

[2] *ST* I, pp. 280–1.

[3] Anders Nygren, in *Agape and Eros*, is the chief spokesman of this view. Karl Barth, who has criticized Nygren's thesis quite harshly, nevertheless agrees with him on this point and even insists on 'the merciless severity of the antithesis' (*Church Dogmatics* II 2, Edinburgh, T. & T. Clark, 1958, p. 747).

[4] *Op. cit.*, p. 282.

which lies within the divine sphere, and he can love himself through man's self-love because there is an eternal identity of the human and the divine which is ultimately unbroken. God does not love man, made in his image and fallen into sin, when he loves his own eternal image in man. His love is strictly eternal self-love.[1]

A love in which the divine loves the human only in so far as the human is divine is a parody of New Testament *agape*. Yet no other result can come from a definition of love as the reunion of the separated. For the definition has been framed to fit into a Universe conceived in terms of *eros*, where the part seeks to be absorbed into the whole by means of an upward movement in which the part, as lower, becomes drawn into the higher from which it has fallen. Within such a Universe there can be no room for *agape* or disinterested care for another for his own sake, and what takes the place of *agape* is merely *eros* inverted. The whole, as higher, is now conceived to be drawing the part into itself. But there is no alteration in the movement, no descent of the higher to the lower, and no desired end except to realize oneness. Tillich describes the perfection of love as 'self-love in the sense of *agape*',[2] which means, of course, self-love as it is when *eros* reaches its complete fulfilment and separation has been finally overcome. In keeping with his starting-point he looks away from the world in which *agape*—care for others—can be realized. While theologians who separate *agape* from *eros* find the heights of love in the message of Christianity telling us about what God has done and how we may love because we have been loved, he speaks of man finding his fulfilment in his highest good and learning to distinguish genuine self-love from seeming self-love.

So in the system *eros* takes over love, and love takes over faith. Everything is decided from behind, as Kierkegaard suggested must be the case when system reigns. The system insists that we

---

[1] Contrast Barth's account of God in his love for men: 'He does not seek Himself, let alone anything for Himself, but simply man, man as he is and as such, man himself. And God does not in any sense fall short of Himself when he loves in this way. In this self-giving to man He is God in all His freedom and glory' (*op. cit.*, p. 750).

[2] *Loc. cit.*

judge nothing from the perspective of our human existence, because if we do we shall see amiss and fail to discern what is 'really' there. We must beware of the term 'faith', which will most certainly mislead us unless we learn to look behind it, discovering in consequence that faith is essentially ultimate concern and ultimate concern identical with the urge to overcome existential estrangement. In learning to look behind appearances we discover the hidden realities toward which appearances point but which are not to be found in them. We start, imagining mistakenly that we need a faith to guide us in our existence. But, if we are wise, we go on to realize that what we 'really' desire is to recognize the hidden power within us and to learn to love ourselves as part of the eternally divine.

It is now possible to look over the whole area of secondary revelation in Tillich's system and find out how *eros*-faith functions in it. Religion was found to be necessary in the first place because human knowledge is limited in existence. Man inhabits a split world in which reason is parted from its depths. The rational word, which ought to give man knowledge of the truth, is limited in actual reason and does not always sound clearly. At the same time, the depth-dimension of reason, although displaced, is still accessible to man and reaches him through the revelation which he receives through the practice of one or other of the religions of mankind. In the exercise of faith, man is grasped by the ground and abyss of being and meaning, the manifestation of mystery being declared in the experience of ecstasy. The power which grasps man in 'the revelatory situation' is the strength of the urge of *eros*, driving him out of existential estrangement into union with being-itself. This means that he is made aware of the Ground of his being, both in its positive and negative aspects, experiencing his unity with that Ground beyond existence in time and space. Such an experience of mystery is necessarily joined to religious activities, because it is in the myths and cults of religion that humanity seeks to approach the mystery of life. Where words addressed to man's actual reason fail owing to the fact that in existence reason has lost its depths, there symbols generated in man's religious life may strike home with meaning.

Secondary revelation stands under primary revelation and is interpreted in terms of the latter. Thus the mystery which is expressed in the symbols of religion is a mystery whose essential nature is already understood. The symbols which are indispensable for the individual believer—he could not believe without them—are primarily ciphers (or 'mere signs' as Tillich would say) for the philosophical theologian, who reads off their signification with ease since he is certain that they symbolize some aspect or other of a Universe explicable in terms of *eros*. The system does not obtain guidance from any religion or from all of them, but it first constructs its 'idea' of religion and afterwards sits in judgment over the religions of the world, showing what is right with them and also where they fail to measure up to the prescribed 'idea'. In *Dynamics of Faith* Tillich writes about 'the many contrasting types of faith', and then goes on to discuss 'faith in its true nature'.[1] When inquiring about the truth of faith he is not concerned with Christian faith or the faith of tree worshippers—that will have its place after the guiding principles have been established and the realities of the situation exposed. The system is bent on establishing the genus *religion* under which, in due time and whenever convenient, the various species of religion can subsequently be grouped.

This is terrain which I have already travelled. My main point is already embedded in the term 'secondary revelation'. But what is new is the information that religious faith is to be fitted by the system into a world-view controlled by the concept of *eros* ('Love is the power in the ground of everything that is . . .'[2]). *Eros* rounds out the picture of the Universe already sketched in by the doctrine of the *logos* with its union of the divine and the human.

According to this picture primary revelation, born of the indwelling *logos*, comes to man in ontological shock and brings him, at one and the same time, knowledge and love of God together with knowledge and love of self. All man needs in an *eros*-ruled Universe is the quality of awareness. Let man but

---

[1] Chapter 5, 'The Truth of Faith', *op. cit.*, pp. 74 ff.

[2] *Ibid.*, p. 114.

be aware of what lies 'beneath', 'behind', or 'through' the opacity of existence, and he needs no arguments to bring him to God. He is aware of God in becoming aware of his own actual finitude and potential infinity.[1] Revelation flows from human awareness of being indissoluably united with the divine, for:

> '. . . man discovers *himself* when he discovers God; he discovers something that is identical with himself although it transcends him infinitely, something from which he is estranged, but from which he never has been and never can be separated.'[2]

The belief that *eros* controls reality, moreover, gives confidence that there can never be a break in the essential divine-human unity. We need not merely trust that God is a God of love, holding our faith in subjectivity, as Kierkegaard believed faith must be held. Kierkegaard indeed taught that the relationship discovered in faith, whereby the individual meets his God, could not be compared to anything else. But Kierkegaard was wrong, says Tillich, because love to God is one instance among others—even if it is the supreme instance—of that uniting love seen at many different levels but always the same:

> 'Infinite passion for God as described by Kierkegaard is, no less than the sexual passion, a consequence of the objective situation, namely of the state of separation of those who belong together and are driven towards each other in love.'[3]

Here the entire subservience of religious faith to metaphysical theology is clearly presented. The system is interested in the symbols of faith only in so far as it knows that it—and it alone—can interpret properly the reality toward which these symbols point. When the Christian gospel brings the message, 'God so loved the world . . .', the system replies that the Christian believer is symbolically acknowledging the objective situation, namely, the openness of finite being to receive the infinite

[1] *ST* I, p. 208. See also the whole section headed 'Human Finitude and the Question of God', pp. 204 ff.

[2] 'Two Types of Philosophy of Religion' in *Theology of Culture*, edited by Robert C. Kimball (Oxford University Press, New York: 1959; London 1960), p. 10. The italics are in the original.

[3] *Love, Power, and Justice*, p. 27. See also the Postscript to this chapter: 'The Objective Situation and Experience'.

because of the eternal unity of all beings within the divine Ground. The system goes on to add that this truth is, of course, common ground for all genuine religions, although Christianity has given it full expression. And the lesson to be learnt is that Christian theology must discover how to interpret its message in such a way as to reflect and not to distort the objective situation.

Kierkegaard tells us that he wrote his *Concluding Unscientific Postscript* in order to answer the question of the individual's relationship to Christianity.[1] His conclusion is that Christianity can be described rightly only when it is seen as an existential communication to be received in subjectivity and inwardness Tillich starts from the other end, establishing on systematic principles what he is sure can be demonstrated to be objectively true. He asks whether Christianity is, or may be, the truth. After finding out what truth is, the first question must be, by this procedure, Can any faith communicate truth? Inquiry then brings the assurance, 'Faith is an essential possibility of man, and therefore its existence is necessary and universal.'[2] The road is now open for an approach to Christianity itself. And it is not surprising that the little book in which Tillich deals with this particular issue should carry the title *Biblical Religion and the Search for Ultimate Reality*. He takes for granted that the problem to be faced is basically how philosophy can come to terms with religion, and, in the second place, how the desired agreement can be reached when the religion in question is one in which all ideas are presented in the special language and thought-forms of the Christian scriptures.

In making out his case that the philosopher has no reason to fall out with the Christian faith Tillich not only admits, but also emphasizes, how differently the philosopher speaks from the spokesmen for faith whose words are the content of the Bible. But all is resolved—or so he argues—by the category of ultimate concern. The religious believer takes faith for his ultimate concern while the philosopher takes being-itself for his. Since it is illogical to suppose that there are two ultimate concerns, the solution is simple: 'the one comprises the other.'[3]

[1] *Op. cit.*, pp. 18–19.   [2] *Dynamics of Faith*, p. 126.
[3] *Op. cit.*, p. 59.

Unfortunately, the rather important matter of which comprises and which is comprised is obscurely stated. Although the reader is told that faith 'comprises itself and the ontological question'[1] —which sounds as though faith controlled ontology—he is told also that

> 'The ultimate concern of the believer is concern about that which is really ultimate and therefore the ground of his being and meaning. He implicitly asks the question of ultimate reality.'[2]

Here the 'really . . . and therefore' gives the case away, showing how an ontological interpretation of reality controls the exposition given of the content of faith. Not for one moment does Tillich consider the possibility that the believer may not agree with the ontologist concerning what makes an ultimate concern ultimate, but instead he proceeds to define true ultimacy in ontological terms. It is hardly surprising, therefore, that he should discover ontology to be implicit in faith since the discovery is based entirely on his own definitions. If faith is ultimate concern, and ultimate concern is concern over one's being and meaning, and concern over one's being and meaning is asking the question of ultimate reality: *if* all this is so, then faith 'implicitly' asks the ontological question. Faith can also be said to comprise itself and the ontological question since, whatever else faith is, it is by definition ontologically orientated.

One interesting feature of the argument in this book is that it is silent on the subject of the need to keep philosophy and theology separate. It makes no attempt to explain or to justify the 'theological' aspect of the ontological quest which it so strongly emphasizes. The ontologist and the believer are shown from the start involved in the pursuit of the ultimate and the infinite:

> 'In both biblical religion and ontology an ultimate concern is the driving force; in both of them the "No" of doubt is taken into the "Yes" of courage; in both of them a participation in concrete experiences and symbols gives content to question and answer; in both cases an ultimate trust in the power of being makes human

[1] *Op. cit.*, p. 61; also p. 60, 'Faith comprises the ontological question.'
[2] *Ibid.*, p. 59.

surrender and search possible. This analogy of structure keeps one side open for the other.'[1]

Such an explanation makes it clear that, in the terminology of the *Systematic Theology*, both sides are theologies. The 'analogy of structure' goes so far as to include on the ontological side philosophical conversion and philosophical revelation parallel to the conversion and the 'opening of the eyes' experienced in the realm of faith.[2] Having arrived at this conclusion, Tillich appears to consider his demonstration of the compatibility of biblical religion and the ontological quest to be almost complete. Yet what exactly has been proved? The most obvious answer to this question would seem to be that ontology has been exhibited as an activity having fully developed theological pretensions and, on that account, as a possible rival to biblical religion. That the concrete experiences and symbols of the ontologist will yield a similar content in ontological theology to that found in the theology appropriate to biblical religion is nowhere shown to be the case—and, after all, this is the point at issue. If they say different things, biblical religion and ontology will be in conflict no matter how much they may resemble each other in their way of delivering their separate messages.[3]

Of course, if the fence erected by the system contains all there is to know, any conflict is unthinkable. An infallible principle of truth and an inerrant idea of theology will then guarantee that the symbols of the believer (properly interpreted) never contradict the concepts and the symbols of the ontologist. But it is altogether too simple to say that religious believers must accommodate their beliefs to make them agree with what the ontologist says because ontologists see things as they 'really' are. No *a priori* pronouncement can decide whether the faith

---

[1] *Ibid.*, p. 63.   [2] *Ibid.*, pp. 64–6.

[3] Kraemer, arguing that Tillich has demonstrated nothing more than 'formal external similarities', confesses himself to be 'frankly amazed that a thinker of the stature and stupendous erudition of Tillich disposes so lightly of the problem' (*op. cit.*, p. 429). He proceeds at once to summarize the *diss*imilarities. Tavard, noting that in the system 'faith tends to become the stuff of all life' and thus to lose all determinate meaning *as faith*, comments: '. . . a philosophical description of being and concern is altogether distinct from a theology of faith and grace' (*op. cit.*, pp. 43, 50).

proclaimed by biblical religion is the same as *eros*-faith ('faith in its true nature'). Only a direct comparison between the Christian gospel and the content of Tillich's philosophical theology can decide the issue.

The chapters that follow will be devoted to this task of comparison. However, since Tillich maintains that his Method safeguards the interests of both faith and ontology, permitting neither to intrude on the other, I shall first stop to examine whether the claims he makes concerning correlation can be substantiated before going on to consider other aspects of the relation between the system and the Christian gospel.

Postscript: The Objective Situation and Experience

One of the puzzles in the system which has exercised critics greatly is the place occupied in it by experience.

Johnson, noting the change in Tillich's description of experience, which in his early writings was said to be a 'source' of theology but later was re-named a 'medium', calls attention to the peculiar rôle assigned to this medium.[1] It is to be no passive vehicle of communication, for it is expected to 'transform' as well as to relay. Experience, says Tillich, 'determines the interpretation of what it receives'.[2] As 'what it receives' includes the biblical message, Johnson observes that the medium, rather than the message, thus becomes the actual creator of the system's theological norm. The content of the biblical message is filtered through the medium, and what comes out is not what went in. Johnson's dissatisfaction at this point is shared by Tavard, who quotes Tillich's words about the medium of experience not being a source and yet having 'productive power'. 'In this position,' Tavard comments, 'I fail to see a perfect consistency.'[3] Tavard fears that by means of his transforming medium Tillich is permitting individual experience to set aside the Christian message as this is confessed by the whole Church.

[1] *Op. cit.*, pp. 133 ff.   [2] *ST* I, p. 46.   [3] *Op. cit.*, pp. 24–5.

Going further than either Johnson or Tavard, Zuurdeeg bluntly asserts that the system is an 'experience theology' and that Tillich's explicit denial that experience is ever a source of theology is contradicted by his practice.[1] The doubts expressed by the two other critics become for him proven objections against the system.

Zuurdeeg's analysis seems to me to be correct but incomplete. In the first place, it fails to show why Tillich should wish to repudiate his implicit theological foundation; and, in the second place, it sheds no light on what Tillich means by a 'medium' which is not—and yet is—a 'source'.[2] Nevertheless, it provides an important clue to the solution of both these problems when it explains that all appeals to experience 'disclose the specific character of the convictions of the persons who voice their experiences. . . . Starting from experience, therefore, means to assume that a starting point, very arbitrary in itself, possesses a kind of objective authority.'[3] This explanation is important in view of the stress laid by Tillich on what he calls *the objective situation*.

For Tillich the objective situation is the reality described by the *logos* philosophy. This reality is authoritative in his eyes, being guaranteed by his ontological analysis and productive of ontological truth—primary revelation, in my terminology. (Zuurdeeg, incidentally, dismisses Tillich's ontological analysis as the forced result of his being tacitly committed to a semi-Hegelian system.)[4] Now, if we adopt such a view of the objective situation, clearly we are committed to an 'experience theology' in the sense that for us revelation issues wholly out of our experience.[5] Our theology tells us that faith is not believing in anything outside us but is an immediate certainty springing

[1] *Op. cit.*, pp. 156 ff.

[2] Although now insisting that experience must be called a medium and not a source, Tillich says that so to name it 'denies the assertion that experience is in no sense a theological source' (*loc. cit.*). It would seem that a change of terms does not mean, in this case, a change of mind.

[3] *Op. cit.*, pp. 157–8.

[4] *Ibid.*, p. 158.

[5] 'Revelation is first of all the experience in which an ultimate concern grasps the human mind . . .' (*Dynamics of Faith*, p. 78).

from the reality of the power of being in us. At the same time, while we know that revelation comes through experience and never comes without it, we know too 'the weak, interrupted, distorted character of all religious experience'.[1] For the objective situation is that experience is ambiguous, since it belongs to life and thus shares in the contradictions of existence. In one sense, experience is a source: without the experience of being grasped by the Ground of our being we would not know what faith is. In another sense, experience is not a source but a medium through which we encounter the *eros* drawing us to seek our true being and meaning. We can see, then, why Tillich dislikes the word *experience* and prefers the 'colourless' word *awareness*.[2] Experience is yours and mine; it refers necessarily to individuals or to a collection of individuals But awareness is not limited to existence; it can be predicated of man-as-such. Experience brings doubt as well as certainty But awareness of the Unconditioned is the absolute certainty proof against all doubt; it is an awareness reflecting the objective situation and transcending every individual experience.

The above analysis explains how it is possible for Tillich to expound an 'experience theology' and yet to deny that his theology is derived from experience It also explains a point that both Johnson and Tavard find curious, namely, that Tillich insists that the transformation wrought by experience on what it receives must not be intentional.[3] This is Tillich's way of saying that, while the individual is not free to interpret the Christian message according to his individual tastes, he is bound to accept an interpretation in terms of the objective situation (i.e. as the *logos* philosophy directs). He who simply repeats the message without transforming it has not been made aware of the Unconditioned reaching him through the symbols of his religious faith; he has failed to find in experience a theological source On the other hand, he who makes his own transformation has set up his individual vision in defiance of the objective situation; he is thinking to find certainty elsewhere than in awareness of the Unconditioned, overlooking the truth that experience is no more than the feeble medium through

[1] *ST* I, p. 52.   [2] *Theology of Culture*, pp. 22 ff.   [3] *ST* I, p. 46.

which man is brought into contact with that which is beyond experience.

The assumption behind the belief that unintentional transformation is safe but intentional harmful is that the objective situation reveals itself to man unless man blocks the revelation by turning away from the Unconditioned towards conditioned existence, for the power of *eros* works silently in man's spirit. Linked with this assumption is Tillich's opposition to natural theology.[1] He thinks it impossible to prove God's being or his nature by arguments, since this is to try to measure the infinite on the scale of the finite and to seek for some ground on which to establish the Ground of our being. Rather, awareness of the divine is the precondition of all valid reasoning. We can make assertions about God only on the basis of an *analogia entis* pointing to the infinite that sustains all finite beings by its presence in them.[2] Therefore, if we labour to prove God we shall never arrive at anything but an idol. If we have no intention of producing him at the end of an argument we shall find him in all our thinking.

To Tillich it seems inconceivable that anyone should fail to recognize the objective situation. Yet what is authoritative for him may well seem arbitrary to others, who will not agree to being told what they 'must' think in order to make contact with reality. In fact, only those will accept his views concerning the objective situation who are prepared to accept his starting-point in an 'experience theology' or, as it may perhaps be termed more accurately, a theology of mystical awareness.[3] Others will find their authority neither in experience nor through it but in the Christian message which comes to their experience and addresses them as individuals. Such persons will maintain that not even man-as-such is aware of the objective situation, but those alone who hear the Word of God.

[1] *Ibid.*, pp. 203 ff.   [2] *Ibid.*, pp. 239–40.
[3] Tillich himself speaks of 'the mystical *a priori*'—see below pp. 134–7.

VI

CORRELATION

IN MY first chapter I argued that the method of correlation did not represent the whole of Tillich's methodology and was by no means the most important part of it.[1] My contention seems to be borne out in part by the fact that it has been possible to discuss large areas of the system without more than a few passing references to the Method. My concern now is to show why Tillich has chosen to stress that his system uses correlation as its method. The reason, I believe, is not hard to discover if we observe the claims that he makes for it.

The method of correlation has been chosen, Tillich says, in order to solve the apologetic problem of 'Christianity and the modern mind'. It aims at achieving a synthesis, a union of the message of Christianity and the concrete temporal situation in which the message must be received:

> 'It tries to correlate the questions implied in the situation with the answers implied in the message. . . . It correlates questions and answers, situation and message, human existence and divine manifestation.'[2]

The Method has been prompted, so the reader is told, by a consciousness of how previous attempts at achieving a synthesis of faith and knowledge have broken down because no way could be found to guarantee the independence of both elements within the proposed alliance. Either the demands of knowledge ('the modern mind') disregard traditional doctrine ('the perennial message')—as happened in nineteenth-century Protestant liberalism after Schleiermacher—or else orthodoxy rises and

---

[1] See above, p. 27.
[2] *ST* I, p. 8. It should perhaps be said that when Tillich here mentions *synthesis* he puts the word in quotation marks (*ibid.*, p. 7).

asserts itself by disowning the claims of knowledge and out-lawing philosophy from the realm of faith—as happened in the neo-Reformation theology of Karl Barth. The danger to be avoided, then, is subordination. Two elements are to be held in equilibrium, and neither element is to be put under the power of the other. This requirement seems to be met in the concept of correlation.

In view of the problem to be solved, the method of cor-relation sounds promising; but it still has to be proved to be workable. In any attempted correlation different elements are placed over against one another in an effort to find some connection between them. Yet whether this activity is justifiable we cannot tell until we know enough about the elements in question to know what relationships in fact unite them. For instance, astrology correlates the fortunes of individuals and the movements of the heavenly bodies. But although the method of correlation in astrology has been used down the centuries for the purpose of casting horoscopes—and is still widely trusted—rational thought today has no interest in horoscopes because it finds no reason for believing the pattern of human lives and the pattern of the starry sky to be directly related in any way. So the discovery that astrology uses the method of correlation is wholly irrelevant when it comes to assessing the worth of horo-scopes. What matters is whether we grant, or do not grant, that correlation in this area is possible.

The possibility of correlation in the case of empirically verifiable facts is something to be investigated experimentally. Is there a genuine correlation between, say, collecting postage stamps and having a tendency to commit suicide? Statistics can be compiled to answer such a question, if not certainly, at least with a high degree of probability. But experimental methods are restricted to the empirical world and to empirical problems. Therefore it is by no means enough to say that one kind of apologetic theology uses the method of correlation. The method is a technique, not a principle of demonstration, and techniques are successful or unsuccessful. The theological technique of correlation can be successful only if the possibility of theological correlation is an actual possibility reflecting an actual relation between the elements correlated. Otherwise it remains as unproductive as the technique of the wise men of Gotham who, trying to fish the moon's reflection out of the water, cast their nets all night but pulled nothing to land.

All that Tillich can claim for his Method for adapting Christianity to the modern mind is that, *provided faith and knowledge go together*, then the Method will display this intrinsic relation. The 'answers' he wishes to fit to his 'questions' will fall into place if there is a place ready to receive them, and whether there is or is not such a place is the point at issue. Yet apparently whether faith and knowledge go together is not a matter which Tillich leaves to be decided anywhere. He has already decided the question by adopting the *logos* philosophy, a philosophy founded on the assumption that humanity and divinity join in the rational word, thus bringing together faith and knowledge as two sides of a single coin. So, if his view of the Universe is correct, his Method also will be productive. Of course, the same thing could have been said about the wise men of Gotham. It was not their method that was at fault but their fundamental assumptions.

However, Tillich leaves out of account that he has assumed anything. Unlike the famous recipe for jugged hare beginning, 'First catch your hare', he limits his descriptions to the last stages of the cooking-process and says nothing about how the hare came to be available for jugging. That is why I argued earlier that his Method is only one part of his total theological method and that the first and basic stage in his actual method is to set up an 'idea' of theology as authoritative. In setting up his authority in the sphere of the metaphysical he has decisively chosen to subordinate religious faith to ontological analysis, so that, strictly speaking, correlation becomes impossible. He has chosen the way of subordination, so that the even balance of elements *suggested* by the term 'correlation' goes by the board. His correlation is now the bringing together of elements which have been previously forced into agreement and on that account can be most readily correlated! That such is the procedure which Tillich has followed can be seen when the details of his Method are examined.

Central to Tillich's presentation of his Method is the metaphor of question and answer. The Method, he insists, correlates questions and answers. But consider for a moment what happens when a question and an answer are correlated. Questions and answers can be correlated only when a common view of the Universe is shared by the one who asks and the one who answers. To take a simple example, the question 'Why am I feeling this pain?' can appear in correlation with the answer 'You ate too much for dinner' or in correlation with the answer 'Your enemy is using witchcraft to hurt you'. Which answer will, in fact, be taken to be a correlative of the question depends upon the way in which the causes of pain are conceived by the person asking the question. The questioner who assumes a relationship of physical effect to physical cause will not accept an answer assuming a relationship of physical effect to magical cause, and *vice versa*. Given the 'unacceptable' answer, he will be likely to retort, 'That's no answer!' or 'Speak when you have something sensible to say!' Every question actually contains presuppositions limiting the possible answers that can be made to it, and before we can reply intelligently we need to know the context in which the question has been asked (i.e. the mental horizons of the questioner). It may very well be that we cannot reply to the question at all until it has been rephrased in order to exclude implications which to our mind 'beg the question'. The classic question of this type is 'Have you stopped beating your wife?' Yet no question can avoid question-begging in some degree, as we can understand by considering such varied questions as: 'Do you trust God to guide you?'—'Haven't you any manners?'—'Where are you going?' These questions may easily be followed by such replies as: 'I don't believe in God'—'Manners have nothing to do with it'—'I'm not going anywhere.' In this event they have not been answered at all. The replies have been addressed to the questioner but not to his question, and they amount to a demand that the questioner rephrase his question to make it acceptable to the other party. Before this happens there may well be an argument involving any topic under the sun as the two involved try to reach a common understanding.

Stated in terms of correlation, the lesson to be drawn from these examples is that no question and answer can be correlated unless the congruity of answer with question is assumed. Whenever we speak about answering a question we are declaring that we believe the question we are asked to be a possible one to answer because we accept the view of the Universe implied in it.[1] If we apply this criterion to Tillich's identification of the human situation with a question and the Christian gospel with an answer, the result is illuminating. Tillich says that he will solve the problem of Christianity and the modern mind (or, in more general terms, the problem of 'message' and 'situation') by the method of correlating 'questions' implied in the situation with 'answers' implied in the message. And this may seem at first glance like an excellent piece of apologetic strategy. To produce Christianity as the answer to the questions asked by the modern mind must surely take the ground from under the feet of the unbeliever who argues that Christianity cannot meet the needs of intelligent people today. Yet, if answering the questions of the modern mind means accepting the view of the Universe possessed by the modern mind, the strategy seems to be of doubtful worth. It may well be that it is exactly the questions which the modern mind asks that prevent it from making sense of the message of Christianity and encourage it to dismiss the Christian gospel as irrelevant. Equally, if we take Tillich's alternative term, 'situation', it is by no means proven that the Christian message is the answer to the question asked by the human situation. We may believe, if we are Christians, that Christianity is the answer to the particular problems confronting us. But to believe that Christianity answers our problems,

---

[1] Although this sounds slightly fantastic, I believe that it corresponds exactly to the facts of experience. For example, the leading questions of the have-you-stopped-beating-your-wife type which would be disallowed in a court of law are questions which actually posit a Universe where history is different from history in the Universe which common experience (and the law) knows. The question assumes a Universe where I beat my wife, although this may not be a historical fact in the everyday world. But very many questions do not involve mainly matters of fact, being questions of the type of 'Do you like Haydn's quartets?' These are the most human questions, because they are intended to elicit a view of life rather than to obtain information.

and will answer other men's problems as well is a very different thing from saying that it can be demonstrated that Christianity as such answers the human situation as such. After all, the human situation does not go around saying, 'The Christian message answers the very questions I am asking.' So what actually is happening is that Tillich is expecting us to accept a theory about the human situation (i.e. the Platonic-Hegelian view set out in the system) and demands that the message of Christianity shall conform to the mental horizons obtaining in this theory.[1]

Certainly, Tillich does not shrink from stating dogmatically that the Christian 'answers' derive their meaning from being answers to a particular sort of 'question'. He puts it in this way:

> 'The answers implied in the event of revelation are meaningful only in so far as they are in correlation with questions concerning the whole of our existence, with existential questions.'[2]

Unless the reader is hypnotized by the word *correlation* he cannot help noticing that here the suggestion of equality belonging to the word has been turned into a means of disguising a process of subordination. The event of revelation—the content of the Christian gospel—cannot say anything for itself; it must merely answer such questions as are asked, supplying the kind of answer expected of it. This is to put the gospel in the position of a prisoner in the power of an inquisitor. But what exactly are the 'existential questions' to be answered? Undoubtedly they cannot be existential questions in the Kierke-gaardian sense of 'existential'. For Kierkegaard an existential question would be one asked by an existing man out of his own encounter with existence, and such a question could as soon be

[1] When he talks of 'situation' Tillich makes it clear that he does not mean the situation 'of the individual as individual' or 'of the group as group', but 'the totality of man's creative self-interpretation in a special period' (*ST* I, p. 4). This applies equally to his references to the 'modern mind'. He does not concern himself about the vagaries of fashions in thought or about individual case-histories. He is interested solely in the basic situation of man-as-such which appears with particular emphases at particular times. The 'situation' at any one time expresses the *objective situation* (see above, Postscript to Chapter V) as reflected in one cultural environment.

[2] *Op. cit.*, p. 61.

concerned with the whole of existence as the shouts of a man struggling for his life in the water could be communicating information about the whole of the ocean. Besides, the context shows that these questions are asked by the man who is concerned with being and non-being, having experienced ontological shock. So it appears that the so-called existential questions which the Christian gospel has to answer are simply elements of the system having to do with the system's analysis of man's essential nature and the conditions of finite being. This conclusion is confirmed altogether by the more lengthy explanation of the Method, which runs as follows:

> '. . . it makes an analysis of the human situation out of which the existential questions arise, and it demonstrates that the symbols used in the Christian message are the answers to these questions.'[1]

From this explanation the reader is left to form his own conclusions as to what would happen were the Method not available to interpret the Christian message, which, being in symbolic form, must require a competent interpreter. Presumably, without the help of the Method, people might even fail to realize that the message *was* symbolic, leading to superstitious notions. In that event the Christian message would not be only meaningless but also positively misleading.

Turning now to look at the Method in action, we can see how ontological analysis dominates and determines everything. For example, the system sets about the task of demonstrating how God is the answer to the questions raised when analysis discovers the quality of 'finitude' in human existence. Tillich writes:

> 'In respect to content the Christian answers are dependent on the revelatory events in which they appear; in respect to form they are dependent on the structure of the questions they answer. God is the answer to the question implied in human finitude. This answer cannot be derived from the analysis of existence. However, if the notion of God appears in systematic correlation with the threat of non-being which is implied in existence, God must be

[1] *Op. cit.*, p. 62.

called the infinite power of being which resists the threat of non-being. In classical theology this is being-itself.'[1]

The most obvious conclusion emerging from this argument is that, when the Method is applied, Christians have been given a precise definition of what God 'must' be called. Other things in the argument are more obscure. For instance, Tillich states that the analysis itself cannot produce God as the 'answer' to its 'question'. Yet elsewhere he goes on to speak of the 'question' of God. The question of God, he says, is the question implied in being, so that the finitude of being drives us to the question of God.[2] Thus it seems that God is already contained in the question before any answer is supplied. On this evidence, the Method does not actually draw a definite line between questions and answers. The questions in the system anticipate the answers required. This fact makes it difficult to accept the claim that the philosophical 'questions' give the form of the theological 'answers' while the content of the latter is derived from religious revelation. Surely, when God is called the infinite power of being to resist the threat of non-being, a most definite content is being given to the word *God*—a content derived wholly from the definition of God as being-itself over against finite existence. There is no evidence to suggest that the Christian message about God revealed in Jesus Christ, or any other specifically Christian statement, enters the picture at all. So in this example it is far from obvious whether any content whatsoever has been borrowed from the 'answer'. True, the word *God* comes from the area of religious faith (not necessarily Christian faith), but it remains empty of content until it is identified with *being-itself or the absolute*.

In short, the whole effort to demonstrate that there are on one side analytical questions and on the other side religious answers, that the two are quite independent and yet happen to agree so well that they can be correlated with the happiest results, and that correlation is the sole theological method employed: this effort appears increasingly barren and incredible as it is displayed. It is manifestly artificial, because both questions and answers derive from a single source and reflect

[1] *Ibid.*, p. 64.   [2] *Ibid.*, p. 166.

their origin at every turn. How is it that the notion of God, when it appears in correlation with the threat of non-being, yields the notion of being-itself? Presumably it is because being-itself, or the infinite power of being which resists the threat of non-being, is already known to be a necessary concept: for without it there would be little point in speaking of the threat of non-being. Indeed all problems vanish when the confusing talk about correlating questions and answers is removed and the theological method is taken to be that of so interpreting the language of religious faith as to make it conform with a particular ontological system. Then the procedure reveals itself as one which takes words found in the vocabulary of religious faith and uses them in the service of the system, assuming that they are pictorial approximations (symbols) to the various ontological terms which the system contains. Thus the sentence I have been considering would be better understood were it to be rephrased along these lines: 'If the word *God* is to be introduced into a world-view conceiving existence to be threatened by non-being, then *God* must stand for the infinite power of being which resists the threat of non-being; so that wherever the word *God* appears it is to be understood in the sense of being-itself.' In the sentence as revised everything is straightforward. There is no problem of interpretation, except perhaps the one of how the proposed meaning of the word *God* is to be reconciled with the message about God proclaimed by the Christian gospel.

Another example will help to show how the Method takes nothing from the Christian 'message' and everything from the system or 'analysis of the human situation out of which the existential questions arise'—how little, that is, the Method deserves the name of *correlation*. This example has to do with the Christian belief that God is the Living God. This means, says Tillich, that there exists a biblical symbol conveying the assurance that God lives in so far as he is the Ground of life. If we ask how we come to know that the biblical message is a symbol indicating that God lives in no other way except as being the Ground of life, or if we ask why the symbol cannot properly describe God as he is in himself, we are told that the reason is because, 'The ontological structure of being supplies the material for the symbols which point to the divine life.'[1] This explanation indicates clearly enough that the biblical message is being interpreted in terms of ontology, yet we are immediately assured that this does not mean that a doctrine of God is being derived from an ontological system, for information about God comes from the 'existential knowledge of revelation' alone. Nevertheless, such an assurance is very little of an indication that ontology is not controlling the entire situation. The revelation referred to here has nothing specifically to do with Christian revelation but is the concept mentioned a few lines earlier under the title of 'existential intuition'. When he speaks of the existential knowledge of revelation Tillich means the consciousness of potential infinity, the encounter with ontological shock, the pull of *eros*-faith, the concern with being and meaning, and all the other 'knowledge' which is bound up with his ontological view of the Universe. What he affirms is simply that primary revelation is not sufficient without secondary revelation, or (to use his own terminology) that the philosopher's intuition of the universal *logos* is always formed by his commitment to a particular *logos*. Far from shifting his appeal away from the authority of his system to the authority of the Christian message, he calls on the authority of another part of the same system for the support he desires.

Thus it matters little whether God is described as the answer to the question implied in human finitude or whether he is said to be the question implied in being. In the system questions and answers interpenetrate as do the 'levels' of philosophy and theology. The system is a comprehensive treasury of knowledge, at one and the same time supplying answers and asking questions. Obviously, there is no need to correlate what is already united, and so the Method is brought into play only when statements from the Christian message are brought on to the scene, having been summoned to answer the questions asked by the system. Then 'correlation' begins. The statements from the Christian message are declared to be symbols, the

[1] *Ibid.*, p. 243. The discussion falls within the section headed, 'God as Living', pp. 241–52.

real meaning of which is revealed in the material supplied by the system. Interpreted in this way, the Christian statements duly answer the questions asked—they are given no other choice. For it is the system that speaks from beginning to end, and the Christian 'symbols' expound exactly what the system decides is their 'true' message.

The unity of question and answer in the system is assumed by the explanation Tillich gives about what is involved in asking questions and receiving answers. He writes:

> 'One can rightly say that man is the being who is able to ask questions. Let us think for a moment what it means to ask a question. It implies, first, that we do not have that for which we ask. If we had it, we would not ask for it. But, in order to be able to ask for something, we must have it partially; otherwise it could not be the object of a question. He who asks has and has not at the same time.'[1]

Now, this kind of question-asking is a very special kind, one leading from having-and-not-having into really having and from knowing-and-not-knowing into truly knowing. The average individual who asks a question (e.g. 'How many miles to Babylon?') and receives an answer ('Three-score and ten') experiences no such radical transition. Very likely he will pause only to ask another question ('Can I get there by candlelight?'), and the answer to his second query ('Yes, and back again!') may or may not satisfy him and end his questioning. For an individual does not wish to *have* in the sense which the system assumes, and by the same token he *has* more than the system suggests. He has enough for his purpose when he stops asking, and he has something even before he starts asking—something upon which he builds when his questions are answered. If he asks the question, 'How far?' he knows about distance here and there, without knowing about the particular distance of his concern. If he asks the question, 'Can I?', he knows about his own capacities, without knowing whether his capacities will be adequate for the task before him.

Within the system conditions are very different. There

---

[1] *Biblical Religion and the Search for Ultimate Reality*, p. 11. Tillich's explanation here is close to Plato's in the *Meno* and the *Phaedo*.

questions are not asked by individuals who ask for more or less, for this or that, and who stop asking when they personally are satisfied. The system transfers the experience of asking a question from the individual man to philosophical man, from the curious person who asks all the questions he feels like asking to an abstraction capable of asking in the last resort only one question—namely, the question of being. In Plato's *Symposium* Socrates describes *eros* as being a daemon, half-human and half-divine, the child of Poverty and Plenty; philosophers also, says Socrates, fit this description. And Tillich, carrying the thought of Socrates one stage further, asserts: 'Man is by nature a philosopher, because he inescapably asks the question of being.'[1] So man-the-questioner himself reproduces the characteristics of *eros*. He has and he has not, and the urge of *eros* possesses him. Offspring of Poverty and Plenty as he is, he is driven to probe the mystery of his strangely divided nature.

Here Tillich's exposition of man's essential possession of the power to ask the question of being links up with the Platonic doctrine of recollection. Man knows in eternity, but in the world of time and space he partly forgets and must learn to remember once more: this is Plato's teaching, shaped by his myth of the pre-existent soul. Unlike Plato, Tillich stresses the utility of thinking as abstractly as possible and so does not use the poetical image of *recollection*, but he speaks out of exactly the same background when he talks of man's power of asking questions. The ability to ask questions belongs to the reality of participating in divine omniscience and of having essential, although not actual, knowledge of what one wants to know. Tillich's man-the-questioner is man cut to fit one special theory. The system deals solely with 'man in his finitude', or that being who would be God were he infinite, but who, because he is not God, is continually asking about his true being and meaning.[2] To speak accurately, it is finite being—in man—which really asks the ontological question about the Ground of being to which it belongs and from which it is separated.[3]

[1] *Ibid.*, p. 9.   [2] *Ibid.*, pp. 11–12.

[3] 'Finite being is a question mark. . . . It asks the question of the "ground of being" . . .' (*ST* I, p. 209).

In other words, asking the question of being actually means engaging in ontological analysis or thinking in terms of the system, for the question of being is asked in this manner only by the philosopher who accepts the system's distinction between being and existence. Such a viewpoint abolishes the individual questioner and makes all ordinary questions human beings ask irrelevant. Instead of investigating what happens when we ask questions the system has interpolated its own question, insisting that there can be no other worthy of attention.

Furthermore, the system has gone on to supply its authoritative answer to the question it raises, for the question of being is answered in the concept of being-itself. Indeed, there could be no system in the first place were there no presupposition concerning the unity of question and answer, i.e. did not the system present for acceptance a unitary view. Tillich indicates as much when he says:

> 'Symbolically speaking, God answers man's questions, and under the impact of God's answers man asks them. . . . This is a circle which drives man to a point where question and answer are not separated. This point, however, is not a moment in time. It belongs to man's essential being, to the unity of his finitude with the infinity in which he was created . . . and from which he is separated. . . .'[1]

In non-figurative language, the point of no separation is the postulate of the system, since the system would immediately fall apart if the essential unity of the finite and the infinite were to be denied. The circle is the system itself, built upon the postulate of essential divine-human unity. And the God who answers the questions he has caused men to ask is the concept of being-itself, a concept requiring essential unity to co-exist with actual separation in a state of being which both has and has not.[2]

Once we are told about the 'circle' within which his Method operates, we can appreciate why it is that Tillich never doubts

---

[1] *ST* I, p. 61.

[2] The condition of at once having and not having is the condition of both philosopher and theologian (according to the system) and it opens up the ideal of theonomy. See the Postscript to this chapter: 'The Unity of Question and Answer'.

the possibility of correlation. He has *a priori* knowledge of the validity of the Method because system-known tells him that questions and answers, situation and message, human existence and divine manifestation are essentially one. He tells us that the Method grew out of his earlier definition of theology as theonomous metaphysics,[1] and it is only as we hold in mind this background that the term *correlation* will cease to confuse us. For nothing but the assumption that the truth contained in religion finds its sufficient explanation in the *logos* philosophy can justify the process of taking biblical or doctrinal statements and claiming that these are symbols of ontological concepts. Yet the technique of substituting one set of terms for another—on the pretext that the substituted set gives the 'real' meaning of the discarded set—is the whole of Tillich's chosen Method. Only thus is the Christian message made to yield the 'answers' demanded by the system.

Tillich claims that his Method has always been used, consciously or unconsciously, by systematic theologians.[2] As evidence he quotes from the opening of Calvin's *Institutes*:

> 'The knowledge of ourselves is not only an incitement to seek after God, but likewise a considerable assistance toward finding him. On the other hand, it is plain that no man can arrive at the true knowledge of himself, without having first contemplated the divine character, and then descended to the consideration of his own.'[3]

He says that here we are given 'the essence of the method of correlation'. Plainly, however, this is quite a different 'circle' from the one in which Tillich operates, for it founds its analysis of the human situation upon the Christian revelation of God. Tillich starts from the postulate that 'Man cannot receive an answer to a question he has not asked.'[4] Calvin starts from the postulate that 'we should learn from Scripture that God, the Creator of the universe, can by sure marks be distinguished

[1] 'Author's Preface', *The Protestant Era*, xlii; see also above pp. 59, 70.
[2] *ST* I, p. 60; *ST* II, p. 16.
[3] *ST* I, p. 63 n. 20.
[4] *ST* II, p. 13. See also *ST* I, p. 65.

from all the throng of feigned gods'.[1] Tillich is concerned with what happens when man considers his own essential nature, when he is 'alone with himself'. Then it is that, he believes, man considers his essential avenue to truth, discovering that, 'The question implied in human finitude is directed toward the answer: the eternal.'[2] Calvin is concerned with what happens when men 'establish their complete happiness in him [God]' and 'give themselves truly and sincerely to him'. He adds significantly that those who consider the question, 'What is God?' are merely toying with idle speculations.[3] No contrast could be greater, and it is hard to see how there is any connection between the Method that Tillich employs and 'correlation' in Calvin. The sole similarity seems to be the very superficial one that both believe that knowledge of God and man are somehow linked. There the likeness between the two thinkers begins and ends. Calvin most certainly does not allow an analysis of the nature of man to set up any 'questions' for faith to answer. The Christian gospel both provides the answers we should know and the questions we should ask.

The chief cause of the startling contrast between Tillich and Calvin is that the latter shows himself to be a true 'existentialist' in the Kierkegaardian sense, bringing together God and the existing individual on the basis of the individual's passion for eternal happiness.[4] Again, anticipating Kierkegaard in another direction, Calvin denies that 'essential' knowledge of God is relevant for the Christian. While Tillich believes that it is man's concern about his true being which causes him to be 'liberated

[1] *Institutes of the Christian Religion*, Book I, Chapter VI, 1: Library of Christian Classics (Westminster Press and SCM Press) XX, XXI, 1961, p. 71.

[2] *ST* II, p. 15.   [3] *Op. cit.*, I, II, 1 and 2: p. 41.

[4] Kierkegaard, whose theology comes out of the Lutheran tradition, hardly ever mentions Calvin; the similarity between the two stems from their common loyalty to traditional Christianity. In this connection it is interesting to find that George H. Tavard, contrasting Tillich's theology and that of Chalcedonian orthodoxy from the perspective of Roman Catholicism, more than once quotes Calvin to show how far Tillich has departed from the central affirmations of the Christian message (*op. cit.*, pp. 28, 42, 51, 80–1). He could very easily have discovered similar statements in Kierkegaard.

and able to see true reality' and gives him experience of 'a saving transformation and an illuminating revelation',[1] Calvin allows no revelation except that which comes with the believer's inward acceptance of the Gospel. Following the argument of the first two chapters of Romans, the Reformer concludes:

> '. . . at the same time as we have enjoyed a slight taste of the divine from contemplation of the universe, having neglected the true God, we raise up in his stead dreams and spectres of our own brains.'[2]

In short, even the most superficial comparison between Calvin and Tillich teaches that, so far from Calvin expressing the 'essence' of Tillich's chosen Method, the Reformer expresses necessity for turning the Method inside out before it can be of service to Christianity. The Method builds upon the belief that truth is reached through the union of 'existential intuition' and 'cognitive analysis'—the former being identified and described by the latter, allowing a system to be built in which everything has its proper place and is shown in its 'real' nature. And the faith behind the Method is that, when man makes use of the Method to understand how 'true reality' can transform his experience and illumine his being, this is because he is aware how the divine can conquer the contradictions of existence. From its different viewpoint, the theological approach typified by Calvin maintains that God's choice of the way in which he has access to men's consciousness has been revealed in the Christian gospel, that this way is the way of free grace, and that from the side of man grace is experienced in the gift of faith. Tillich-type theology trusts in the divine power which maintains being. Calvin-type theology trusts in the divine grace which creates faith and forgives sins.

Here the stage is set for a direct confrontation of the two types, and the issue to be settled is: can the forgiveness of sins be identified with the conquest of the contradictions of

---

[1] *Biblical Religion and the Search for Ultimate Reality*, p. 65. Note that here Tillich asserts that awareness of the ontological question is 'an opening of the eyes, a revelatory experience'.
[2] *Op. cit.*, I, V, 15: p. 69.

existence? It is a vital issue—perhaps *the* vital issue—in the relationship between Tillich's system and Christianity.

Postscript: The Unity of Question and Answer

In the *Systematic Theology* 'asking the question of being' is a metaphor for engaging in ontological analysis within the frame of reference provided by the *logos* philosophy. When the analysis is complete and the doctrine of the *logos* philosophy has been expounded, the 'answer' arrives. This metaphorical mode of speaking introduces unnecessary confusion. It is not altogether easy to see why we must ask the question of being under the impact of the answer we receive or why we must be driven to a point where question and answer are not separated. On the other hand, there is no great effort of mind required to assent to the proposition that a metaphysical theory, once accepted, determines both the solution of problems and the manner of their posing. We should know where we stood if Tillich told us frankly that the 'circle' where question and answer are joined in ultimate unity is the fenced-off area circumscribed by his ontology and that his system does not permit us to move outside it.

Why Tillich does not tell us this but rings the changes on the metaphor of question-and-answer instead is because he wishes to argue that he is exhibiting two distinct elements and, without distorting either, proving that they are made for each other. Hence his stress is laid on correlation as the necessary method for theology to employ because it favours neither faith nor reason, allowing each to say its own say. He insists that his Method enables him to show that Christian answers fit questions asked by those who seek the truth apart from revelation and religion generally, thus meeting once and for all the challenge, 'Is there any way to unite the opposite ways of ontology and biblical religion?'[1] Here both the motive and the strategy are obviously the same as in the issue of the philosophy-theology

[1] See *Biblical Religion and the Search for Ultimate Reality*, p. 56.

relation which I investigated in my third chapter. Indeed, the
issue of synthesis arises again, almost unaltered, in connection
with correlation. This is hardly surprising since it is the basic
claim of the system to be properly apologetic—i.e. to mediate
between Christianity and the modern mind, satisfying equally
the philosopher and the Christian theologian.[1]

Tillich himself, as well as his critics and interpreters, makes
some relevant comments on the balance (or lack of balance)
between 'questions' and 'answers' in the system.

Tillich's observations concern the systematic approach as
such, but they can be applied also to his understanding of his
Method. He writes:

> 'But there is a real danger felt by those who are uneasy about
> the system; namely, that its form becomes self-sufficient and
> determines the content. Should this occur, the truth is moulded
> till it fits the system.'[2]

His reply is that in expounding his system he begins each main
section 'with an existential analysis of the question to which the
theological concepts are supposed to furnish the answer'.
Unquestionably, Tillich's admission is candid and direct, for,
above all, the content of the system is the point at issue. Yet his
defence is less than satisfactory on at least two counts. First, the
notion of a presuppositionless 'existential' analysis is a chimera.
The 'essentialist' character of his actual analysis is evident at
every turn. (As he himself has said, it could not be otherwise if
one tries to build a theological system.)[3] Second, the Christian
message does not answer the questions put to it until it has been
declared to be symbolic and has been translated into the terms
of the system . . . moulded to fit.

---

[1] So Tillich calls apologetic theology 'answering theology', a theology
answering the questions raised by the human situation. See *ST* I pp. 31,
and 6–8.

[2] *The Theology of Paul Tillich*, p. 330.

[3] See above, p. 38. Tillich 'existential' analysis is most probably modelled
on Heidegger's example. The first part of the latter's *Sein und Zeit* purports
to give an analysis of the meaning of existence without going outside man's
existence itself. Yet Heidegger thinks of man as the clue to metaphysics
which, like Tillich, he identifies with the question of being. Like Tillich
also, he has agreed that he is not an existentialist but an ontologist.

Tillich's self-justification can do little to lay to rest the doubts of those who are uneasy about the system and mistrust his Method. Hendrik Kraemer, probably the most outspoken among the critics of the system, does not consider the claims of correlation as such. Instead, he bases his argument against the validity of the system on Tillich's statement that theology starts from a 'mystical *a priori*' and then proceeds to add to this the criterion of the Christian message.[1] Beginning with the same observation, Robert C. Johnson seeks its bearing upon the Method. Johnson notes that 'the orientation point, and the basis of the mutual dependence within the correlation, is one logically prior to the Christian revelation', and he concludes that, on this account, 'there is no assurance or guarantee that the questions with which Christian theology deals are Christian questions—and even less that they are *the* Christian questions'.[2] He sees a strong affinity between the theologies of Schleier-macher and Tillich, based on their common starting-place in the 'mystical *a priori*'. Thus he writes:

> 'Each builds upon the initial assumption of an "inside knowledge", an immediate, pre-reflective knowledge of an immanent ground of unity that is both logically and ontologically prior to the separation involved in all human cognition and existence.'[3]

Johnson's precise understanding of the basic unity underlying the 'questions' and 'answers' of the Method—a unity based on the system's 'orientation point' in ontology—makes it difficult to understand why he should hesitate at all over the issue of synthesis.[4] He finds that Tillich's system requires 'questions' and 'answers' which are at once independent and dependent.[5] In just the same way, the system requires a 'philosophy' and a 'theology' showing interpenetration and yet distinct from each other; for, as correlation is possible solely when it rests on the presupposition of an orientation point, so the philosophy-theology relation of the system rests on the same presupposition. The point to which man is driven (according to the system) is

---

[1] *Op. cit.*, pp. 419–20, 427–8, 445. Kraemer points out (p. 445) that the effect of *adding* the Christian message to a given concept is to subjugate the message to an ontological philosophy of religion.

[2] *Op. cit.*, p. 119.　　[3] *Ibid.*, p. 69; see also p. 118.

[4] See above pp. 76–7.　　[5] *Op. cit.*, p. 118.

the point of perfect theonomy. Here questions and answers are one, and so are philosophy and theology. Actually, man is driven to this point if—and only if—he accepts the *logos* philosophy. Nothing drives him there except the assumptions of one particular metaphysics.[1]

Tillich's Method has been defended by Edward Farley, who expounds in his *The Transcendence of God* what he terms the Principle of Correlation.[2] Denying that correlation is based on synthesis, Farley argues that the Principle is derived from the later Schelling in his revolt against Hegel's belief that religion and philosophy share the same content—which belief is the one based on synthesis. Having put his case for Tillich's thinking being considered a true alternative to Hegel's 'identity ontology', this critic adds, in a footnote, that he holds that Tillich in fact uses his speculative theory of the divine to judge religious revelation, although 'this is not the intention or an inevitability in the method of correlation.'[3]

Now it seems a little odd, if Tillich is adopting Schelling's Principle, and if Schelling decisively broke with Hegel's way of synthesis, that the Method expounded in the *Systematic Theology* should fall once more into some kind of 'identity ontology'. Furthermore, Farley produces no evidence to back his claim that the result discovered in the *Systematic Theology* is not an inevitability in the Method. He stresses the notion (taken from Tillich himself) that the Principle of Correlation must not be blamed for the shortcomings of any particular theology based on the Principle. Yet this belief in correlation as a universal method serving different theologies is a belief that fails to see correlation for what it is. For correlation is the product of one philosophical outlook and fits no more than one type of theological system. Without realizing it, Farley illustrates this fact admirably when he explains why it is possible to apply the

[1] Though used in other circumstances, Professor Emmet's words apply very well in these: '. . . I do not see that Tillich has done more than to say that if we do not make these assumptions it will be so much the worse for the *logos* philosophy which he favors . . .' (*The Theology of Paul Tillich*, pp. 207–8)
[2] Section 3, Chapter III (Philadelphia, Westminster Press, 1960: pp. 97–102).
[3] *Ibid.*, p. 233.

Principle of Correlation improperly. He writes, 'But this merely stresses that theology itself has its being in existence, and will reflect estrangement.'[1] Such an explanation takes for granted that Tillich's definitions of *being, existence* and *estrangement* are authoritative explanations of reality, and therefore point to the 'real' nature and function of theology. Farley has adopted Tillich's ontology and also, by implication, his idea of theology. Having once embraced the system, he can hardly refuse to remain with it; he can quarrel with it in detail, but not in essentials—and the unity of question and answer, situation and message, philosophy and theology, is the essential basis of correlation. Therefore, if he desires a theology that shall not sit in judgment on Christianity, he will have to choose a Principle which does not have (in Johnson's terminology) an orientation point logically prior to the Christian revelation.

It is instructive to find that Farley suggests the Principle of Correlation to be the result of Tillich's trying to combine Hegel with Kierkegaard.[2] He does not mention that Kierkegaard gives reasons why such a combination must prove unworkable, yet his defence of correlation, in fact, demonstrates how sound the Kierkegaardian diagnosis is. According to Kierkegaard, a system must assume that truth flows out of itself. In connection with correlation, the truth which the system lays down for acceptance is the unity of divine-human reason underlying all existing divisions. The system knows that theonomy precedes philosophy and theology. It knows that the questions the ontologist raises are prompted by divine revelation. Therefore it knows that any religious statement—if it is to be counted as revelation at all—must 'really' be the answer to the 'real' questions of existence, i.e. ontological ones; and this systematic truth is exposed by means of correlation, i.e. translation of religious terms into ontological ones. Because the Principle of Correlation is based on the assumption that the meaning of revelation is known apart from the Christian message and applied to judge the latter, Farley's separation of Schelling-Tillich from Hegel is

---

[1] *Ibid.*
[2] *Ibid.*, p. 102.

beside the point, theologically speaking. A correlation ontology, just as much as an identity ontology, posits the rule of speculation over faith. Kierkegaard knew what he was doing when he refused to find in Schelling a genuine 'existentialism' that had cast off the shackles of Hegel's essentialism.

VII

SALVATION AND CREATION

WITH THE last chapter ended one stage in my inquiry. The foundations of Tillich's system have been exposed, and it is now possible to see how system-built develops out of system-known. Since the chief difficulty in reading Tillich is in disentangling his terminology and, particularly, in finding out how much is assumed in his definitions, the way ahead should be to some extent easier going. For, once the reader is aware of what actually is involved in the method of correlation (and in the question-and-answer metaphor used to expound it, with such confusing results), the sting of the system is drawn. While other parts of the system wait to be explored, they can be related to that which is already known, and seeming ambiguities and obscurities will mostly disappear. The next area of the system which opens up for inspection is its understanding of the nature of the Universe, its beginning and its final goal, as this relates to human existence.[1] This raises the problem of how the system regards the Christian doctrines of Creation and Redemption, thus advancing my inquiry into the stage where system and gospel can be compared and contrasted much more directly than has been possible so far. An immediate point of contact—and conflict—comes, as I have already indicated, in connection with the concept of forgiveness.

It is impossible to think about forgiveness without asking whether the system, which takes as its terms of reference essential and existential being, moves at all in the same dimension as Christianity, which speaks of God's love and man's sins. Up to the present I have been concerned to show how the system does not actually correlate 'situation' and 'message' but

[1] Broadly speaking, this area coincides with the second volume (and third part) of the *Systematic Theology*, 'Existence and the Christ'.

instead draws both sides of the so-called correlation out of the all-embracing vision of the *logos* philosophy, assuming that the Christian message can be interpreted to agree with this vision. Now it is time to ask whether the translation of the Christian message into the terms of the system is (*a*) arbitrary but possible, or (*b*) both arbitrary and inconceivable. The first steps toward finding which alternative is correct has to be to notice whether the vocabularies of the system and of the Christian message overlap significantly.

On the matter of whether his system finds place for the concept of forgiveness, Tillich's own view is quite explicit:

> 'The question implied in human finitude is directed toward the answer: the eternal. The question implied in human estrangement is directed toward the answer: forgiveness.'[1]

This confidently stated thesis, however, does not wholly fit in with the principles of the system. There is no difficulty about the first sentence, for, by the system's definition, the eternal is a quality negating finitude and expressing the infinity of being. Thus the answer to the question of human finitude is, beyond question, the eternal: *eros* draws the finite to the infinite—or, more accurately, to the eternal Ground of both finitude and infinity. But the second sentence, on the other hand, creates problems. The answer to the question of human estrangement must be some quality negating estrangement. And within the system it is the power of being which negated estrangement by manifesting the totality which is man's true being. And this power of being is represented in existence by *eros*, or love as the desire for reunion with the source of being. In the world of time and space 'the estranged is striving for reunion', and the concept of reunion is one that has 'ontological ultimacy'.[2] So it is evident that the proper answer to the question of human estrangement must be some manifestation of the reuniting power of being. But forgiveness is not a suitable vehicle to carry such a manifestation. Forgiveness has to do with restoring a

---

[1] *ST* II, p. 15.

[2] *Love, Power, and Justice*, p. 25. Compare too the statement, 'Love as the striving for the reunion of the separated is the opposite of estrangement' (*ST* II, p. 47).

relationship rather than with reunion within a totality. Forgiveness is impossible without someone who forgives and a forgiven individual.

It appears that what has happened in this instance is that Tillich has reached outside his system and appropriated a word out of the vocabulary of Christian faith, setting it then within his system where it is out of place but nevertheless served the purpose of drawing together his system and the Christian gospel. That the Christian word actually is out of place and that the seeming agreement of system and gospel has no foundation in fact is not hard to prove, for one has only to look elsewhere in the system to find the required evidence. In the matter of forgiveness, Tillich has emphatically stated that this quality, so far from being the inclusive 'answer' to the 'question' of estrangement, is no more than one amongst many of the *appearances* of the reality of man's need to be reunited with his source. Not forgiveness itself, but that reality toward which forgiveness points, is the answer that the system actually gives to the question of estrangement. For example, man's experience in his situation in the twentieth century makes him realize, says Tillich, that forgiveness is not a living symbol able to meet man's religious needs—

> 'The question arising out of this experience is not, as in the Reformation, the question of a merciful God and the forgiveness of sins. . . . It is the question of a reality in which the self-estrangement of our existence is overcome, a reality of reconciliation and reunion, of creativity, meaning, and hope. We shall call such a reality the "New Being", a term whose presuppositions and implications can be explained only through the whole system.'[1]

This statement is clearly much more consistent than the one which ties forgiveness to estrangement. The New Being is as well suited to negate estrangement as forgiveness is ill suited. (After all, the term has been invented to serve this need and no other!) The New Being is a quality of being, it is manifest as a power, and it reunites us with the source of our being in so far as we participate in it. Furthermore, it is not tied to the

[1] *ST* I, p. 49.

personal realm. It does not require any particular individual in relation to it, either to give or to receive it.

Exit forgiveness, enter that toward which forgiveness points! Tillich elevates this term of his invention to the position of 'norm' of all theology—the New Being is our ultimate concern. It is therefore, by implication, the final answer to human estrangement. Here is a 'theological answer' exactly corresponding to the system's 'existential question'. There is no doubt that this question and this answer are not divided, for they have every appearance of growing out of the same view of the Universe.

Most conspicuously, the message brought by the New Being is a message arising out of Tillich's theonomous metaphysics. It is a child of the system and has no necessary connection with the Christian gospel. Tillich seeks to supply a link between this concept and Christianity by asserting that the New Being is manifest 'in Jesus as the Christ'.[1] What he means by this claim is an issue on its own, and I shall deal with it as the subject of the next chapter. But a prior issue is the relation of the New Being to the message of Christianity in general. If the Christian gospel is understood as the message of the New Being, so we are told, an answer will be given to the question implied in our situation and in every human situation. With the metaphor removed, this statement reads to the effect that, if Christianity is interpreted in the terms which the system employs, the resulting message will meet the requirements which the system declares to be essential requirements in a genuine religion. In other words, unless the Christian gospel means what the system wants it to mean, it will have no message acceptable to the system. The importance of the Norm of the system is therefore beyond all doubt. The New Being has unquestioned authority within the system. In fact, when Tillich introduces his Method, he explains that the 'answers' implied in the Christian message are produced by systematic theology 'under the norm'.[2] Thus it

---

[1] *Ibid.*, pp. 49–50.

[2] *Ibid.*, p. 64 (italics in the original). The other conditions for obtaining 'answers' are, according to Tillich, to take them '*from* the sources' (the Bible and culture) and '*through* the medium' (human experience).

appears that the possibility of correlation is assumed altogether because the Norm of the New Being has been previously chosen and the compatibility of that Norm with Christianity taken for granted.

It cannot be denied that the choice of this particular Norm has taken a very great deal for granted. And this brings back into the picture the concept of forgiveness. For, according to the system, forgiveness may sometimes (e.g. in Reformation times) be the message which meets the human situation, and sometimes it may not (e.g. in the twentieth century). But the New Being is the perennial message which always meets every human situation. It is the essential message while the other is the accidental. Therefore the relation between the New Being and forgiveness, as the system asserts it, gives the pattern of the relation between the message of the system and the Christian gospel. The symbols of the Christian gospel must follow where the Norm leads, and the problem for Christian theology is precisely whether it is possible for the gospel to follow the system and still remain the gospel. By setting the concept of forgiveness and the concept of the New Being over against each other, I hope to find a ready solution to the problem. What holds for this piece of the system should hold throughout.

In the theology which makes forgiveness the centre of the Christian message, the fact of God's forgiveness of man is something which we could not know apart from his self-revelation through his chosen people, a revelation culminating in the Incarnation and the Cross. Forgiveness of sins, says Calvin, is that 'which believers obtain, not through any merit of their own, but through the sole mercy of the Lord'. Forgiveness is 'the way to approach God and the means that . . . preserves us in his kingdom', being the sure foundation on which 'rests and stands our salvation'.[1] Calvin's type of theology assumes that forgiveness comes to individuals, not on account of what they are but *as* they are.[2] It assumes that, since they are

---

[1] *Instruction in Faith* (Philadelphia, Westminster Press, 1942), p. 53.

[2] This distinction forms the basis of the doctrine of man found in the two contrasting types of theology. For Tillich, man is *essential* man, an entity to be discovered 'behind' or 'beneath' the appearance of individuals existing in time and space, never simply men as they are observed but man-as-such

individuals, forgiveness reaches them as news—something entirely unexpected and unforeseeable. And it assumes that the news of forgiveness is news for them as individuals, concerning their eternal happiness. As Calvin repeats, 'it is always necessary that we be justified by something outside of ourselves', a statement leading on to a confession of what justification means for Christians:

> 'Finally, we must thus affirm that the company of Jesus has such a value that because of it we are not only received freely as just, but our very deeds are considered just and are recompensed with an eternal reward.'[1]

Underlying this theological outlook there are two prime elements. The first of these is the reality of the individual in existence. And the second is the separation of *agape*—God's outreaching and self-giving care—from *eros*—the unifying love striving to restore the part to the totality of which it is a part. The first element is necessary, otherwise the Christian Church could not be a communion or fellowship. The unity of the Church does not spring from any quality belonging to man-as-such but because it is a communion of believers, each of whom has been called into the fellowship. That the individual is a reality follows as a corollary of the Christian doctrine of Creation (which I shall be considering shortly), and the nature of the Church is, of course, closely linked with Creation and the Fall. This first theological element leads naturally to the second, for God's love is that kind of love which meets real individuals and their individual needs. Like Christian fellowship—the fellowship created by God's love through the Spirit—this love is not something which follows from the nature of man-as-such. As Anders Nygren says:

> 'We look in vain for an explanation of God's love in the character of the man who is the object of His love. . . . In relation to man,

as the philosopher knows him. A theologian of the opposite type may also speak (as Barth speaks—see above p. 105 n. 1) of 'man as such', but he means man as existing, where any individual, as an individual, represents all his fellows.

[1] *Ibid.*, p. 45.

Divine love is *"unmotivated"*. When it is said that God loves man this is not a judgment on what man is like, but on what God is like.'[1]

Such a love cannot be a longing for reunion, an *eros*-urge in which like reaches out to embrace like. On the contrary, it is a caring which is, in Nygren's terms, spontaneous and un-motivated. It is a caring which watches over another for the good of that person and which is characterized, not by any longing, but by patience (Isa. 65.1, 2) and unsleeping vigilance (Psalm 121). Neither this second theological element nor the first one became controversial issues until comparatively modern times. Yet Kierkegaard's category of 'the individual before God' has its roots in Luther's teaching that faith is not faith unless it is 'for me and for thee', and Nygren's separation of *agape* and *eros* is an implicate of the Reformation rejection of the idea of merit. Both elements are unmistakable in Calvin. He starts from the assumption that the only thing that really matters in deciding what men are is whether they turn away from their Creator or turn towards him in 'personal religion'.[2] And he certainly would have agreed with Nygren's statement that to speak of God's love is to say nothing about man. His continual theme is that we cannot use our ideas of what is right and wrong in order to judge the behaviour of God, and even blasphemously to challenge his goodness. Taking it for granted that God's love is seen above all in the forgiveness of the Cross, he bases all his arguments against the Roman doctrine of merit on the axiom expressed in his question: 'First, what is forgiveness but a gift of sheer liberality?'[3]

Calvin's treatment of forgiveness is worked out against the background of the Apostles' Creed. The biblical phrase 'the forgiveness of sins' affirmed in that Creed sums up, in a simple but direct manner, why the elements of individuality and *agape* separated from *eros* have become prominent issues for Christian theology. For the phrase indicates that here is an experience where an existing individual finds *his* sins forgiven,

[1] *Agape and Eros* (London, SPCK, 1947), pp. 75–6.
[2] *Op. cit.*, p. 17. The French word Calvin used was *piété*.
[3] *Institutes of the Christian Religion* (III, IV, 25): p. 651.

And forgiveness of sins is also an experience where individuals encounter Another, in a relationship which has not been of their seeking. But neither element is to be found in the theology based on the New Being. According to this theology, which is concerned with the overcoming of existential estrangement, man discovers *himself* in becoming aware of the power of being-itself. But note that no one sees his own individual face when man-as-such becomes aware of himself. For this 'self'-discovery is not really an event in time and space. In order to know the meaning of man, the finite must know the infinite to which it is joined, which means that it is divinity which knows itself in humanity. In awareness there is no encounter between the unlike. There can be no one to meet or be met, because awareness is awareness of some*thing*—

> *Man is immediately aware of something unconditional which is the prius of the separation and interaction of subject and object, theoretically as well as practically.*[1]

Once such an awareness is granted, religious revelation concerning man's relationship with God becomes irrelevant. For awareness is by itself a full and sufficient revelation of God the Unconditional. Revelation of God's love becomes irrelevant likewise, since God—being that which precedes the existence of subject and object—needs must love himself as the unlimited Ground of all that is. Forgiveness of sins cannot matter in the end, because, in that case, the Unconditional would have to bow to the conditions of a world where real individuals need to be forgiven for real sins.

Starting from opposed world-views, the two theologies not unnaturally see themselves as threatened from opposite quarters. Only 'artificial barriers,' according to Tillich, are able to stop 'the searching mind' from asking the question about the being of God, the truth of estrangement, and the New Being.[2] Unquestionably, he means by 'the searching mind' the mind driven on by the urge of *eros*, the mind on the quest for being and aware of itself as participating in being-itself, the

[1] *Theology of Culture*, p. 22 (italics in the original).
[2] *ST* II, p. 12.

mind already knowing itself to be infinite potentially while finite actually. Such a mind cannot be deflected from asking the truly philosophic question, which is 'the question of man himself'.[1] No restriction can be contemplated, because the fact that the question is asked means that the answer is, in principle, present. If the mind driven by the urge of eros reaches out in quest of the truth, this is on account of the presence of the divine mind thinking through it and taking it up into the divine truth. Once man by means of self-questioning desires to know, he is from that point driven to ask the right questions and cannot stop until he embraces the really real. Exactly at this point, however, the theology based on forgiveness of sins cries, Halt! Calvin, who says that we come to some slight knowledge of God only to pass him by and set up some 'phantom of our own brain', roundly condemns all those who 'estimate God not by his infinite majesty but by the foolish and giddy vanity of their own mind'.[2] Tillich-type theology cannot but see this as an 'artificial barrier' seeking to prohibit the philosophic eros. Calvin-type theology is bound to view theonomous metaphysics as the pursuit of a 'phantom' deriving from the human mind's 'giddy vanity'—what Kierkegaard called 'an essay in the comic' and 'thinking fantastically'.

Of course, Tillich-type theology does not admit the rejection of philosophic eros by Calvin-type theology, because it does not admit that a kergymatic theology such as Calvin or Kierkegaard supported is a possible one. Tillich would put the query to Calvin—How we can know God so as to estimate him by his infinite majesty unless we possess an immediate awareness of the infinite? He would probably suggest that, in thinking that man's enlightenment can come solely through God's revealed Word given to Israel and the Christian church, Calvin is ignorant of the systematic understanding of the sources of faith. By the same token, therefore, Calvin fails to realize that the concrete symbols of the Judeo-Christian religion cannot have more than a relative validity.[3] Yet is it not the very willingness of the Tillich-type theology to have the Christian message

[1] ST II, p. 13.   [2] Instruction in Faith, p. 18.
[3] 'They [Judaism, Islam, and Christianity] are intolerant and can

stand in a relative position to its own absolute authority that leaves the Christian believer hesitant in thinking that it can be called *Christian* theology? Tillich's philosophical theology is so very certain about what exactly the Christian symbols 'really' mean that the significance of the Christian gospel seems to crumble away piece by piece whenever his system's statements are closely examined. I have tried to show that, from its context within the system, the New Being as the overcoming of estrangement cannot possibly be taken as the equivalent of forgiveness. I shall now look especially at the term 'estrangement' in order to find out how Tillich goes about relating the term to the Christian term 'sin'.

'Estrangement is not a biblical term,' writes Tillich, 'but is implied in most of the biblical descriptions of man's predicament.'[1] Once again the reader will note the use of the word 'implied'. The biblical descriptions of man as a sinner imply his existential estrangement if—and only if—the Bible is not in the last resort interested in the individual and his needs but teaches (implicitly) the unity of the divine and the human in the urge of *eros* within man-as-such. Supposing this to be true, three notable consequences ensue. The first of these is that we cannot take seriously the biblical teaching which states that the nature of sin is revealed by the presence of God's law and by our failure to obey that law. Instead, sins are to be taken to be expressions of one sin, which is the 'sin' of failing to have unity with God. According to the system, 'It is not disobedience to a law which makes an act sinful but the fact that it is an expression of man's estrangement from God, from men, from himself.'[2] The second consequence is that man's individual responsibility to God is depersonalized, becoming the misfortune of finite being in finding itself to be less than divine. How far this depersonalizing process goes is not always apparent at a first glance. For example, we may read that 'unbelief' for Protestant Christianity 'means the act or state in which man in the totality

become fanatical and idolatrous. . . . The self-criticism of every faith is the insight into the relative validity of the concrete symbols in which it appears' (*Dynamics of Faith*, p. 123).

[1] *ST* II, p. 45.   [2] *Ibid.*, pp. 46–7.

of his being turns away from God';[1] and we may accept the explanation under the impression that here 'man' means the existing individual. But actually the statement has nothing to do with individual decision, for it concerns the self-realization in existence of finite being. And the 'turning away' is not a hardening of the heart which refuses to meet God in his self-disclosure. It is the condition consequent upon man's entering into his destiny in time and space, actualizing himself as finite being and thus losing 'his essential unity with the ground of his being and his world'.[2]

The first and second consequences of accepting the term 'estrangement' in place of 'sins' leads on to the third, which is the most important one, since it shows how the system interprets the religious concept of salvation. Because estrangement has no place in the dimension of personal relationships or individual encounter, but moves entirely within the impersonal realm where the part is real only by virtue of its participation in the whole, it is axiomatic that it is not John Smith or Mary Brown who stands in need of salvation. Rather, it is the estranged part which needs to be saved into the whole (i.e. made actually what it is essentially). From the point of view of the system this means that the world of time and space is waiting to be saved into the Ground of its being, so that it need be no longer the 'split' world we know, a world where essential and existential being are two levels of being. Salvation means the healing of a cosmic wound and relates to man only because man is part of the Universe of being and that part in which the split comes into consciousness. Man is the wound supplied with a voice, a voice to be raised in complaint and dissatisfaction. Man, with his ability to ask questions about the Ground of his being and meaning, reveals most openly 'the situation of being related to and excluded from infinity'.[3] Man shows the nature of the split world, agonizes over it, and, in proclaiming that he

[1] *ST* II, p. 47.

[2] *Loc. cit.* Note that the prime mark of man's 'unbelief' is the fact that he asks questions. Did man not ask questions, all would be well—man would be God (cp. *Biblical Religion and the Quest for Ultimate Reality*, p. 12).

[3] *Ibid.*, p. 31.

cannot endure the contradictions of existence, points to the sole remedy by means of which it may be overcome.

To sum up: the first consequence of admitting that the biblical description of man's predicament involves estrangement is loss of the biblical emphasis upon human disobedience; the second is loss of the biblical teaching concerning man's individual responsibility for unbelief; and the third is loss of the biblical account of God's reconciling action in saving those who believe through faith. Since the rebellion of mankind is replaced by the deficiencies of created nature, both the law of God and man's ingratitude and disobedience fade into the background, and the foreground is monopolized by an unbiblical preoccupation with the predicament inherent in inhabiting a world of finite beings and by an unbiblical hope in the salvation which will achieve 'victory over existence'.[1]

On the issue of salvation, the theology of the New Being misrepresents the Christian gospel both negatively and positively. The negative misrepresentation comes to the fore in a claim to the effect that, if salvation be understood in terms of healing, this is an adequate interpretation.[2] It should be obvious enough that, with salvation restricted to this one metaphor, that part of the biblical message is ignored which declares how salvation is first of all God's gracious action in seeking out the lost and rescuing them. In Tillich's ordinary usage 'healing' means nothing more than impersonal 'reintegration'. Thus a typical sentence in the *Systematic Theology* asks the rhetorical question:

> 'But if final revelation is unable to heal the splits of cognitive reason, how could it heal the splits of reason in any of its functions?'[3]

By implication this sentence assumes that 'healing' does not come to existing individuals but to the totality of the rational order which is disrupted under the conditions of existence. And,

---

[1] *Ibid.*, p. 165. Johnson points out that Tillich's theology constantly, by *a shift in the question*, changes the biblical message (*op. cit.*, p. 122). Here the shift is from overcoming *the world* to overcoming *existence*—a very different thing.

[2] *Ibid.*, p. 166.   [3] *ST* I, p. 154.

if this be the case, then Tillich's words appear not merely to ignore much that Christian faith asserts about salvation but also to propose something very difficult to reconcile with the Christian gospel in general. Inadequate statement thus shades into the proclamation of 'another gospel'.

Consider, for instance, how the system which has erected the New Being in Jesus as the Christ into the Norm of systematic theology can, on occasion, drop all reference to the Christ, and still be certain of the power of the New Being present in the Universe:

> 'The New Being is not dependent on the special symbols in which it is expressed. It has the power to be free from every form in which it appears.'[1]

The positive misrepresentation of the Christian message of salvation is brought to a focus here, for the claim to be able to do without the 'appearance' of Jesus Christ conflicts completely with the biblical claim that 'there is salvation in no one else . . . no other name . . . by which we must be saved' (Acts 4.12). Yet the system denies any conflict. From its own standpoint it has merely taken Christianity under the protection of its authority and demonstrated that the kerygmatic claim of the latter, when symbolically interpreted, is true—or, as Kierkegaard would say, up to a point true. After all, the system can argue that it does not propose *any other name* as Saviour. The New Being is not a name but a power independent of any and every name. Nevertheless, the New Being has effectively displaced the name of Jesus as the only Saviour. When the truth of Christianity is thought to 'imply' the New Being, then truth has ceased to lie with a message about the Incarnate Son of God and has been transferred to a message about the real structure of the Universe. Salvation becomes the breaking through into time and space of the power of essential unity conquering existential estrangement; or, to put the same thing less technically, the power of the New Being within man is eternally witnessing to the wholeness of being that lies behind appearances, undoing the harm done at the creation of our split world by 'healing' it into unity.

[1] *ST* II, p. 165.

At the point where creation rather than mankind is made the principal object of salvation, there the Christian doctrines of Creation and the Fall are turned inside out. Instead of a good creation spoilt through man's disobedience, the system seems to posit a creation the very existence of which is productive of all evils, a creation needing to be saved from itself. This aspect of the system is too startling to be overlooked. It has been challenged by several of the contributors to the volume *The Theology of Paul Tillich*, most directly and most fully by Reinhold Niebuhr in his essay, 'Biblical Thought and Ontological Speculation in Tillich's Theology'. And Tillich has replied to Niebuhr's criticism not only in the same book[1] but also in the second volume of the *Systematic Theology*.[2] He concedes that Niebuhr's 'reproach' that he identifies finitude with evil and turns Creation into the Fall is understandable, but denies that it is justified. On the contrary, he maintains that his system holds that the created universe is 'good in its essential character'.

This sounds reassuring until the reader remembers that creation for Tillich is the transition from essence to existence, and that in existence everything is estranged from what it 'essentially' is. Existence, our state in the world of space and time is not good. It is not evil. It is self-contradictory.[3] Therefore, when Tillich tells us that creation is essentially good, he is actually saying that creation is good in so far as it is not creation.

Nowhere else, perhaps, is the ambiguity of Tillich's language so seriously confusing as it is here. Although he denies that the created world is evil, he argues—consistently with his position—that evil is the necessary accompaniment of a created world as such. He expresses this in the formula which he defends in his reply to Niebuhr, namely: *actualized creation and estranged existence are identical*. There is no existence in time and space which is not estranged existence, and therefore Creation and the beginning of the Fall coincide. The two are 'ontologically' the same although 'logically' different. Suppose,

---

[1] *Op. cit.*, pp. 342–4.   [2] *Op. cit.*, p. 44.

[3] 'Being is finite, existence is self-contradictory, and life is ambiguous' (*ST* I, p. 81); this is Tillich's description of what *actuality* entails. (See above, p. 66.)

then, that the reader accepts Tillich's formula. What follows? He now knows that a created world (one where being is finite) can never be anything other than a place where evil breeds. And he knows that evil cannot be found anywhere else except in that actualized creation where it is at home. True, he does not have to say that finitude is itself evil, but instead he confesses that 'the transition from essence to existence is a universal quality of finite being'.[1] Like an Aeon in a Gnostic system, finitude functions as a middle link in a chain which begins with the Incorruptable and ends in corruption, each successive link losing some of the perfection belonging to the one above it and thus both losing some of the perfection belonging to the one above it and also producing some additional imperfection in the one below it. Finitude is 'mixed' with non-being and 'limited' by it.[2] But existence, the next link in the chain, is decisively 'estranged' from being, though still belonging to it. Nevertheless, if finitude and existence are separate links, they are also linked together. In the *Systematic Theology* evil is described both as the destructive consequence of man being disrupted from his essential unity with being-itself (i.e. his predicament in estranged existence) and also as the destructive consequence of man being determined by his finitude.[3] Basic evil, however, must always lie in the fact that actual finitude is necessarily estranged existence too. It does not lie in finitude as such, for, in the order of logic, finitude can never determine man's true nature, which is essentially infinite. To use Plato's metaphor of the Cave—altogether appropriate here—finite being builds the cave and places man in it, with the result that, so long as man lives in the cave, he lives among shadows. But only because he is subject to estranged existence will man be tempted to imagine that he is forced to remain inside the cave of shadows. Not the fact of the cave walls round about him but the fact of the distortion of his nature, encouraged by the enclosing walls, makes him remain in the cave. At any time he may 'come to himself' (*via* ontological shock) and be awakened to the reality of the light of eternity outside the cave of finitude.

Accepting Tillich's formula, then, does not mean identifying

[1] *ST* II, p. 36.　　[2] *ST* I, p. 189.　　[3] *ST* II, p. 66.

finitude and evil—even though this is escaped by the hair-breadth of a logical distinction ontologically meaningless. It does mean having to think of Creation and the Fall together as one complex making up the predicament from which we have to be delivered. But all efforts to have the Christian view of the Universe fit comfortably inside the concepts of the system are doomed to failure in the end. The pother about whether the system views Creation as good or bad, whatever is said on either side, can never be settled satisfactorily. The point is that Tillich cannot accept Creation itself as being a reality. Just how he does regard it comes out of his presentation of the biblical account of Creation and the Fall.

As usual, he assumes that knowledge gained from contemplating the universal human situation provides the key for understanding the 'real' significance of the biblical symbols. The third chapter of Genesis may seem on the surface to be about the disobedience of Adam and Eve rather than about the transition from essence to existence, but 'hidden behind' the psychological and ethical form of the story lies a cosmic myth. Describing as it does the true gospel of man's predicament in story form, this cosmic myth has 'universal validity' or, at the very least, a claim to such a status.[1] Needless to say, the true gospel does not appear obviously in the biblical record but is 'implied' in it. No one can read the story, Tillich remarks, without realizing the 'cosmic presuppositions and implications of the Fall of Adam'. But he goes on at once to say that the myth giving the best exposition of the truth implied in the story of Adam is Plato's myth of the Transcendent Fall of the souls. The Transcendent Fall, he urges, should be taken seriously by theology since it has been supported by so many philosophers, Christian and non-Christian, who 'have recognized that existence has a universal dimension'.[2]

Quite so. And theology equally well might take seriously Kierkegaard's reminder that existence must be revoked in the eternal without remainder before a speculative system can round itself out. The most conspicuous feature of Tillich's

---

[1] *Ibid.*, p. 37.
[2] *Ibid.*, pp. 37–8. See also *The Theology of Paul Tillich*, p. 343.

attitude to Creation is his turning away from everything particular towards whatever has a 'universal dimension' and thus a claim to 'universal validity'. When he insists that the 'real' message of Genesis is to be found in the Platonic understanding of human existence he is rejecting the Hebrew tradition, with its doctrine of Creation, for the Greek tradition, which notoriously lacks any corresponding doctrine.

Speaking in terms of the system, Tillich says that 'the transition from essence to existence'—either Creation or the Fall, that is, depending upon how one looks at it—'is the original fact'.[1] What may not appear at once is the precarious standing of any fact, whether original or derived, in a system considering the true meaning of anything to be its universal dimension. Already, before stressing that the phrase 'the transition from essence to existence' describes the fact-of-facts, Tillich has pointed out that it is mythical in form. Although less obviously mythical than the Genesis story, and in spite of the abstract terms which it contains, it is 'a half-way demythologization' of the myth of the Fall. It is still mythical in character, because it has not succeeded in purging itself of 'the temporal element'.[2] Tillich does not stop to point out that this same phrase is also an imperfectly demythologized statement of the myth of Creation—perhaps he thinks that this is sufficiently clear from his references to the 'symbol' of Creation. But, what is more important, he nowhere hints as to the bearing of what he says about myth on the status of *facthood*. The original fact—the fact giving birth to all other facts—has been declared to be a myth, and this means that the reality of Creation has been specifically denied.

A myth opens out eternal truths to reason through the telling of a story in which the truths appear disguised as events. But, since the literal meaning of a mythical story is patently absurd, man is led to grasp the reality lying behind the disguise, and thus to separate truth from error. By equating original fact with mythological statement, Tillich has propounded the

[1] *ST* II, p. 36. And a few pages later, '. . . theology must insist that the leap from essence to existence is the original fact . . .' (p. 44).

[2] *Ibid.*, p. 29.

doctrine of man's existence in a shadow world, a world only adequately presented in the Platonic myth of the Transcendent Fall of souls. Existence is the original myth—a myth not told but acted. Acts themselves, of course, must be equally mythical. The myth of Creation leads us directly to the myth of the world of time and space, of finite being which appears as individuals, a self-contradictory world where nothing can appear as it really is. Since reality (being) is hidden in time and space, it can be hidden nowhere else than behind the fact of existence. Accordingly, when we drive being out of its hiding-place by means of the rational word (or else by experiencing the depth of reason in ecstacy), the hiding-place is our least concern. Just as we read myths in order to discern the meaning through the narrative, so the facts and acts of our experience have value for what can be glimpsed through them. Where reality is truly known (i.e. after ontological shock), there experience becomes transparent to its depths and the factual world is seen to be a surface phenomenon obscuring the really real.[1]

It is inevitable, therefore, that a system based on such a doctrine of man's existence should regard the universal dimension of everything so exclusively that the individual, the personal and the existential dimensions vanish. Faith and love in man and God become the divine loving itself. Creation and salvation are transformed into the reading of a myth; not only do we live our life as a tale that is told but also none except the uninstructed or the superstitious accept the tale as a true story. Thus when Tillich declares that theology should include both the moral (the individual and personal) and the tragic (universal)

[1] The two unpublished parts of the system ('Life and the Spirit', 'History and the Kingdom of God'), when they appear, will show to what extent Tillich succeeds in harmonizing his views of 'the really real' with the factual basis of the Gospel. But any true agreement seems out of the question. As Jules Laurence Moreau has written: 'In the end, neither Bultmann nor Tillich seems to be able to avoid the category of eternity as opposed to time; to this extent the myth of the beginning and the end, the creation-eschatology myth, is truncated and forced into an alien structure. Tillich, particularly, cannot seem to evade the idealistic categories which so deeply underlie his system; this must be admitted, despite the brilliance and complexity of the most competent systematic theologian to have produced a system in our day' (*Language and Religious Language*, Philadelphia, Westminster Press, 1961, p. 177).

elements in its statements about man and his existence,[1] he gives a reassurance unsupported by actual performance. On the contrary, by also demanding the 'interpenetration' of the two elements, he makes certain that the tragic-universal shall swallow the individual-moral. His system divides sin from moral responsibility. Sin is 'really' the universal state of estrangement[2] and evil the universal consequence of that state.[3] Salvation too loses any moral reference when it becomes the universal effect of a saving (i.e. healing or uniting) power discovered within the estranged state,[4] where 'structures of healing and reunion of the estranged' balance 'structures of destruction'.[5]

Instead of the biblical question, 'What must I do to be saved?' Tillich has substituted the question, 'How can man best pursue the quest for the New Being upon which he is universally engaged because he is man?' And he answers his own question by a two-part answer. The first part of the answer is tacitly assumed rather than argued. It arises out of his assumption that it is possible to posit an authoritative idea of theology, and it is summed up in the thesis that man is immediately aware of the Unconditional. This part of the answer says, in effect: 'Man knows the truth about his existential predicament through primary revelation. By this means, he has absolute certainty that his quest is for the New Being and nothing else: he is driven by *eros* to join himself to that which he has never left. He knows too that the New Being, while found in all effective symbols of religious faith, is not limited to any one of them.' Such an answer shows that, while salvation is central to his system, Tillich's theology shares no common ground with the biblical concept of salvation. It is not only a question of the emphasis being upon cosmic rather than upon personal salvation, for this in itself would raise no unsurmountable barriers. The real division stems from the fact that the system does not accept the biblical *cosmos* in which the individual person truly exists and out of the midst of which human beings

---

[1] *Op. cit.*, p. 39.

[2] 'The disruption of the essential unity with God is the innermost character of sin' (*ibid.*, p. 48).

[3] *Ibid.*, pp. 60–1.   [4] *Ibid.*, p. 86.   [5] *Ibid.*, p. 75.

cry out for salvation. The world the system contemplates is a different world from the world of the biblical creation-story, and, very naturally, the same type of salvation will not serve both worlds—the condition of each is unalike.

The second part of the answer which Tillich gives to the question of how the New Being is to be found is an answer given in explicit terms; it is the Norm laid down by him for systematic theology: 'The New Being in Jesus as the Christ as our ultimate concern'. Whether this answer is compatible with the Christian gospel is the next issue to be considered.

VIII

THE CHRIST

ANYONE WHO considers abstractly the theological issue of salvation must first find out what there is to be saved before he can profitably inquire into the process whereby saving becomes effective. After that, he may go on to the third question of what it is that can start the saving process and bring it to a successful conclusion. Christian faith takes another course. Because it confesses trust in 'Jesus Christ our Saviour' (Titus 1.4), it begins where the other ends. And Christian theology, for the most part, follows the order of Christian faith. It starts with the given fact of a Saviour, and, as a consequence, takes for granted that salvation is an act of God carried out through the Incarnate Son of God on behalf of men. The last thing it comes to develop is a rationale of the process of salvation. In the history of Christian theology, self-conscious theories of the Atonement came late on the scene and are still the centre of much dispute.[1]

The *Systematic Theology* illustrates perfectly the fully abstract approach. Starting from the ontological analysis of existence as estranged, it proceeds to explain the saving process as a reuniting of that which is estranged, a healing of a split universe. It next deduces from this analysis what the agent of salvation must be. 'Out of this interpretation of salvation, the concept of the New Being has grown,' is its comment.[2] The New Being is

[1] Anslem's *Cur Deus Homo* is an example of a serious attempt to bring an abstract approach to bear on the Christian doctrine of the atonement, proceeding by first taking Jesus Christ out of the picture (*remoto Christo*). But Christ is never really forgotten. The argument is drawn to the Cross rather than leading there, and the whole is set in a profoundly biblical conception of Divine Righteousness and human sin.

[2] *ST* II, p. 166. Note also the statement of the general principle of how the Christ is known: 'Christology is a function of soteriology. The problem

158

the result, because the terms of the analysis demand two things of the agent: (*a*) that it be a power to bring about wholeness, and (*b*) that it be a power identical with the power of the whole. The name *New Being* expresses both qualities of power. 'Being' identifies the power with being-itself, the creative Ground of being, the eternal, infinite and unbroken wholeness. 'New' denotes a change from (factual) estranged existence to (essential) wholeness.

At this point the Method is brought into action. The Christian confession of 'Jesus Christ our Saviour' is produced in correlation with the question of the healing of estranged existence. (This is the process of extracting answers from Christian beliefs by placing them under the Norm.)[1] And this means that Jesus as Saviour is identified with the power ever uniting the split world. Henceforth, the title of the Christ in the *Systematic Theology* is said to be 'the bearer of the New Being'. The system is prepared to guarantee the truth of the Christian claim that salvation comes through Jesus Christ, basing its proof upon its capacity to demonstrate that the New Being indubitably appears in him. Its guarantee is unconditional but subject to the proviso, already noted,[2] that the New Being has the power to be free from every form in which it appears.

After discovering the medium of salvation (the New Being), the system completed its systematic task, properly so called. It discovered an authoritative truth enabling it to declare what every theology 'must' say concerning this medium. But, by going on to identify that medium with the Christian Saviour, the system has done more than affirmed the theonomous metaphysics on which it is based. It has passed from primary to secondary revelation, from *system known* to *system built*, and from the area of certainty (as the system conceives certainty) to the area of ambiguity. In this area the system realizes that there is a risk. The risk is not that its analysis may be mistaken so that it asks the wrong question—no such thing could be considered. The risk is that a wrong answer may be given to its question

of soteriology creates the christological question and gives direction to the christological answer' (*ibid.*, p. 150).

[1] *ST* I, p. 64; see also above, p. 141.   [2] See above, p. 150.

by an inadequate religious faith.[1] In the present context, the New Being may have been attached to the wrong religious symbol. It may be, after all, that the Christ whom Christians worship is not the bearer of the New Being. There is no possible way to eliminate this particular danger, since nothing appertaining to the factual world can be other than doubtful. Yet, if the system accepts this one inevitable risk, it does not have to hold in doubt anything else. Knowing the essential truth about salvation, for example, it can easily examine the various theories of the Atonement current in Christian theology and conclude that each has 'a special strength and a special weakness'.[2] As an authoritative and inclusive source of truth, the system can sit in judgment over all partial and *ad hoc* attempts to reach the truth.

The system which fits the message of Christ as Saviour within its inclusive theory of salvation makes that theory hinge upon the ontic unity of power and reality. This unity has been presupposed from the first, for one of the names which Tillich applies to being-itself is the name of 'the power of being'. However it is important to notice that the New Being, the power conquering existential estrangement, is also a 'new reality'.[3] From the standpoint of the system the bearer of the New Being is a full reality as the Christ. The system can take the religious title of 'Christ' or 'Messiah' and interpret it as a symbol representing the New Being.[4] But it also has to take into account that this title was bestowed by his followers upon one particular man, called Jesus. It was the coming of the New Being in conjunction with a single individual that made the New Being a 'new reality' for the first Christians and that makes it still new for Christians today. But Jesus is simply an individual, and no overcoming of the human predicament can come from an individual as such. Jesus the individual lived under the conditions of existence and was immersed in all the

---

[1] On the subject of 'the risk of faith' see *Dynamics of Faith* Chapter 6, section i, 'Faith and Courage' (pp. 99 ff.).

[2] *ST* II, p. 171.   [3] *Ibid.*, p. 92.

[4] *Ibid.*, Chapter I, E.4. 'The Symbol of "Christ": Its Historical and Its Transhistorical Meaning' (pp. 88–90).

contradictions of that state. Therefore Jesus cannot bring salvation. Only the Christ can save. Yet the Christ saves when the Christ is found in conjunction with the man Jesus. So what actually saves is Jesus *as the Christ*. Hence the full formula in the *Systematic Theology* spelling out the Norm laid down by the system is: 'The New Being in Jesus as the Christ as our ultimate concern.' The symbol of Jesus as the Christ is guaranteed by the system completely so far as the Christ-element is concerned. It is guaranteed so far as the Jesus-element is concerned only after the risk inherent in all statements made about the world of time and space has been taken into account.

The system's assumption that the sole possible faith is faith in Jesus as the Christ has implications which spread far out into the theological field. It provides the chief Christological difficulty that appears when Tillich 'correlates' his system and the Christian message. The difficulty which the system does not surmount is the gulf it has made between the universal and the factual, a gulf which becomes most obvious at the point where Christian faith looks back to its Founder, an individual who (faith claims) once existed. This gulf is certainly not bridged in the concept of the New Being. By proposing to heal a split world through the mediation of the Christian Saviour, the system has driven a wedge between the Eternal Christ, in whom is the power of the New Being, and the man Jesus, who was born in the reign of Augustus Caesar, lived in Nazareth and died on the Cross. It denies the apostolic preaching which asserts that the One whom God has made 'both Lord and Christ' is, necessarily, 'this Jesus' (Acts 2.36).

The system cannot avoid coming to this conclusion, which follows logically from the premiss that salvation is participation in a power-reality which is suprafactual. Tillich has no hesitation in presenting the logic of his position:

'. . . one must say that participation, not historical argument, guarantees the reality of the event upon which Christianity is based. It guarantees a personal life in which the New Being has conquered the old being. But it does not guarantee his name to be Jesus of Nazareth.'[1]

[1] *Ibid.*, p. 114.

In the above statement the link between the universal and the factual has been snapped in two, with the result that the reader is left with an indubitable Christ of faith and a problematic Jesus of history. Yet, is there not a link of some sort implied in the suggestion that, if perhaps not 'the man Jesus', still some other personal life has embodied the New Being? The answer to this question is soon given, but it is hardly reassuring. The link which Tillich proposes is not actually any personal life as such. Instead, the guarantee is transferred to the 'picture' of a personal life—which is not the same thing at all. Tillich writes:

> 'The power which has created and preserved the community of the New Being is not an abstract statement about its appearance; it is the picture of him in whom it has appeared.'[1]

The more the system is unfolded, the wider yawns the gap between the universal and the factual, and the harder becomes any reconciliation with the Christian gospel. If the participation guaranteeing Christianity involves a picture rather than a person, then the Norm for systematic theology ought to be spelled out as the New Being through the picture of the Christ arising out of some life—probably that of Jesus of Nazareth. For this is what the phrase 'Jesus as the Christ' evidently means. The truth of all religion lies in the universal power of the Ground of being, says the system, and is mediated through symbols (i.e. 'the Christ'). Faith—that is *eros*-faith or the hidden power within ourselves—can guarantee this truth, 'because its own existence is identical with the presence of the New Being.'[2] Thus the truth that shines through every symbol, being

[1] *Ibid.* At this point the connection between Tillich's outlook and that of Schleiermacher is very evident. For Schleiermacher the 'picture' or 'impression' of Jesus as it affected the minds of the disciples was the root of Christian faith. He argued that, since all depended upon the 'enduring influence' of that which the disciples felt within them, the historical events in the life of Jesus which the creeds emphasize (especially the Resurrection and the Ascension) are no part of the certainty of faith. Although the parallel between the two theories of the relation of faith to personal existence is so close, Tillich does not acknowledge any indebtedness to Schleiermacher in this area. Elsewhere he admits that his Christology has 'some traits' in common with Schleiermacher. (See below, p. 171.)

[2] *Ibid.*

universal, reveals itself as immediate evidence. It is wholly real, and 'tested by its transforming power'. In other words, the New Being—or Christ-power—or *eros*-urge—guarantees itself. But nothing in existence can be guaranteed, existence being by definition self-contradictory. Therefore, when the New Being appears under the conditions of existence, we know that it has appeared but never, with any certainty, when, where or how. We cannot locate the universal in time or space. Nevertheless, we must connect the presence of the New Being with particular temporal and spatial impressions 'in and through' which its power reaches us. In this way we come to accept reality in a 'picture' which may very well fail to correspond with any empirically known fact and yet be more real than the totality of empirical facts. For this 'picture', while looking like something factual, is able to bring us into touch with the universal.

It is essential for the system that the universal and the factual shall never meet directly. That is why Tillich finds it necessary to insert the 'picture' of an individual life as that through which the Christ-power is communicated to man. The 'picture' of one human life is not itself a life or a reproduction of a life but simply analogous to a life.[1] And it serves as an occasion, not as a cause, of the manifestation of the power of the New Being. It has 'creative power, because the power of the New Being is expressed in and through it'.[2] In fact, a 'picture' of a personal life plays a part in the economy of the system exactly parallel to that of a myth. Just as man, imprisoned in his earth-bound existence, makes use of fabled narratives in order to learn more than bare facts can tell him, so he makes use of pictures (perhaps incorporating myths) drawn more directly from existence in that they are founded on the biographies of individuals. Myths represent eternal truths under the guise of events. Pictures of personal lives communicate creative power under the guise of personal communion. But neither events nor person-to-person relationships have being at the level of the 'really real'. That is why myths and pictures are needed, so that 'in and through' what appears in existence man may be led to the reality lying 'behind' the surface of things. Both myths and pictures take

[1] *Ibid.*, pp. 114–15. [2] *Ibid.*, p. 115.

their form in the human mind and raise in that mind the 'truly human' question of man's own being and meaning. It was in the minds of the disciples that the 'picture' of Jesus as the Christ took shape, and today this same picture is recreated, out of the biblical record, in our own minds. It is the identical picture, possessing the same universal validity and unchanging, inexhaustible power. Quite otherwise, the existence of a man called Jesus of Nazareth is a problematic event, an event for historical research to inquire into but a matter of indifference for faith. The really real has no traffic with the merely factual. Faith deals with the universal dimension of existence, with that dimension which is communicated in myths and in pictures in such a way that reality grasps us in the depths of our being. The system knows where faith operates and what it can and must say—

> 'Faith can say that the reality which is manifest in the New Testament picture of Jesus as the Christ has saving power for those who are grasped by it, no matter how much or how little can be traced to a historical figure who is called Jesus of Nazareth.'[1]

Although the system loses—or is prepared to lose—Jesus of Nazareth in order to demonstrate the certainty with which the Christ may be known, it gives a central place to what has always been central in traditional Christianity, namely, Peter's confession at Caesarea Philippi. This point of meeting is also the point of greatest contrast between the system and the Christian gospel. Both assert with Peter, 'You are the Christ' (Mark 8.29). And neither means what the other means when it uses these words. For traditional Christianity the event at Caesarea Philippi marks the giving of the original testimony to the fact that Jesus was recognized by his followers to be what he was: the Christ of God. But for the system the event at Caesarea Philippi points to the eternal truth that a power-reality has been made manifest in existence. For traditional Christianity the continuity of the Church is demonstrated in the fact that it continues to confess what Peter confessed. But for the system

---

[1] *Dynamics of Faith*, p. 88. Compare also: 'Historical investigations should neither comfort nor worry theologians. Knowledge of revelation, although it is mediated primarily through historical events, does not imply factual assertions . . .' (*ST* I, p. 130).

the continuity of the Church is demonstrated in the fact that it continues to experience what Peter experienced. Aulén has remarked, 'What is essential to faith is to see God "in the despised man Christ" (Luther)'.[1] In opposition to such an outlook Tillich protests against using 'Jesus Christ' as though it were an individual name and not the combination of a name and a title: ' "Jesus Christ" means—originally, essentially, and permanently—"Jesus who is the Christ".'[2] His system cannot look at any man individually, for it knows man solely in general terms (i.e. man in his essential nature and in his existential estrangement). And when it looks at Jesus of Nazareth it sees not the despised man but 'the fact to which the name of Jesus of Nazareth points', declaring that 'the basic Christian assertion' is that 'Essential God-Manhood has appeared within existence and subjected itself to the conditions of existence without being conquered by them.'[3]

From this it is abundantly clear that the system does not think that the Christian gospel is in itself more than the raw material out of which a satisfactory faith can be constructed. In Kierkegaard's phrase, the system believes Christianity to be up to a point true. It believes that it is not enough to confess the name of Jesus, since the important thing is to assert the fact to which the name of Jesus points. The orthodoxy of Chalcedon, declaring Jesus Christ to be *very God and very man*, is itself only preparatory for the true knowledge of Essential God-Manhood. And confession of belief in the Second Person of the Trinity who was born, suffered under Pontius Pilate, and rose from the dead is, when rightly interpreted, an adequate foundation for an awareness that this Essential God-Manhood has appeared in existence. Of course, the operative word here is 'appeared'. Essential God-Manhood appears in existence because it cannot properly belong to it—it cannot enter into the ambiguities of life in any true fashion. No individual historical event can convey properly universal truths. But universal truths can appear 'in and through' events.[4]

[1] *The Faith of the Christian Church* (London, SCM Press, 1954), p. 210.
[2] *ST* II, p. 98.   [3] *Loc. cit.*
[4] In the New Testament, the only use of the word 'appears' is in describing specific instances when the Risen Lord was visible to his followers.

How little events in the empirical world can have to do with the universal truths which are the system's concern is best illustrated in Tillich's exposition of the meaning of the Resurrection. He calls his interpretation the 'restitution theory'. According to this theory the 'real' meaning of the Resurrection is one aspect of the triumph of being over negativity, namely, the conquest of transitoriness. The 'picture' of Jesus was so united with the disciples' experience of the power of the New Being that, even after death, the person of Jesus continued to have 'the character of spiritual presence', a presence 'raised above transitoriness into the eternal presence of God'. This was the event which was soon 'interpreted through the symbol "Resurrection" which was readily available in the thought forms of that day'.[1]

This theory is not put forward as sharing the authority of the system, but as a likely guess. That is only natural, since the actual content of any historical event must always be something neither fully proveable nor ultimately of real concern in the eyes of the system. However, if the guess is not required by the system, it is fully in accord with it. It is completely indifferent to all that makes an event an event in time and space (what happened and where and when it happened). Not only does the Restitution Theory leave out all reference to the human body of Jesus but it takes away any necessary connection with his death. The Restitution, we are told, may well have preceded the confession of Peter at Caesarea Philippi. Such a surprising conclusion is, nevertheless, strictly logical. It merely follows the system's assumption that the 'restitution of Jesus to the dignity of the Christ' is something which impinges upon the minds of the disciples. It is not merely a psychological interpretation of events as 'inner' events 'in' the minds of the disciples.[2] Tillich rejects a psychological interpretation of the Resurrection, and the reason is not hard to understand. When one places the events subjectively inside the minds of men instead of objectively in the empirical world, the empirical order is still supreme. The minds of the disciples believing in a Risen Lord are still individual, believing minds.

[1] *Op. cit.*, p. 157.   [2] *Ibid.*, p. 156.

But Tillich is not interested in either the subjective or the objective side of the empirical order. He is interested solely in the universal dimension of things which his system recognizes as the only source of truth, whether on its objective side as the structure of being or on its subjective side as the awareness of the Unconditional. He does not think it important that once, somewhere, somehow, one man rose from the dead or was believed by other men to have done so. But he does think it important that at one time or another, somewhere or other, somehow or other, a group of men realized for themselves an eternal truth and experienced a spiritual power. It matters little, in the long run, what prompted their experience. What matters is that we can share their experience, knowing it to be a universal human possibility. The first Christian disciples saw the essential unity of the power of the New Being and they possessed a 'picture' of a human life (Jesus of Nazareth, they said—were they right?) and knew that 'in eternity they belong together'.[1] They discovered that, however transitory life may seem to be, it has an eternal dimension in it. And we may make the same discovery for ourselves by sharing the same experience of power-reality.

We may—provided, of course, that we look to the same 'picture' of the life of Jesus of Nazareth and share the religious symbols of 'Christ' and 'Resurrection'. But perhaps our faith is centred in some other complex of religious symbols and connected with some other revelatory foundation. We may see our ultimate concern expressed in the Mosaic law, perhaps, or in Mohammed the prophet, or in Buddha the Enlightened One.[2] In that case, we share the same power, only differently mediated. Nevertheless, among all varieties of religious revelation, the Christian revelation can be systematically demonstrated to be the complete and final revelation. It is not essentially different from any of the other forms of revelation (the New Being is not tied to any form), but it is better. And it is better because it exhibits a unique formal perfection. It is the only one among religious revelations to take as its medium of revelation a human life, and thus it is the only one to join

---

[1] *Ibid.*, p. 157.   [2] *Dynamics of Faith*, p. 88.

together the absolutely concrete with the absolutely universal.[1]

Here Tillich displays exactly what his interpretation of the 'event' at Caesarea Philippi involves. Peter's confession, 'You are the Christ', means for him that being has been grasped and driven out of its hiddenness in a particularly effective way. Different religions, as a matter of experience, have taken a host of objects, inanimate and animate, to stand as their 'mediums of revelation'; and what could be more natural, seeing that everything that exists partakes of being-itself and thus can become a route leading to the revelation of *theos*![2] But the system knows that, although all revelations are equally valid in so far as they exhibit esctatic reason, some are superior to others because their mediums of revelation are more 'transparent for the ground of being and meaning'.[3] And the system also knows that man has a unique status in the Universe on account of being 'that being in whom all levels of being are united and approachable'.[4] So it is obvious to the system that a religion finding its revelation of *theos* in man must have a medium of revelation possessing the greatest 'transparency' possible. For this reason the system cherishes Christianity. What is pre-eminent in this religion is not indeed the Christian belief that Jesus was the Christ of God who rose from the dead. Such a belief may be mistaken and is not, in any case, within the realm of ultimate concern. The system cherishes Christianity because it sees that this religion, through the mythological symbols proclaimed in its creeds, unites the universal and the concrete (i.e. the divine and the human). The attitude of the system, of course, is decided, not by what individual Christians or Christian churches think they believe, but by the theological reading of Christianity which the system proposes when it says that Christians 'really' believe in the New Being revealed in the 'picture' of a human life.

The system has to maintain its interpretation of Christianity in face of the constant theme of the New Testament that the message to be proclaimed concerns 'this Jesus' who is Christ and Lord because he died and rose again from the dead. Tillich overcomes this difficulty by interpreting the 'symbols' of the

[1] *ST* I, p. 16.   [2] *Ibid.*, p. 118.   [3] *Ibid.*, p. 120.   [4] *Ibid.*, p. 168.

New Testament so that they point away from the particular events of first-century Palestine to the universal dimension of existence, as in the case of the Restitution Theory of the Resurrection. However, he finds some direct support for his views in John's Gospel, with its description of the Logos. He believes that, when this Gospel says that the Logos became flesh, this means 'that the principle of divine self-revelation has become manifest in the event "Jesus as the Christ".'[1] Here is one more instance of Tillich hanging a crucial argument upon nothing better than a misleading similarity of terms. While it is true that John's Gospel uses the term 'logos', it does not happen to be the case that this term can be equated with the principle of divine self-manifestation as that principle stands in Tillich's theonomous metaphysics. Tillich's *logos* theology asserts that God is only properly known in the rational word that grasps being and brings to light the true name of Deity. For the Fourth Gospel, on the other hand, God is made known by the only Son, who is Jesus of Nazareth, the son of Joseph (John 1.18, 45). And the phrase 'become manifest' in Tillich's system does not in any way represent the same thing as 'tabernacled among us', the phrase of the scriptural record (John 1.14). In short, the Logos in the New Testament does not support, any better than anything elsewhere in the same writings, Tillich's belief that the Christian message has to do with Essential God-Manhood instead of with 'God in the despised man Christ'. And the attempt to prove that it does merely exploits ambiguity.[2]

Emil Brunner has written:

'The peculiar fact about Christianity—and one which gives great offence—is this: it is absolutely concerned with an external

[1] *Ibid.*, p. 16.

[2] Hendrik Kraemer has some interesting things to say in this connection in his section 'Universal Logos and The Word made Flesh' from the last chapter of *Religion and the Christian Faith* (pp. 437–9). He points out that Tillich's claim that the Christian theologian believes that wherever the universal *logos* is at work it agrees with the Christian message (*ST* I, p. 28), begs the question altogether. Such a claim assumes that Tillich's ontological analysis is the proper work of the universal *logos*, as no other philosophy can be, and also that the Christian message actually does agree with Tillich's ontology—which is just the point at issue!

historical fact. . . . To be "made flesh" means among other things an actual state of presence, sensible, external, non spiritualized . . . "flesh" means the brutal solidity of the facts of sensible existence.'[1]

It is exactly this that the system must at all costs deny. It is unthinkable that the Logos should *actually become* flesh, instead of merely appearing 'in and through' it. Thus Tillich reacts sharply against the doctrinal term 'Incarnation', which, he says, 'is practically impossible to protect from superstitious connotation'.[2] So he interprets the Incarnation of the Word as the manifestation of a principle, causing the solidity of sensible existence to melt and resolve itself into a dew of universality. *Becoming flesh* cannot mean what a 'myth of transmutation' would make it mean, so it 'must' mean the participation of being-itself in existence. Instead of the Incarnation, therefore, the system produces the 'concrete universal' of God-manhood. The concept of the concrete universal, of course, is one produced by philosophical Idealism, rising out of the view that, as everything partakes in the Absolute, so the Absolute is clearly an Absolute which differentiates itself. The true universal includes the concrete; and, conversely, the concrete includes the universal.[3]

It would be a grievous error to suppose that the concrete universal manifesting the universal *Logos* ('the concrete *logos*', as Tillich calls it) can ever, in any circumstances, be itself a particular or individually existing actuality. On the contrary, what is concrete *represents* the particularities of existence in so far as they are universal. The New Being, for instance, is known concretely; but it is known 'in and through' a personal life, not as a personal life. The scandal of particularity in Christianity is avoided in the system by substituting the picture of Jesus of Nazareth for the factual reality of the Incarnate Lord. The Christ-event is not an event in time and space but a mani-

[1] *The Mediator* (London, Lutterworth Press, 1934), pp. 153–4.

[2] *ST* II, p. 95.

[3] So Tillich argues (*ST* I, p. 17 n. 5), concluding: 'Christian theology moves between the poles of the universal and the concrete and not between those of the abstract and the particular.'

festation of the eternal and the infinite in existence—a light of universality shining in the darkness of particularity and not conquered by it. In such a context, Luther's phrase 'the man Christ' is a meaningless combination of words. The Christ who manifests himself in existence does not exist—how could the New Being be estranged from itself? Instead, the Christ-principle appears in existence and is recognized in its Christ-power. This a whole world of difference—literally—from actually existing. It is a picture-existence, or something analogous to actual existence but safely beyond all the self-contradictions of particularity. So when, in the picture-language of myth, Paul speaks of God sending forth his Son when the time had fully come (Gal. 4.4), the system knows that this myth points to the eternal truth that man-as-such can be grasped by the Ground of his being and meaning through the concrete symbols of his ultimate concern. And for Christians this means that their faith in the Christ-event is not misplaced, because it makes manifest for them the hidden power within themselves ... *no matter how much or how little can be traced to a historical figure who is called Jesus of Nazareth.*

Admitting that his Christological position resembles the idealistic teaching of Schleiermacher, Tillich points up the difference between them. Schleiermacher's concept of Christ as 'essential man' (*Urbild*), he explains, holds true humanity in transcendence over existence, while his own New Being shows how 'essential man' participates in existence. It does more— 'Essential God-Manhood points to both sides of the relation and this in terms of eternity.'[1] This contrast does not seem to take into consideration Schleiermacher's insistence upon the actual presence of God manifested through the God-consciousness of Jesus; but, in any case, Tillich's stand is no less clearly idealistic than Schleiermacher's. He takes his stand on the eternal manifest in, but not dependent upon, time and space. Jesus can be known as the Christ and Bearer of the New Being only because he sacrifices 'himself as Jesus to himself as the Christ',[2] a sacrifice allowing the 'medium of final revelation' to appear when the bearer 'becomes completely transparent to the

[1] *ST* II, p. 150.   [2] *Ibid.*, p. 123; and *ST* I, p. 137.

mystery he reveals'.[1] Nothing else but idealism would support a revelation in terms of eternity, leaving men with a colourless medium instead of with a living Lord. It can produce a Christ-power discovered in a Christ-event, but it cannot produce a Saviour of whom an individual may say, 'I know whom I have believed' (II Tim. 1.12). Good news of salvation resolves itself into an awareness of the reality of Essential God-Manhood, and Jesus of Nazareth vanishes at the point where the absolutely universal meets with the absolutely concrete.

In order to know the power of God the New Testament thinks it sufficient to know 'Jesus Christ and him crucified' (I Cor. 2.2). But in Tillich's system Christ and the Cross are religious symbols standing in the shadow of a higher knowledge, for secondary revelation needs to be interpreted in the terms laid down by primary revelation. The New Testament recognizes 'one mediator between God and men, the man Christ Jesus' (I Tim. 2.5). The system is quite certain of the essential unity between God and man independently of the Christian revelation. And when the system does turn to consider the man who bears the name of Jesus, it is not from interest in him but from interest in what may be gained through him. He is valued, not for himself, but for what he brings with him.[2] This is where the clash between the gospel and the system is at its most intense. The presuppositions of his theonomous metaphysics prevent Tillich from accepting the unity of the person whom the New Testament knows as the Lord Jesus Christ. Jesus is the Christ only to the extent that he is not Jesus. This saviour is very different from the one who was named Jesus because he would save his people from their sins (Matt. 1.21). He was not born into the world; he appeared in existence. He did not triumph over sin and death by his Incarnation, Cross and Resurrection; he conquered existence under the conditions of existence. He is not the Son of God who died and lives forever to intercede on behalf of his brethren; he represents the divine-

---

[1] *ST* I, p. 133.

[2] Brunner points out how so much of modern interpretations of Christ, since the time of Schleiermacher, has left the traditional Christian path of concern with the mystery of the Person of Christ and regard him only as 'the Bearer of something else' (*op. cit.*, pp. 266 ff.).

human unity which always persists, even in estranged existence. Sins and the sinner vanish in such a gospel, which limits the kind of Christ it will accept by the kind of salvation it desires.[1]

Since the person of Christ and his saving work stand at the heart of the Christian message, my inquiry into how the system and the Christian gospel confront each other is now in principle complete. At the same time, not all the terms of the confrontation have been stated adequately; and, if the outlines of the system have been sketched in, some of the important details may still remain a little vague. I will now turn to see how Tillich's choice of an interpretation of ultimate reality 'in terms of the Eternal' brings him into conflict with the 'existential' outlook of Christianity, an outlook concerned to emphasize the reality of the individual existing in time and space.

[1] It is in relation to Christology that the system exhibits most openly its divergence from traditional Christianity, and some of the sharpest criticisms of Tillich's thought have been directed here. An early essay, 'A Reinterpretation of the Doctrine of the Incarnation' (*Church Quarterly Review* CXLVII 1, January–March 1949) and the first volume of the *Systematic Theology* together drew critical comments on his Christology. Among these were: 'Contemporaneous Protestantism and Paul Tillich' by Gustave Weigel (*Theological Studies*, June 1950), 'The Jesus of History and the Christ of Faith' by Robert C. Johnson (*Theology Today* X 2, July 1953), 'The Place of Christology in Contemporary Protestantism' by Maria Fuerth Sulzbach (*Religion in Life* XXIII 2, Spring 1954). George H. Tavard's *Paul Tillich and the Christian Message* is the first full-length study of Tillich's Christology, written in the light of the second volume of the *Systematic Theology*. Tavard's conclusion is: 'Between 1949 and 1957, the date of *Systematic Theology* II, his doctrine has not evolved. . . . From the point of view of Christian orthodoxy, it is just as weak now as it was then' (*op. cit.*, p. 129). In fact, Tillich's Christology could hardly evolve without disrupting the system of which it forms a part, and the main lines of the system were laid down before he came to America. Tavard's belief that, if the system is true, '. . . we could, frankly, have managed without the Messiah' (*ibid.*, p. 104) was anticipated six years earlier by Arthur C. Cochrane, who wrote on the basis of the first volume of the *Systematic Theology*, 'The truth is that the revelation of God in Jesus Christ is not essential to Tillich's system' (*op. cit.*, p. 90).

IX

SELF-TRANSCENDENCE AND THE PERSONAL

KIERKEGAARD believed an existential system to be a contradiction in terms, yet he remarked that the speculative philosopher who created the system wished to be an existing individual at the same time as he abolished existence. The speculative philosopher thought that he could eat his cake and have it too. He thought that he could be an individual without subjectivity, an individual who existed *sub specie aeterni*.

The whole of Tillich's system is based on the claim that it is possible—and necessary—for man to escape from subjectivity and arrive at the 'really real'. Only if reality is accessible is it worth while to philosophize:

> 'From the time of Parmenides it has been a common assumption of all philosophers that the *logos*, the word which grasps and shapes reality, can do so only because reality itself has a *logos* character.'[1]

And Tillich finds this assumption so unquestionable that he can declare that man is by nature a philosopher. Therefore he trusts ontology to put him into touch with reality and interprets everything in terms of the universal and the eternal, using the system as the fitting means by which to come to the knowledge of the whole. But he does not forget about the empirical world. He speaks often about particular people, things and events. He places a high value upon history and culture, which are the realms, after philosophy and religion, in which his chief interests lie. On this account it is very important to find out whether he can escape the charge of inconsistency which

[1] *ST* I, p. 75. Compare also: 'Words are the results of the encounter of the human mind with reality' (*ST* II, p. 19).

Kierkegaard brought against speculative philosophers. Does his system in any genuine sense look beyond the universal dimension of things? Has he found some way of inserting within his system that which Kierkegaard said must cause the collapse of every system?

My investigations so far do not lead to any reason for supposing that these questions can be answered in the affirmative. Tillich's claim to have altered the Hegelian tradition so that it now embraces the Existentialist protest against Idealism seems to have a shaky foundation, while the chief difficulty that I have found throughout in placing his system alongside the Christian gospel is his persistent refusal to admit the reality of the world of existence. The evidence here is incomplete, because the two final parts of the *Systematic Theology* are not yet available and their titles ('Life and the Spirit' and 'History and the Kingdom of God') indicate that what they contain would be most relevant to this particular issue. Nevertheless, although not rounded out, the system is clear enough in its total effect. And the total effect of the system's relation to the Christian gospel adds up to a denial of the reality of existence.

However, no final answers can be given until statements of Tillich's concerning the general nature of his system have been considered and what he has to say about the particularities of existence has been reviewed in the light of these. The statements focus round the term 'self-transcendence'.

This is a term which Tillich often uses as a distinguishing badge for his system, speaking either of 'self-transcending realism'[1] or of 'self-transcending naturalism'.[2] In the first volume of the *Systematic Theology* it appears as the quality in man which proves his unity with being-itself and makes him capable of experiencing ontic anxiety,[3] while in the second volume the self-transcendent view of God and the Universe is contrasted with the supernaturalistic and naturalistic views.[4] The meaning of the term is most quickly defined in this last connection. To

[1] 'Realism and Faith', *The Protestant Era*, pp. 74–92.
[2] *The Theology of Paul Tillich*, p. 341.
[3] *Op. cit.*, p. 191.
[4] *Op. cit.*, p. 7.

call the world self-transcendent is to say that 'within itself, the finite world points beyond itself.'[1]

Nothing unfamiliar here! The way of self-transcendence is the way which discovers God as the Ground of being. The finite points to the infinite, going 'beyond itself in order to return to itself in a new dimension'.[2] The Universe is one, but split into different levels of being. The capacity for self-transcendence in everything finite announces the unity of the Universe beyond the split, thus being the objective counterpart of the subjective experience of ecstasy. Yet if the ideas connected with self-transcendence are familiar, the context in which the term is set brings light upon the subject of Tillich's resistance against the suggestion that metaphysics deals with a world-behind-the-world. This is what it seems to him that the common theistic reading of the Universe does. It establishes 'a supernatural divine world alongside the natural human world'.[3] So Tillich thinks that naturalism, which sees no place for a God other than the Universe, is right in rejecting supranaturalism. The error of naturalism, in its turn, is to draw its understanding of the Universe too narrowly, neglecting the self-transcendence of the finite.

The way of self-transcendence makes common cause with naturalism over the rejection of supranaturalism. Neither will admit the right of any religious faith to claim authority for its message, for both are agreed in having no belief in any revelation which does not issue from man himself. The world accessible to us, and not any spiritual world beyond our ken, is the only real world that they are prepared to consider. This common cause, which Tillich notes, is perhaps even more remarkable than might be thought. It amounts to the fact that both naturalism and Tillich's way of self-transcendence recognize a primary revelation—and a secondary relevation which is subordinate to it. They both refuse to recognize the claims which the world's religions make on their own behalf, but they are perfectly prepared to think that religion has real use and can present truth, though only in an oblique fashion. Religious revelation can never, indeed, convey the message

[1] *Loc. cit.*   [2] *Ibid.*, p. 8.   [3] *Ibid.*, p. 6.

which those who trust in it imagine it to convey, for they take it to be information about the supernatural world. Naturalism and the way of self-transcendence know that there is no supernatural world, so they know that the message of every religion is really truth relating to the natural human world, disguised as a message from the imaginary over-world. So they are not in the least inclined to throw out religion as merely false, since they are prepared to believe that the truth embodied in the message of religion may not be available in any other area of human consciousness. They simply demand the right to interpret that message and demonstrate its 'real' meaning. John Dewey, for example, has his 'idea' of theology just as much as Tillich. Tillich believes that no one, even if he thinks of himself as an atheist, can live without faith in the form of a hidden power within him. Dewey is certain that many people who are actively repelled from all religions on intellectual and moral grounds 'are not even aware of attitudes in themselves that if they came to fruition would be genuinely religious'.[1] Both thinkers interpret the message of religious faith in terms of the 'natural human world' as they conceive this world. Thus Tillich finds that what Christian theology calls salvation is the healing power of being-itself conquering the negativities of existence. And Dewey explains how, if the religious function were only rescued from the supranaturalism of the religious,

'The idea of invisible powers would take on the meaning of all the conditions of nature and human association that support and deepen the sense of values which carry one through periods of darkness and despair to such an extent that they lose their usual depressive character.'[2]

The interpretations wear a different outward form, but they spring from a common conviction, one expressed by Dewey when he says that the 'actual religious quality in the experience . . . is the *effect* produced'.[3] Dewey, like Tillich, believes in a New Being, 'a reality of reconciliation and reunion, of creativity,

[1] *A Common Faith* (New Haven, Yale University Press, 1934), p. 9.
[2] *Ibid.*, pp. 14–15.   [3] *Ibid.*, p. 14.

meaning, and hope'.[1] Only, he looks for it in a different place.

Naturalism and the way of self-transcendence certainly stand together in a common front against the recognition of authoritative revelation. They support each other in the conviction that the only Universe—there can be no more than one *uni*verse—is known to man; therefore to seek for anything at all beyond that which man can (in principle) grasp through his own efforts is a waste of time and a misuse of intelligence. But over the question of what man knows the two views are, of course, completely divided. In this regard Tillich's choice of the terms 'self-transcending realism' and 'self-transcending naturalism' appear to be difficult to disentangle. They resemble such awkward combinations as sympathetic egotism or universal nationalism. It might be possible to look for some justification for the choice in the precedents provided by the *mystical realism* of the Middle Ages and the *pantheistic naturalism* of Spinoza. But probably one of the most potent reasons for adopting these terms is that they successfully avoid any suggestion of the unpopular label of *idealism*.

In exploring the system from a philosophical angle, such critics as Dorothy Emmet and John Herman Randall, Jr mention that the rôle which idealism plays there is more evident than acknowledged. By the same token, how thoroughly the way of self-transcendence leaves behind the empirical world is one of the things which the system keeps in the background, or at least does not labour to declare in plain and unambiguous fashion. Yet the very language of the system contradicts the realistic and the naturalistic outlook, being language that is highly metaphorical and that presses into service expressions largely meaningless if taken to be descriptions of natural events or empirical data. What happens to finite being, when (following the self-transcendent route) it 'goes beyond itself' in order to 'return to itself in a new dimension', is something that cannot be recorded by observation; this event plainly evades the perspectives of naturalism and realism as these are

[1] *ST* I, p. 49. Interestingly enough, Tillich himself sheds light in this agreement when he says, 'Idealism and naturalism differ very little in their starting-point when they develop theological concepts' (*ibid.*, p. 9).

commonly understood. While these latter theories try to deal with the whole of reality, the system rejects absolutely any programme of this kind, adopting instead the idealistic programme of delineating reality as a whole. It sees true reality as mediated, not through the senses, but through immediate awareness. Here is the only Universe given us to look at— hence the need for metaphysical speculation, or *looking with open eyes*—and it is a Universe which is real because it finds its reality in the Unconditioned, in being-itself or the absolute.

If the Unconditioned is where reality is found, however, then the conditioned world we live in cannot be fully real, but real solely to the extent to which it inheres in the Unconditioned. Therefore, in so far as we take our existence to be the true reality, we are deluded by shadows. This means that knowledge and faith are exactly the opposite of that which they are taken to be by the ordinary individual whose thinking is governed by naturalistic or supernaturalistic presuppositions. True, knowledge is still the indubitable and faith is still trust in the unseen. But now the indubitable is that which lies beyond the world of time and space, while the 'surface' of the empirical world is that which is not beheld with the eyes of speculative certainty. Thus Tillich explains:

'The immediate awareness of the Unconditioned has not the character of faith but of self-evidence. Faith contains a contingent element and demands a risk. It combines the ontological certainty of the Unconditioned with the uncertainty about everything conditioned and concrete. . . . The risk of faith is based on the fact that the unconditional element can become a matter of ultimate concern only if it appears in a concrete embodiment.'[1]

It is our trust in anything concrete that makes our beliefs a flimsy support on which to lean. Unless we keep our feet firmly established upon the Ground of our true being and meaning, it

[1] *Theology of Culture*, pp. 27–8. In the *Systematic Theology* Tillich avoids speaking of being-itself as the Unconditioned (see *The Theology of Paul Tillich*, p. 340), but he holds fast to the concept of the unconditional in all encounter with reality. It is the unconditional element which makes possible the 'mystical *a priori*' and underlies ultimate concern.

may be that the illusions of the empirical world will lead us on to our destruction by causing us to seek the unconditional element where it cannot be found, and so we may end by accepting that which is not unconditional at all. We may be led far away from true concern (concern for unity with the Ground of our being) into fanaticism and superstition, where we deny the validity of all other faiths except our own; or we may be driven from the depth-dimension of existence into scepticism and materialism, where we deny that life contains more than the individual sees 'with his own eyes' on the surface of the world of time and space. Looking at secondary revelation, then, Tillich finds that there is no substitute for religious faith. Being the kind of creature he is, man cannot see the true world except by making use of religious myths and rites to help him rise from what he thinks he can see to what is truly real. But there is always the danger that religious faith will be perverted and turn aside from its real purpose. In that case it will encourage people to accept shadows in place of substance.

On the side of its attitude to religious faith, this view coincides with the naturalistic outlook. Dewey too would condemn superstition and scepticism as perversions of the religious function. But, although Tillich and Dewey alike regard the secondary revelation of reality through the channel of religion to be essential, because they claim to know the really real over against which the results of religion should be measured, they adopt diametrically opposed positions when it comes to explaining what is substance and what is shadow. Here Dewey's naturalism altogether contradicts Tillich's self-transcending naturalism. For Dewey, the purpose of all religion which is healthy and not debilitating in its effects is the unification of the self through 'the idea of the integration of the shifting scenes of the world into that imaginative totality we call the Universe'.[1] Dewey believes that the adjustment of the individual to 'the totality of conditions with which the self is connected'[2] is the real end of man's being, therefore in his estimation religion is chiefly a matter of the right employment of the individual's imaginative capacities. The whole into

[1] *Op. cit.*, p. 19.   [2] *Ibid.*

which the self is to be taken up is not in the least a real entity. This is where faith comes in. Faith constructs an imaginative world which—just because it is not real—contributes to the creation in reality (i.e. the empirical world) of conditions which enable the individual to adjust himself to the real conditions around him. There is a risk in faith, of course. This risk is, again, the opposite of Tillich's concept of the risk of faith. Dewey conceives the risk inherent in religious faith to be the creation of mistaken action in the world through the choice of wrong ideals. If faith follows any dream which does not correspond to action which is morally creative, then the self will not be unified and fitted for decisive action in the shifting scenes of the present world.

When he elaborates his theory of religious faith Dewey pauses briefly to attack those who think that ideals can be anything more than imaginative constructions. He writes:

'It is argued that the ideal is already the final reality at the heart of things that exist, and that only our senses or the corruption of our natures prevent us from apprehending its prior existential being. Starting, say, from such an idea as that justice is more than a moral ideal because it is embedded in the very make-up of the actually existing world, men have gone on to build up vast intellectual schemes, philosophies, and theologies, to prove that ideals are real not as ideals but as antecedently existing actualities.'[1]

There speaks the advocate of naturalism, sweeping to one side supernaturalists and self-transcending naturalists alike. He can do so because he is certain that reality is in the empirical order and that 'the imaginative totality we call the Universe' is simply a product of that order. Equally certain that he sees reality, Tillich finds that the totality we call the Universe is grounded in the reality of being-itself, and that we can know anything about empirical existence solely because it points beyond itself to the structure of being. The two visions of reality are mutually exclusive. Dewey starts from individual existents in a shifting setting. Tillich starts from structured Whole rooted in a transcendent Ground. The self upon which

[1] *Ibid.*, p. 21.

Dewey concentrates his attention is, so far as Tillich is concerned, a surface phenomenon, a question-mark asking about its being. The place to start when we genuinely want to find reality is not where we encounter individuals in time and space but where we are immediately aware of that which is given us in the structure of being:

> 'The question is not whether selves exist. The question is whether we are aware of self-relatedness. . . . A self is not a thing that may or may not exist; it is an original phenomenon which logically precedes all questions of existence.'[1]

It is naïve to accept anything as it seems to be before we learn to 'distinguish between its surface and its deeper, more real levels'. But there is no stopping even at the deeper levels of existence while we still imagine that particular existents are real:

> 'No thing, however, is isolated from all other things. And, the deeper the levels into which we enter, the less possible it is to consider them in isolation from each other and from the whole of reality.'[2]

There is no stopping, in fact, until we have arrived at 'the ground of all levels'. But by then we have long since ceased to think of ourselves as individual selves, realizing that the real core in us belongs to 'the living-substance in which all living beings participate'.[3] The reality of this living substance cannot be doubted, for it is rooted in being-itself as the Ground of life.

In short, Tillich's self-transcendent naturalism contradicts the naturalistic understanding of reality. It belongs to the idealistic camp. Similarly, in spite of the so-called existentialist revolt against Hegelianism, it has remained in the 'classical tradition' upheld by essentialist philosophers (including Hegel). While Tillich has rejected Hegel's dialectic as a principle for interpreting the Universe, accepting in its place inspiration from Schelling's Positive Philosophy, yet the result is no departure from idealism. For Schelling's modification of

[1] *ST* I, p. 169.
[2] *Biblical Religion and the Search for Ultimate Reality*, pp. 12–13.
[3] *Ibid.*, p. 13.

Hegel does not break with the idealistic claim to grasp reality as a whole. The speculative basis of truth is maintained, although it is widened from the *pure thought* of Hegel so as to include *revelation*. There is no surrender here to existential categories, because revelation is defined in essentialist terms. To the idealistic view, revelation is not something coming from a realm inexplicable to the thinker. According to Tillich, revelation is ecstatic reason, or reason in its depths; and therefore it falls into its place within the whole, so that the system-maker (who delineates the whole) easily incorporates it within his circle of ideas.

Tillich criticizes Hegelian idealism for identifying ontological reason directly with revelation and for failing to see that existential estrangement has also to be taken into the picture.[1] This seems to suggest that he repudiates idealism in general and the revelatory power of ontological reason in particular. In fact, all that he denies is the theory that ontological reason is the sole source of revelation. His view is that, since the rational word does not appear in its wholeness under the conditions of existence, it has to be supplemented by the revelation of mystery. He proposed to add a 'theological' vision to the 'philosophical' one, or (in my terminology) to place secondary revelation alongside primary revelation. In the cave of shadows which is existence we must learn to listen to the wisdom speaking through divine-human reason; yet we must also learn to listen to the same wisdom speaking through rites, symbols and myths . . . knowing that, ultimately, the two are really one.

Keeping to its essentialist presuppositions, self-transcending naturalism interprets revelation, as it interprets existence, on the basis of the *logos* philosophy and thus in terms of mystery (*theos*) instead of in terms of any specific revelation. In stressing the 'existential' or 'theological' element in knowledge Tillich is actually bringing to the fore the mystical element which is a perennial feature of classical metaphysics. (Indeed, most of

---

[1] *ST* I, p. 74. Professor Emmet cites this statement, but at once states her opinion that Tillich's description of ontological reason rests upon idealistic assumptions (*The Theology of Paul Tillich*, p. 207).

the time his term 'existential' simply means 'mystical'.)[1] His system assumes, besides the identity of thinking and knowing, the immediate awareness of the Unconditioned. So it begins by asserting that all religious revelation is founded upon the 'mystical *a priori*'. It refuses to accept the doctrines of any one faith as revelations of the divine or expressions of divine truth. That is why it insists that the symbols of religion (i.e. statements of belief set out in the language of particular faiths) must be *deliteralized* (i.e. interpreted as mythical or figurative expressions of truths expounded by the system as methodological knowledge). And that is why it believes that religious myths must be retained—not because they are either literally true or else an analogical approximation to truth, but because they provide 'a vehicle of religious expression'. Without myths, religion would be devoid of its language.[2] Here the assumption is that there is only one religion. The true idea of this one religion is authoritatively set forth in an essentialist analysis carried out along the lines laid down by a *logos* philosophy using the perspective of self-transcending naturalism. Self-transcending naturalism knows that myths have power to induce an experience of the holy through which the revelation of mystery takes place. It knows too that no other revelation is possible. Hence it disallows any other claim to exhibit genuine revelation, reducing all expressions of such claims to myths which 'really' do not mean what they say.

Because self-transcending naturalism is mystical-essentialist and not religious-existentialist it cannot break out of the circle of idealism. For example, Tillich states Hegel's belief that the truth is the whole, immediately adding, 'But no finite being has the whole.'[3] If this warning had been made by Kierkegaard, the conclusion would have been drawn that, on this account, no system can hope to stand. Since it is impossible for us to see the totality of things *sub specie aeterni*, we must be content to be existing individuals who see only glimpses of eternity and can know the Eternal God solely through faith in his revelation of

[1] Occasionally this identification is almost explicit. Thus he writes: 'Metaphysical knowledge is existential; even in . . . Aristotle it has a mystical element' (*ibid.*, p. 157 n. 9).

[2] *ST* II, p. 152.   [3] *Ibid.*, p. 72.

himself in Jesus Christ. But Tillich never considers exchanging the objective awareness of the Unconditioned for the subjective inwardness of faith (or what he would call a misunderstanding of religious symbols through failure to deliteralize them). He never doubts the possibility of anticipating wholes in the construction of systems yielding methodological knowledge. The fact that man does not have the whole does not lead Tillich to doubt anything, but instead it leads him to assert with complete confidence that doubt belongs to the essential being of man! It is surely not difficult for the reader of the *Systematic Theology* to see what Kierkegaard meant when he said that the speculative philosopher wishes to be an individual, but an individual without subjectivity, an individual who exists *sub specie aeterni*. Tillich's individual exists. There must be an individual to read the *Systematic Theology* and to agree (or disagree) with what he finds there. But, if he agrees and accepts the system he finds there, he is freed from *real* doubt. He knows that every existing man must experience doubt, but he knows also that this doubt is the other side of essential faith or being grasped by the power of being-itself. Therefore he is able to see himself, not as an existing being—experiencing doubt—but as he really is, *sub specie aeterni*. Once he embraces the system he is no longer merely an individual. He is one who is aware of his essential being, knowing that he participates in ultimate reality through his capacity for self-transcendence. He knows that through self-transcendence he can go beyond himself and return to himself on another dimension. He is, with this knowledge, no longer an individual bound to subjectivity. He has another dimension to move in.

To this description of how the individual is lost in the universal dimension of man-as-such, Tillich would almost certainly object that the individual's knowledge of what it means to be man-as-such does not mean losing his individuality but enriching it. Instead of looking at himself, with a surface view of the Universe, as a mere individual, each man can now understand the true wonder of what it means to be a human being. His personality is not in the least merged into an undifferentiated whole, but it is now seen to have unexpected levels of reality as it participates within the structure of being and learns how to realize its infinite potentialities. Nor does acceptance of the system leave behind the personal God which is so prominent a feature of the Christian religion:

> 'Being includes personal being; it does not deny it. The ground of being is the ground of personal being, not its negation. The ontological question of being creates not a conflict but a necessary basis for any theoretical dealing with the biblical concept of the personal God.'[1]

To this defence there can be only answer, which can be given in the form of a question, namely, Can there be true personal being without true individuality?

If this question is posed directly to Tillich's system it will turn into the question, Is self-transcendence compatible with the notion of real individual selves? And the system seems always to stop short of admitting the reality of anything individual or particular. The 'self' in the finite being which is self-transcendent serves only to point beyond itself to the infinite in which it participates—it is real only in its universal dimension, and therefore it has to 'go beyond itself' in order to return to itself in that dimension. This is not surprising, because the individual self can have reality only if it stands as a self in a real existence. Real existence is, however, exactly what the system cannot recognize, existence being self-contradictory in the systematic view. Tillich defines existence in terms of 'standing out' (*existere*, to stand out) of non-being.[2] In existence objects stand out of non-being, but also remain in it—if they stood out of non-being altogether they would have realized their essential being altogether and would no longer belong to the level of existence but would *be* as God *is*. But what makes anything stand out of being at all is not its existential selfhood but its participation in being beyond existence. An actual tree, for instance,

> '. . . stands out and exists only because it participates in that power of being which is treehood, that power which makes every tree a tree and nothing else.'[3]

Thus treehood alone is real. Individual trees are not.

[1] *Biblical Religion and the Search for Ultimate Reality*, p. 83.
[2] *ST* II, p. 20.   [3] *Ibid.*, p. 21.

Such an outlook upon existence leads to the belief that the whole of the created Universe is no more than an appearance caused by looking at things from the self-contradictory perspective of finite beings fallen into existence. This belief follows, as I have already outlined, from Tillich's understanding of the two levels of being, essential and existential, and the implications of the belief are made plain in his approach to the Christian doctrine of Creation. The two levels of being represent eternal distinctions, and therefore even the philosophical description of the origin of the material Universe (or the Fall of souls) as 'the transition from essence to existence' is not real but 'a story to be told'.[1] The system regards this story as either a myth or a fact—from the point of view of the system the two categories are on the same level. Neither is real, in the sense that both belong to the level of self-contradiction which is the level of existence. That fact and myth belong together is, in fact, the key to Tillich's conception of the myth. In the ordinary way, people say that something is 'only symbolic', contrasting the status of symbols with the status of actual, empirical facts. An individual king, they believe, is more 'real' than the crown that symbolizes his kingship; for the actual metal crown that can be worn and is as 'real' as its wearer is not, of course, itself the symbol—the symbol is a 'mere idea'. But for the system, with its idealistic devaluing of the surface level of experience which it believes to have no enduring being, symbol and myth possess more reality than facts do. So Tillich argues that people should never say 'only a symbol', but they should say 'not less than a symbol'.[2] For him a symbol has reality, whereas a fact is a 'mere fact'. Facts, if they are no more than facts (i.e. if their significance is purely individual and they display no signs of having a universal dimension), are nothing but flickering shadows on the face of eternity.

This explains why an event in time and space, such as the crucifixion of Jesus, gains its significance for the system not by being an actual event but by being a symbol and part of a myth having 'universal symbolic significance'.[3] It is not

[1] *Ibid.*, p. 29.
[2] *Dynamics of Faith*, p. 45; see also *ST* I, p. 131, and *ST* II, p. 9.
[3] *ST* II, pp. 153–4.

because this event happened at a historical moment and involved an actual individual, Jesus of Nazareth, that it should occupy a central place in Christian faith. Its importance comes from being an event 'elevated' to universal and timeless meaning by virtue of its ability to serve as a symbolic focus for an eternal truth. Its symbolic value is indicated by the presence in the history of religious mythology of other dying gods. But its unique value arises because no other myth centres on the picture of a personal life and so can signify Essential God-Manhood. This myth corresponds to the necessary 'idea' of religion, as the system conceives religion necessarily to be, namely, 'the all-embracing function of man's spiritual life'.[1] Thus an event is given meaning and reality not in virtue of its being a fact but in virtue of its being a myth.

Where events mean nothing as events, it is hard to see what place there can be for personal being. Persons are beings whose lives are made up of events, who move on the factual plane of existence, who are born, struggle, and die, and whose biographies can be compiled only when the event of their earthly life is actually over. Instead of the system including personal being within its ontology, it would seem to be (in the phrase attributed to Mr Sam Goldwyn) definitely *included out*! Tillich's claim that his system does not conflict with the biblical concept of the personal God is irreconcilable with the biblical insistance that God is known through his mighty acts. 'In all its expressions,' writes Tillich, 'theology refers to the divine mystery—the mystery of eternal being'.[2] This sentence is correct if mystical awareness is taken to be the final source of our knowledge of God. But theology is not just concerned to express deity as mystery, if it is Christian theology. In fact it does not try to probe into the mystery of eternal being at all. The mystery of God's eternity is simply acknowledged by Christian theology to be something which is beyond man's comprehension, and what theology tries to express is God's self-revelation as Creator and Redeemer. Christian theologians, like Christian believers in all walks of life, are concerned to speak about

[1] *ST* I, p. 15.   [2] *ST* II, p. 91.

> The One eternal God
> Whom heaven and earth adore,

and this God can be adored by his creatures only because he has entered into a relationship with them. A deity who is the creative and abysmal Ground of being can make itself immediately known by pervading reality as the Unconditioned. But the God who is Creator has conditioned himself to meet with his own creation, and such a God is known through this divine condescension alone. He reveals *himself*, and reveals himself to *men*.

The reality of God's relationship with his world means taking particularity with complete seriousness. For God did not merely create the possibility of the transition from essence to existence; on this view, he created a real world. And, the moment that creation is taken to be a symbol representing the eternal distinction between eternal states, then the God who moves on the personal dimension is effectively negated. This particular deliterization of symbols—so necessary to the system —eviscerates the Christian gospel. It is exactly the same with the event of salvation in the Incarnation, Cross and Resurrection. It is not enough to know that the manifestation of Essential God-Manhood under the conditions of existence brings us experience of the New Being, if we, personally, want to be saved. We may be told that this manifestation heals us into our true being and satisfies the whole of human reality. But we, individually, need more than this. We need to hear of 'the Son of God who loved me and gave himself for me' (Gal. 2.20). And this knowledge cannot come through participation in eternal being but, as Paul indicates, when we 'live by faith' in the loving and saving Christ. This Christ who is Saviour is the one who says, 'I know my own and my own know me' (John 10.14). Therefore there cannot be belief in this saviour simply by knowing, through power experienced, that there has been conquest of existential estrangement in a personal life. This personal life must be known *as personal*, as the life of 'this Jesus', and not as a picture elevated into the universal and eternal world of meaning, while the individual life behind the picture fades away into the unknown and the unknowable.

Salvation also, in the Christian view, must be an event which saves on account of its being a fact and not merely because it becomes translucent and reveals the Ground of being. The God who meets men personally in Jesus Christ is the God who has acted in specific events:

> Who wondrous things hath done,
> In whom His world rejoices.

Again, the reality of personal being depends upon accepting particularity as real. Tillich advocates looking at the ontological question of being (ontological *speculation*), in which case one must look away from the surface of experience until one reaches the level where individuals have lost their transitory reality. This *looking* is not looking with the eye of faith, which, as Calvin said, sees one particular object:

> 'Since it is clear that Christ is the perpetual object of faith, we cannot know what we receive through faith except by looking to him.'[1]

If Tillich can be charged with not taking the personal dimension of the Christian gospel seriously, he has a counter-charge of his own to press against those who take their stand upon the literal truth of biblical language. He believes his ontological approach to be not only compatible with the biblical message (symbolically understood) but also the necessary basis for any proper understanding of the biblical God. A God who is merely personal, says Tillich, is not the true God, the God who is mystery and eternal power and not simply a highest being.

I have dealt with the heart of Tillich's argument earlier when I pointed out how Tillich's concern that God shall not be made one being among other beings leads to his definition of God as that which precedes the subject-object structure of the Universe.[2] But the point I now have to make is that such a definition, as well as not being one which represents the biblical conception of deity, also contradicts the notion of a personal God. From the perspective of the system, of course,

[1] *Instruction in Faith*, p. 40.   [2] See above, pp. 82 ff.

'personal God' is a symbol, and Tillich speaks of this symbol both as 'absolutely fundamental' and as 'confusing'. He concludes that the symbol can only mean that God is the Ground of everything personal: 'He is not a person, but he is not less than personal.'[1] Unfortunately, such a statement says very little in a direct way, for it cannot be understood unless exactly what the system means by personal is also understood.

Probably the best way to discover the meaning of personality for the system is through its definition of a man as 'finite freedom'.[2] Finite freedom means the power man has to ask questions and receive answers (i.e. to be independent of the divine Ground and yet to remain in unity with it). Tillich adds that it is the quality of finite freedom in the Universe which makes pantheism impossible.[3] Yet the concept would seem to indicate exactly the opposite. Finite freedom is a universal quality—in itself a notion excluding real individuality —and its function is to guarantee that man, even though he falls into the self-contradictions of existence, can never fall away completely from the divine Ground of his own being and meaning. Man essentially participates in deity, or he could have no finite freedom. Therefore man, *as a person*, is never an individual as such; he is always a union of participation and individualization. 'As a self', says Tillich, 'he is an individual person who participates universally.'[4] In other words, man is never outside God, since God is 'the principle of participation as well as the principle of individualization'.[5] And, finally, man's very power of appearing in existence as (on the surface) an individual is itself a proof that he is rooted in the Ground of being and has never left it.

The God who is not a person and not less than 'personal' is, in the system's reckoning, 'the eternal process in which separation is posited and is overcome by reunion'.[6] The sole basis for the appearance of individuality is the eternal truth that there is a differentiation of 'being from being' within God. Therefore, man-as-such (not existing individuals) possesses freedom in a finite way, mirroring the divine process in so far

[1] *ST* I, p. 245.   [2] *ST* II, pp. 8, 31–2.   [3] *Ibid.*, p. 8.
[4] *ST* I, p. 243.   [5] *Ibid.*, p. 245.   [6] *Ibid.*, p. 242.

as his existential predicament will allow. God and man together manifest the personal by exhibiting a process and not simply a pure absolute.[1] The pantheistic nature of Tillich's view of God thus comes fully to the fore—pantheistic, that is, in its denial of a true relationship between God and creation, where individuals are real because God made them and not simply because they participate essentially in being. The same pantheism is exhibited when Tillich, denying that the true Godhood of God can be expressed in the ego-thou relationship of biblical faith, calls for a recognition of the full dimension of deity. He says that we should turn to contemplate 'the mystery of the divine ground', consider 'the infinity of the divine life', intuit 'the marvel of the divine creativity', and adore 'the inexhaustible meaning of the divine self-manifestation'.[2] Here the mystical reverse face of the pantheistic coin is uppermost. From the viewpoint of Christian faith, however, a call to worship God in these terms does not sound especially impressive. Far from seeming to rise above the ego-thou relationship expressed in biblical piety, the terms used by Tillich seem far less rich and less expressive of the holy. *Mystery*, *infinity*, *creativity* and *self-manifestation* are bare words compared with such terms as *The Holy One of Israel*, *The God and Father of our Lord Jesus Christ*, *He that is able to keep you from falling*, and *The Lamb that was slain*.

The God who meets us as individuals within a personal relationship is, for Christian theology, the most exalted God there can be. He is also the God who judges us, for his nature is to be holy and righteousness as well as almighty. It is this moral dimension which is so much lacking in the God of ontology, whose main characteristic is to be universal. God, says Tillich, can never be an object, for he is always subject. That means that, when we are aware of God, God himself is thinking in us. The Unconditional being present, our subjectivity is swallowed up in the pure objectivity of being-itself. Kierkegaard also taught that God was never an object. But the meaning of this was that we could never reflect about God, making him the

[1] See the Postscript to this chapter: 'Non-being in God'.
[2] *ST* I, p. 289.

object of our speculations. It was as though we had taken a picture or a piece of cloth to stare at, only to find that the 'object' of our scrutiny was looking back at us. The Christian gospel, so Kierkegaard argued, has ears and listens to us while we speak.[1] Self-transcendence as a gospel lacks this dimension. Denying that which is particular and individual, it cannot include the dimension of personal being. Tillich may say that ultimate concern is the abstract translation of the Great Commandment.[2] But the point is that this commandment is lost when so translated. To love the Lord our God with all our heart, soul, mind and strength is not at all the same thing as to cherish 'a religious concern which is ultimate, unconditional, total, and infinite'.[3] The direction of our concern is different in each instance, and so the quality of the concern is different too. In being ultimately concerned about our own being and meaning we share in the universal longing of man-as-such to be reunited with his origin, thus knowing the pull of cosmic *eros*. In learning to love the Lord who first loved us and who addresses us as individuals through grace we discover what it means to be members of the family and household of God, thus knowing how great is the *agape* that the Father has shown us (I John 3.1).

[1] *Training in Christianity* (London, Oxford University Press, 1941), pp. 228–9.

[2] *Op. cit.*, p. 11.

[3] *Ibid.*, p. 12. Johnson points out that Tillich's claim that he does not separate form from content in faith is hard to reconcile with his readiness to define theological concepts having an 'undesignated referent'. If his definitions take no account of the content of Christian revelation, how can he still say that his Criteria are derived 'from the whole of the Christian message' (op. cit., pp. 130–1)? To the same general effect, Tavard argues that faith, in the New Testament sense, is *faith that comes by hearing* (Rom. 10.17). But Tillich, because he ontologizes faith, ties faith to awareness of the structure of our existence and leaves us groping. Tavard makes the comment that 'systematic shunning of the objective question (commitment to what?) leaves a bewildering after-taste of word-juggling' (*op. cit.*, pp. 31 ff.).

Postscript: Non-being in God

If the terms of the system are accepted there is and can be nothing, in the last resort, outside God. Even man-as-such is to be understood as included in Essential God-manhood, and therefore the system shows itself to be monistic and quasi-pantheistic. But, in an article entitled 'Some Comments on Tillich's Doctrine of Creation',[1] J. Heywood Thomas has come to a different conclusion. Because of Tillich's way of interpreting *creatio ex nihilo*, so Thomas argues, his system is not monistic but dualistic. The article ends by saying:

> 'What Tillich has done is to make the "nothing" out of which we come a something with fatal power. Hence, as I suggested, we are once more faced with Dualism.'[2]

Now, while it is true that non-being in the system is a *something*, Thomas's thesis entirely overlooks the fact that the system makes non-being a something found within God himself. Tillich expounds this point most fully in *The Courage To Be*, where he states:

> 'Non-being belongs to being, it cannot be separated from it. We could not even think of "being" without a double negation: being must be thought of as the negation of the negation of being. . . . If we speak of the power of being-itself we indicate that being affirms itself against non-being.'[3]

He goes on to explain that it is non-being which makes God a living God, and it is through non-being that God is revealed. The presence of non-being in God means that there is finitude in God, and anxiety as well—though, in the divine being, finitude is eternally conquered by the divine infinity. Without non-being God would be no more than 'immovable self-identity', while with this negation of himself he affirms himself dynamically.

The implications of such a view are far-reaching. Some of them have been indicated by Arthur C. Cochrane, whose

---

[1] *The Scottish Journal of Theology* XIV 2 (June 1961), pp. 113–18.
[2] *Ibid.*, p. 118.   [3] *Op. cit.*, p. 170.

analysis of the triad *being, non-being* and *finite being* raises several important questions.[1] Cochrane points out that the definition of God as being-itself is unsatisfactory, for the system should rather refer to 'the togetherness of being and nothing'. At the same time, being-itself, though put beside non-being, is reckoned ontologically prior to it; and non-being is subordinated to the structure of being. This double vision of non-being—part adversary, part collaborator—seems to Cochrane far from clear. He wonders whether non-being, if included in God, can be taken seriously as a negation of being; and he asks, 'Is not Tillich's nonbeing too dependent on being, and vice versa, for it to be anything but a caricature of *the* power that truly threatens man?'[2]

Cochrane's question is answered from within the system by the axiom that man, although estranged from being, is not separated from it. The dualism which Thomas thinks he sees is a limited dualism only, incapable of disrupting the system's basic monism. There can be no 'fatal power' in non-being because, whether we know it or not, the objective situation is that being-itself is eternally vanquishing non-being. Indeed, being-itself *needs* the non-being it conquers, just as animals need food and kill to eat. Without non-being being-itself could not be what it is. Man's anxiety, therefore, may tend in the direction of despair, but total despair is not possible for man without total loss of his humanity. The one effective power in the Universe is the power manifested in *eros*-faith, and this is the power which (though hidden) remains always in spite of the existential predicament. After all, existence is a predicament merely. Its chief feature is its self-contradictoriness. It contains tragic elements, but it is not tragic. In it the forces of disruption are always balanced—more than balanced—by the forces of healing. Because it is solely through the anxiety born of non-being that we encounter ontological shock and become aware of the power of being within us, non-being is less fatal than friendly. And we do not meet non-being on its own but always

---

[1] *Op. cit.,*—see especially pp. 78, 79–80, 81, 84–8. Cochrane heads his chapter on Tillich, 'Being, Nonbeing, and Being-Itself'.

[2] *Ibid.,* p. 88.

as 'digested' within being. It is God that discloses himself to us in the simultaneous meeting of being and non-being.

In short, non-being is 'something' only when it is an element in God. It can never have any power to threaten man in his true humanity. It is a painted devil, capable only of scaring the child of being and of sending him running back to his own safe home.

Tillich's understanding of non-being in God is (as Cochrane has noted) very close to that of Hegel. While not being able to go the whole way with Hegel in his philosophy of history, Tillich agrees with him wholeheartedly concerning the dialectical movement within the Absolute.[1] He erects what he terms 'trinitarian principles' on the foundation of the dialectic of the finite and the infinite within the divine life. These are supposed to prepare the way for the Christian doctrine of the Trinity, but they presuppose a Hegelian-type Trinity and not a Christian one. As Tavard has noticed,[2] Tillich recognizes a trinitarian God for no other reason than that he finds all life to be trinitarian—meaning by this term that three aspects (three 'moments' within a 'process') of a known reality are presented to our view. And there cannot be life, any more than there can be being, outside the divine life. Hegel believes that when we contemplate the dialectical movement within the Absolute we know all that there is to know. Tillich simply amends this doctrine and states that, although our knowledge is limited in existence, yet our participation in the divine life is assured.

The absence of any true dualistic element in the system accounts for its failure to preserve either the personal or the moral dimension of human life. Sin cannot be a genuine threat to man, for sin is estrangement, and estrangement by definition is never final separation. In any case, there are no *sins*—such a concept as the individual sin is to be found only where persons are considered to have their own separate reality as God-created creatures. By taking non-being into God, the system has guaranteed the dynamics of divinity at the expense of denying reality to the individual life that can be both lost through sin and saved through grace.

[1] *ST* I, p. 275.   [2] *Op. cit.*, pp. 118–20.

X

SYSTEMATIC CERTAINTIES

BECAUSE TILLICH intends his system to be fully systematic, no word, no phrase, no metaphor, and no popular expression remains unaffected—in principle at least—when it is brought within the system's orbit. The authority of the system must extend throughout the entire kingdom of language.

This is the reason why, although Tillich describes theology as the methodical interpretation of the contents of the Christian faith, he finds that most of the leading terms used in traditional Christian doctrine stand in need of drastic *re*interpretation. In fact, it is almost a law that, the more central to doctrine a word or phrase may be, the more certain it is to be marked out for replacement. The word *faith* is apparently among the most unsatisfactory of all,[1] sharing its position as a theological scandal, perhaps, with the words *sin* and *Incarnation*. Whether substitute words can be found, or whether old words will have to go on working even though they have outlived their usefulness, Tillich knows that his theology will not leave things as they were. His Method, especially, calls for

> 'an interpretation of the traditional symbols of Christianity . . . which preserves the power of these symbols and which opens them to the questions elaborated by our present analysis of human existence.'[2]

[1] 'It belongs to those terms which need healing before they can be used for the healing of men. Today the term "faith" is more productive of disease than of health. It confuses, misleads . . . for the time being, the only way of dealing with the problem is to reinterpret the word and remove the confusing and distorting connotations, some of which are the heritage of centuries' *Dynamics of Faith*, Introductory Remarks vii. See also above, pp. 99–100, for further references from the same source.

[2] *ST* I, p. 64.

The system is prepared to open the Christian 'symbols' as oysters are opened to make them ready for eating. Yet it would seem that not only the terms of Christian doctrine but all words whatsoever have to be opened so that the system may have them at its disposal. The authority of the system allows many truths to be known as certainties which cannot be doubted since the system guarantees them. Therefore these certainties ought to be presented in appropriate terms, and this will mean either inventing special technical phrases to serve as a vehicle of communication or else using words and phrases already in existence and having these serve the same purpose.

Tillich employs both methods. A more complete study of his thought than the present one pretends to be would, no doubt, make a detailed study of his terminology in relation to the various certainties proclaimed in his system. My purpose has been less to present the system as a system than to indicate what the system means for Christian theology, and for that reason I have been more concerned to prove its assumptions than to expound its teaching in an orderly fashion. My belief is that, once the main character of the system has been grasped, nothing in it should be unduly perplexing. And yet the reader of the *Systematic Theology* and Tillich's other writings may sometimes fail to recognize how far the process has been taken of interpreting words in order to make them fit the system. So I shall close my study by considering three phrases used prominently by Tillich, each of them leading the reader into some important aspect of the system. The three phrases are: 'on the boundary', 'accepting acceptance', and 'the God above God'. Behind each phrase—and giving it the sense which Tillich intends—lies a certainty assumed by his system but not necessarily easily seen in the phrase at it stands.

'On the Boundary': the Certainty of the Knowledge of the Whole

Tillich often speaks of being 'on the boundary'. This is the general title attached to his Autobiographical Sketch in *The Interpretation of History*, and here Tillich declares himself to stand on several boundaries. To select just three headings out of twelve, he stands On the Boundary Between Heteronomy and Autonomy, On the Boundary Between Theology and Philosophy, and On the Boundary Between Religion and Culture. We might suppose—and Tillich encourages us to suppose—that being on the boundary between two territories indicates a receptive mind admitting no preconceptions. But we soon discover that Tillich being on the boundary means occupying a vantage-point from which the observer can see the whole of an area instead of one small piece of it. He who thus stands in a central position possesses a complete view, whereas the man standing to one side or the other of the border line sees no more than a broken fragment. Thus the former is not less sure of himself than the latter but vastly more sure. No wonder, then, that almost at once we learn that 'the border line is the truly propitious place for acquiring knowledge'.[1]

Such a conclusion may seem odd, for the phrase does not at first sight suggest this meaning. To stand on the border, or boundary, seems so much like being what people call 'a border-line case' ('He's not quite sane, but he's not a raving lunatic either—he's a border-line case') that it is difficult to accept any other interpretation. Surely the reason why the border line is a place for getting to know things must be that it makes one less narrow and dogmatic! Nevertheless, all the evidence points in the other direction. When Tillich speaks of acquiring knowledge he means certainty, not getting to know things in a random and tentative manner.

Valentinus the second century Gnostic gave a prominent place in his system to *Horos*, meaning both 'the boundary' and also 'true definition'. Tillich's metaphor of the boundary is considerably nearer to the Valentinian *Horos* than to the metaphor of the border-line case in ordinary speech. The boundary is where knowledge comes, because for the system truth lies in wholeness; and, without wholeness, true definition is impossible. Indeed, being on the boundary is practically equivalent to thinking in a system. Only it appears that the metaphor

[1] *The Interpretation of History*, p. 3. This sentence is quoted by Tillich from his own work, *Religiose Verwirklichung*. Compare also Tillich's statement in *Theology of Culture*: 'Judging means seeing both sides' (*op. cit.*, p. 51).

emphasizes one special aspect of the systematic task. Since every system tries to anticipate a final whole by uniting all things in heaven and on earth in order to arrive at completeness, every system-maker is always challenged by the existence of two fields of knowledge commonly distinguished from each other. Can he succeed in uniting the apparently diverse? If he can, he begins to round out his system and brings truth into being.[1] If he cannot, his system remains at a standstill facing a roadblock on the path leading to knowledge of the whole. Tillich, in his rôle of Observer On the Boundary, is well able to produce those syntheses demanded by his system. Standing between Heteronomy and Autonomy, he sees what whole is needed to enclose these two—and he announces the discovery of Theonomy. Theonomy functions as a unity that transcends the separate units which it encloses, holding them together as a nut-shell holds together the two halves of the nut and makes the nut a single object. Similarly, Tillich stands between Theology and Philosophy—and discovers The Theonomous Character of Knowing, or Awareness of the Unconditioned. Finally he stands between Religion and Culture. In this case he announces that Religion is the substance of Culture, while Culture is the form of Religion.

Making a synthesis transcending the difference between two fields is, in the last resort, incompatible with standing on the boundary between them. If the synthesis has been fully successful there can be no separate fields and, consequently, no boundary: the supposed two are really one and must *interpenetrate*—to use a favourite word of Tillich's. So it happens that the Observer On the Boundary, standing at his vantage-point where he surveys the total landscape, does not have to choose or compromise. He will not settle for one side or the other, or

[1] For Tillich ontological reason is 'the structure of the mind which enables it to grasp and to shape reality' (*ST* I, p. 75). Thus reason actually creates the truth which it recognizes as it shapes out a rational system. The *logos* in man can bring certainty of knowledge because reality itself has a *logos* character; and so mind and reality plunge into one common mould—mind does not simply trace the shape of a reality external to it. Compare Kierkegaard's words about System thinking that it brings truth into being which was not there before, thus assuming that Christianity is only *to a certain degree true*. (See above pp. 47 ff.)

else accept a little of both. Instead, he rejects the alternatives before him, believing that these are false alternatives ready to dissolve under a synoptic view. Like the mother pleading for her baby before Solomon, he knows that it is better to have no baby at all than to have to agree to take half a baby. An illustration of this point is provided by the common description of Tillich's position as a theology taking a middle way between liberalism and neo-orthodoxy.[1] This is just what standing of the boundary line cannot mean. It is abundantly clear that Tillich is neither a liberal with orthodox leanings nor yet a champion of neo-orthodoxy who has his liberal moments.[2] Rather, he stands above both parties, judging them. He does not believe that the truth contained in either party position is properly grasped by the party itself, just as an actor cannot properly estimate the character he is to play if he has seen merely his own lines but not the whole script.

So, when Tillich says that he stands on the boundary, he is claiming to see the whole in such a way as to be able to correct the partial and astigmatic vision of others who can see no more than a part. He can make accurate definitions because he can ask the right questions and find suitable answers fitting the questions precisely. This claim is the basis for his assumption that the system can freely interpret the material with which it deals, laying down its own terms without fear of being challenged—much less refuted. It underlies his confidence in the system being able to assert authoritatively what the Christian message 'really' means. He is certain that he can reinterpret the Gospel in terms of his system and yet retain the 'power' of the Christian 'symbols', because, having defined what truth is, he cannot imagine that the Gospel can do other than submit to reinterpretation in terms of the objective situation. If Christianity does not actually say what his system says, then it must *imply* it. All of which points up the accuracy of

[1] See, for example, the chapter entitled 'The Boundary Between Liberalism and Neo-Orthodoxy: Paul Tillich' in William Hordern's *A Layman's Guide to Protestant Theology* (New York, Macmillan, 1955).

[2] I shall argue later that Tillich can be called a liberal—see below pp. 230–1. But this is because of an ambiguity in the label *liberal*, and not because Tillich supports any brand of modified or adulterated liberalism.

Kierkegaard's contention that when a speculative system speaks of explaining Christianity it means that Christianity needs to be corrected in order to bring it into line with the assumptions of speculation.

Naturally, Tillich never even suggests that he alters the least part of the Christian message in order to make it fit into his system. In the same way, he avoids giving the impression that his self-transcending naturalism will alter the ordinary understanding of the world very much. He might have insisted that his vision of reality so conflicts with the world-view of contemporary Western man that the lumber in his readers' minds must be cast out. Instead, although attacking present-day nominalism and bias against speculation, he tends to tone down any suggestion of intending to revolutionize our thinking. He speaks about self-transcending naturalism interpreting concepts so that these are simultaneously 'confirmed and negated', 'accepted and overcome', or 'preserved and opened'. This formula—which, incidentally, is derived from Hegel[1]—enables him to suggest that he is not so much changing anything as allowing its real nature to appear. (And, indeed, from the idealistic standpoint this is what he is doing.) Nevertheless, he does not stop to explain why self-transcending naturalism

---

[1] An interesting account of a discussion with Tillich is recorded by J. Heywood Thomas as follows: 'When asked to explain what meaning we could give to the statement that reason was overcome and yet preserved, Tillich very significantly said that the German word "*aufheben*" means both "to overcome" and "to preserve".' Thomas mentions this as an 'excellent example of Tillich's tendency to exploit the ambiguity of language', adding: 'But however attractive the view, it is not one bit sounder because of an accident of the German language' (*op. cit.*, p. 256).

The peculiar interest of this record is that, in exploiting this particular accident of the German language Tillich is walking in the footsteps of Hegel, and Thomas's reaction echoes that of Kierkegaard. Kierkegaard poked fun at what he called Hegel's trick, saying that it illustrated the popular saying about trying to talk with one's mouth full of hot mush. He also accused Hegel of distorting the meaning of the word, since it could not be used in both senses at once (*Concluding Unscientific Postscript*, pp. 199–200). It is also noteworthy that Zuurdeeg does not hesitate about the Hegelian derivation of Tillich's method of handling his ontological concepts. The polar structure of being in his system, Zuurdeeg says, resembles the Hegelian thesis and antithesis in having valid and non-valid aspects. 'The valid aspects have to be *aufgehoben* in a synthesis' (*op. cit.*, p. 158).

requires this double movement, this saying of 'yea' and 'nay' at one and the same time. The movement is actually identical with the one which Tillich attributes to finite being when, in self-transcendence, it goes beyond itself in order to return to itself in a new dimension. And it fits in very well with the metaphor of the boundary line. When the Observer On the Boundary combines two fields of vision into a single whole he does more than add the two together. He superimposes his total perspective upon what he sees, having the same kind of insight into the total situation as a pilot of a helicopter would have if he hovered above a road and saw two cars approaching each other around a blind corner. An even closer approximation to the vision enjoyed by the Observer would be the illustration of a man watching two bees trying to get together when separated by a window pane; while the bees see only each other and thus experience an inexplicable frustration, the man understands their *predicament* (another good Tillichian word) because he knows the qualities of glass.

As I have argued earlier, everything hangs upon whether there is such a panoramic view of reality as the system assumes. In the event of the panoramic view proving impossible for mortal man to reach, the border line will not be the place at which to acquire knowledge and the Observer On the Border will prove to be a fantastic individual. Then the synthesis for which the system labours will collapse and the yea-and-nay saying which it practises will emerge as a piece of highly questionable manœuvring. Outside the Universe conceived by idealism that which is negated can never be accepted, except in an ironic sense. A man who resists arrest, and has to be 'over-come' so that he can be 'preserved' in a prison cell, is hardly likely to admit that prison is where he is most at home; and anything which has to be negated so that it may be synthesized into a whole has had equal violence done to it. In order to make its synthesis the system has to ignore what it does not like and accept only that which suits its purposes. Once the system has taken a thing in hand it can never be what it was before—Tillich admits as much when he explains how finite being, after it goes beyond itself, returns to itself *in a new dimension* (i.e. not as its old self). It is all very well for the system to play the part of Ariel in the *Tempest* and sing a dirge over finite being—

> 'Nothing of it that doth fade
> But doth suffer a sea-change
> Into something rich and strange.'

But the fact remains that the system does not show that the change actually takes place. The system only shows that it does not wish finite being to remain finite. It cannot endure the notion that God may have intended the world to be a finite world, and so has made it that way. Banishing such an unwelcome thought to the limbo of not-to-be-entertained-possibilities, it then proceeds to proclaim self-transcendence as a certainty.

The metaphor of standing On the Boundary emphasizes how the system must always assume its idealistic world-view, arguing continually from this view, not towards it. The border line can be the place where knowledge is acquired simply so long as the system is sure that there is really no line there at all. With this assumption made, the system knows also that all which appears to hinder the border line being abolished must be overcome (i.e. declared to be unreal). Take, for example, Tillich's stand On the Boundary Between Philosophy and Theology. Tillich is certain of the 'mutual immanence' of the two.[1] On the basis of this certainty, he can proceed to correct (or simultaneously overcome and preserve) all other views about the nature both of philosophy and theology. He knows that there is but one grand tradition in philosophy, a tradition stretching from Parmenides to Hegel which identifies philosophy with ontology. Equally surely, he knows that theology must be properly apologetic theology, declaring the *logos* structure of *theos*. And he knows that these views of both fields are indubitable, because they allow philosophy and theology to be united on the basis of the identity of the universal and the concrete *logos*—the respective goals of the philosophical and the religious quests.

---

[1] Tillich is sure about this 'mutual immanence' because he is sure also of the mutual immanence of religion and culture: see *The Theology of Paul Tillich*, p. 336. He has stood on the Boundary Between Religion and Culture as well as On the Boundary Between Philosophy and Theology. Two boundaries—a double certainty!

In all this, the Observer On the Boundary does not have to consider once whether philosophy may not have its centre elsewhere than in ontology, or whether theology may perhaps be more than expressing the mystery of being as revealed through the depths of reason. He starts from the systematic certainty that he possesses the knowledge of the whole. It is a knowledge which overcomes or removes all other knowledge, preserving only what it can open to the questions which it wishes to put. It is even a gospel which can be preached, since the Observer On the Boundary can explain that everyone who has become dissatisfied with his old beliefs is really a man in the boundary-situation who has only to become aware of his situation to find something to live for, whether or not he is attracted to the message of the Christian churches.[1] He who has this knowledge has all he needs both for a theoretical and a practical understanding of life. Indeed, he stands On the Boundary between Theory and Practice.

The specifically religious message of the border line is that the difference between different religious faiths (and between religion preached in churches or temples and religion lived out in solitude by the contemplative and the philosopher) is both overcome and preserved. Tillich explains how Socrates and Paul are really teaching the same lesson when they speak about knowing the good and about knowing Christ, each following his own vision of the New Being. Since 'true knowledge includes union, and therefore, openness to receive that with which one unites', Socrates was speaking about union with that same Source of all goodness which Paul identified with Christ. Both were speaking, in fact, of *gnosis* or that which is 'cognitive, sexual, and mystical union at the same time'.[2]

The certainty that comes from standing on the boundary line which is not really there can well be described, and is perhaps most accurately described, as the certainty of *gnosis*. Probably

[1] See, 'The Protestant Message and The Man of Today' in *The Protestant Era*, pp. 189–204. Here Protestantism is identified with 'the independence of one who finds himself in a situation in which he shares the lot of everything human to be subject to the threat of not-being' (p. 196)—and, of course, to be able to experience the reality found through being in this situation!

[2] *ST* I, pp. 95–6.

because he knows only too well that the term has been long outlawed from Christianity, Tillich uses it very sparingly. Yet he appeals to the theological 'solution' of the Alexandrian school to the problem of reconciling faith with knowledge in order to justify his use of the word and the concept.[1] The Observer On the Boundary is the true type of the gnostic, because he has the higher certainty of direct union with reality which is lacking in the lower, though still valuable, certainty which is mediated through *pistis* (religious faith). The most prominent feature of Tillich's system is the constant elevation of *gnosis* over *pistis*;[2] and it is illustrated most vividly in his contrast between man's direct awareness of the Unconditioned and the indirect message he receives from the symbols of faith. In his awareness of the Unconditioned man meets himself—he is united with the goal he seeks, as is proper when *gnosis* is involved. On the other hand, the symbols of the Christian message (or the message of some other religious faith) are symbols which have to be interpreted—a symbol mediates reality only to the extent to which it is self-transcending, negating itself in its literal meaning and affirming itself in its self-transcending meaning.[3] Religious faith is still mixed with the shadows of existence and, unless adequately interpreted by the light available to the gnostic, leaves the believer in bondage to the surface of experience and unaware of the knowledge which can be acquired at the boundary line.

Paul confessed that it had pleased God to save believers by the 'sheer folly' of the Christian message (I Cor. 1.21—Moffatt). The gnostic does not say that this message is not a message which can bring salvation. But he first lays down the condition that, if he is to listen to any message at all, he must know that it is not a foolish one. A foolish message will be one which does not answer the question which man asks: the question of man himself.[4] So, before he can accept the *kerygma*

---

[1] *ST* I, pp. 153–4.

[2] Hendrik Kraemer notes this point as the reason why Tillich 'is simply forced to treat philosophy in fact as the criterion *de jure* and *de facto*' (*op. cit.*, p. 434).

[3] *ST* II, p. 9. [4] *Ibid.*, p. 13.

which was Paul's gospel of folly he must cease to be a mere believer and know that this *kerygma* is capable of answering his questions and thus of being the source of a revelatory experience. He must know that it is not 'really' folly by standing at the boundary line and making a judgment after seeing both sides, the side of faith—represented by Paul—and the side of *gnosis*, which will enable him to read the symbols of faith out of the 'depth' of his own being. The kind of faith which receives from God what God wills to give is not a live option for the system. Instead, the system assumes that the discovery of God is always on the level of *gnosis*, where man rises to be united with his own essential being and meaning. Man cannot believe anything that he does not already know essentially, and he must refuse the foolishness which would ask this of him. What he must do is to take his own situation as an Observer On the Boundary with ultimate seriousness. In spite of the deceptive surface of life, he may acquire knowledge on the boundary line which will unite him with the truly true and enable him simultaneously to accept and to overcome the universal human predicament.

In so far as Tillich's *Systematic Theology* gives directions to man as to how he may learn to conduct himself in his boundary-situation, it might carry, without any incongruity, the subtitle of 'A Guide to *Gnosis*'.

'*Accepting Acceptance*': The Certainty of Participation in the Whole

A common phrase may be used in Tillich's system, but appear with its ordinary meaning so completely 'overcome' that it is like a fly in amber, caught up and submerged in an alien element. That is what has happened to the phrase 'on the boundary,' which has become so completely a technical term that its associations with popular speech have to be entirely ignored before its technical meaning can emerge. After a different fashion, the system may coin its own phrase and use this in place of some accepted term in philosophy or theology. My second choice from Tillich's vocabulary is an example of this type: a substitute phrase replacing a traditional Christian symbol (to echo the language of the system). The Protestant watchword of 'justification by faith', so Tillich has suggested, can be reinterpreted in the form of 'accepting acceptance'. This thought is developed at length in the last chapter of *The Courage To Be*, a chapter called 'Courage and Transcendence' and subtitled, 'The Courage to Accept Acceptance'. It also finds a place in both volumes of the *Systematic Theology*.

Put forward in *The Courage To Be* as 'the genuine meaning of the Paulinian-Lutheran doctrine',[1] Tillich's phrase raises again the issue of the relation of his system to the Christian conception of forgiveness. The emphasis upon the doctrine of Justification in Reformation theology was the result of Luther's re-discovery in Paul's writings of a forgiveness which is neither deserved nor earned. Tillich himself stresses that the doctrine arose out of the experience of personal encounter with a forgiving God. At the same time, he argues that the experience of being *accepted although unacceptable* is both the real expression of what the Reformers meant and also is wider than the Reformation formula. It has a parallel, for example, in the experience of the psycho-analyst's patient today who learns to accept himself, and, by undergoing this experience, overcomes his guilt. Certainly, Tillich insists, the Reformers had a deeper grasp of the situation than a patient on the psychiatrist's couch is likely to have; for they had a conception of ultimacy in the situation, introduced under the symbol of God. In spite of this fact, he insists that Accepting Acceptance should replace Justification by Faith Alone. The former presents the truth of man's situation in a form which shows it to be what it is. The latter has become 'incomprehensible even for students of theology'.[2]

The first thing that Tillich has to say about Accepting Acceptance is that it is a paradox, for

> 'Accepting that one is accepted is the paradox of salvation without which there would be no salvation but only despair.'[3]

The mention of the word 'paradox' at once brings Kierkegaard into the picture, since he was the first thinker to bring the concept into prominence in connection with the Christian gospel. Kierkegaard believed that the paradox was a necessary

[1] *Op. cit.*, p. 156.   [2] *Loc. cit.*   [3] *ST* II, p. 179.

element in Christian faith, because faith has to do with the individual, an individual who does not *know* and *therefore* believes. Since reason cannot confirm faith or even find grounds for thinking it probable, 'the absurd is the object of faith, and the only object that can be believed'.[1] The Christian gospel with its message of the Word becoming flesh and forgiveness being shown to sinners, is both absurd and paradoxical— 'Christianity is precisely the paradoxical.'[2] In his understanding of Christianity as the absurd, Kierkegaard is following Paul's teaching about the foolishness of the *kerygma*, and his concept of paradox is probably drawn ultimately from Luther's belief that the Gospel could make opposites agree, a belief which underlies his whole theology of Law and Grace, Wrath and Love, Bondage and Freedom, and the other antitheses reconciled in Christ. Thus for him the paradox is not just one feature in the Christian gospel among many; it is what makes Christianity a gospel. And he considered the unpardonable offence of speculative philosophy to be this: that it first agreed to accept the paradox of faith, and afterwards went on to explain it and so abrogate it. The System believes that it can play with the paradox, simultaneously preserving and overcoming it![3] But a relative paradox, a paradox up-to-a-certain-degree, is no paradox, and certainly not the absolute paradox of Christianity.

The relative paradox, denounced by Kierkegaard, re-enters in Tillich's teaching. The need for paradox, he explains, can be rationally demonstrated. The paradox is that which cannot be derived from our ordinary experience but breaks into it from above. *Paradoxical* means 'against the opinion'—namely—'the opinion of finite reason'.[4] In other words, there is no paradox for self-transcending realism. There is a seeming paradox when we fail to take into account the reality which becomes visible whenever reason becomes transparent toward its depths. But, to the systematically informed mind which knows that finite

[1] *Op. cit.*, p. 189.   [2] *Ibid.*, p. 95.
[3] *Ibid.*, pp. 186 ff. It is in this section that Kierkegaard discusses Hegel's 'trick' with *aufheben* (see above, p. 202 n. 1).
[4] *ST* I, p. 56–7.

o   209

being is also self-transcendent, what is paradoxical to finite reason also appears to be what it is, a statement of what is really there to be known.

According to Tillich's system there is really only one paradox in the Christian message: the appearance of the New Being in existence.[1] The paradoxical element here is that existence should be conquered under the conditions of existence. It is paradoxical because it is a transcendent reality. But it is also eminently reasonable for those who accept the system's ontological analysis. They know that man in existence, though separated from being, still belongs to being and partakes of the power of being-itself. It is true that, until they experience the power of faith by being grasped ecstatically by the Ground of their being and meaning, they will not know the paradox to be true for them: that is, they will not be directly aware of the truth of the paradox. Yet they need not be ignorant of its nature, or else the *Systematic Theology* will have been written in vain. That means, of course, that it is perfectly possible to separate out a genuine paradox from a mere jumble of words which offends logical rationality. The paradox is a relative paradox—relative to finite being—and, by means of a judicious use of ontological analysis any enlightened person can find out what transcendent reality is indicated in any particular paradox and judge whether the paradox is true or not.

In a footnote in which he takes Brunner to task for making the offence of logical rationality the touchstone of Christian truth, Tillich remarks: 'This "offense" is neither that of Kierkegaard nor that of the New Testament.'[2] In respect of Kierkegaard's views, at any rate, Tillich's statement is wide of the mark. The distinctive feature of paradox in Kierkegaard's eyes is that it is folly to the Greeks, while the test of whether it is an absolute paradox is decisively 'the absurd'. This does not mean that anything incomprehensible must be a gospel, but it does mean that something comprehended cannot be the Christian gospel. Kierkegaard has put the issue in a brief dialogue:

[1] *ST* II, p. 90. Compare also, *ST* I, p. 57.
[2] *ST* I, p. 57 n. 15.

'But, if such is the case, speculative philosophy cannot get hold of it at all.' 'Quite right, this is precisely what the paradox says; it merely thrusts the understanding away in the interests of inwardness in believing.'[1]

Certainly, nonsense does not bring salvation, and unless the paradox represented a transcendent truth it could not be of concern to anyone. But only a relative paradox can be *known* to be rationally compelling. An absolute paradox cannot be known to be anything except a possible object of belief, and it may be judged to be a foolish one. The only reason for believing in a paradox must be wholly internal to the paradox itself. It is its own authority.

By following the paradox down a trail which ends—once again—at the point where Tillich clashes with Kierkegaard, I may seem to have left the phrase under investigation far behind. Actually, I believe that the main reason for Tillichs' adoption of this particular phrase has been exposed. Tillich prefers Accepting Acceptance to Justification by Faith Alone because the former phrase merely looks paradoxical. It allows him to slip in a relative paradox in place of an absolute one. The forgiveness of sins, as Luther stated it, was a paradox in the full sense of the word: it was against *all* opinion. Luther's theological formula, 'at the same time righteous and a sinner' (*simul justus et peccator*) held on to both sides of the contradiction, nowhere indicating how the two could co-exist. But for Tillich the necessary precondition of having any dealings with a paradox is to know just why it is a transcendent truth and not simply irrational and untrue.[2] The form of his relative paradox, 'acceptance of being accepted in spite of being unacceptable'— in the shortened and more usual version significantly without any visible paradoxical element—has been fashioned to fit neatly into the ontological box that waits ready to receive it; and there need be no anxiety about whether the lid will not be able to be closed down and the fastener snapped into place. Man *is* acceptable because he is essentially at one with being. And he is able to accept acceptance because he can be drawn through the power of *eros*-faith into that unity which he has

[1] *Op. cit.*, p. 195.　　[2] *ST* II, p. 91.

never essentially broken. What makes Accepting Acceptance possible 'is the state of unity between God and man, no matter how fragmentarily realized'.[1]

These last words reveal how Tillich's *paradox of salvation* is never more than a paradox-up-to-a-point. The sinner is not indeed wholly a sinner; he is fragmentarily righteous. And no one could find anything particularly paradoxical in the righteous being declared righteous, however fragmentarily their righteousness is realized. The real point of Accepting Acceptance as a substitute for Justification is this: it retains some appearance of being a paradox, not unlike Justification by Faith Alone, but it allows a major shift to be made away from the doctrine of Justification, with its strong affirmation of the individual's need to meet face to face with a forgiving God who forgives *him*. Then, in place of the stress upon individual belief (which is impossible to disregard in Luther's formula) it emphasizes 'the subjective side, namely, the acceptance'.[2] Such a 'subjectivity', of course, has nothing whatever to do with Kierkegaard's subjectivity which is the inward faith of the individual which believes and does not know. This subjective element is the receiving end of the process of the part being gathered up into the whole by the urge of *eros*. *Accepting acceptance although (relatively) unacceptable* is being 'drawn into the power of the New Being in Christ'.[3] What saves, in this relative paradox, is the New Being; and what draws is *eros*-faith; and who knows all about it is the gnostic who is directly aware of that with which he is immediately united.

The paradox of salvation which the system knows can be summed up by saying that it turns out to be the very understandable process of the healing of a body which, although sick, is in principle healthy, a body where 'structures of healing' are active to counter 'structures of destruction'. To accept acceptance may indeed require the 'courage of confidence'.[4]

---

[1] *ST* II, p. 179.

[2] *Loc. cit.* The 'subjective side' here corresponds to the 'question of salvation' (see, *op. cit.*, p. 80).

[3] *Loc. cit.* (See also p. 166.)

[4] Tillich defines courage thus: 'It is the act of the individual self in taking the anxiety of non-being upon itself by affirming itself, either as part of an

But the most that can be said about the difficulty of accepting acceptance is that the evidence for our being accepted is (because it corresponds with our actual unity with being-itself) fragmentary. The reality of our ultimate unity with the source of our being and meaning, however, is the certainty of certainties—ontologically considered. And, since it is the subject of the one real question which we are asking all our lives, and since the God who drives us to ask the question gives us the power to answer it, there should be small reason for despair. One of the things which might prevent us finding answers, of course, might be if we were to take the symbols of the Christian faith in a literal sense and come to imagine that our ultimate concern was not, after all, with our own being and meaning but with our relationship to a God who forgives sinners. Against such a danger, the substitution of Accepting Acceptance in place of Justification by Faith Alone will provide a safeguard.

Undoubtedly, Tillich believes most intensely that his system teaches no less than the essence of Christianity. It is identical with the content of the Christian message, without the religious supranaturalism which disfigures traditional Christian doctrine. In this connection, Tillich maintains that his Accepting Acceptance guards against the delusion of self-salvation quite as effectively as does Justification by Faith Alone, if not more so.[1] There is no healing of that which is estranged from God, except from the side of God. All self-salvation is idolatrous, including that type which arose in Lutheranism through taking Justification to be a demand for doctrinal assent instead of trust in divine grace. What Tillich says against self-salvation is well said, yet his claim to avoid the pitfall of self-salvation raises doubts. The difficulty here is the same one which is encountered in connection with his claim to include both *agape* and *eros*

embracing whole or in its individual selfhood' (*The Courage To Be*, p. 147). Yet it should be noted that, if courage affirms selfhood, it does not affirm the individual in himself. What is accepted is not anything particular. Accepting acceptance 'is not a justification of one's accidental individuality' (*ibid.*, p. 156). Courage is an element in *eros*-faith (see *Dynamics of Faith*, p. 103), and so it takes its place within the essential unity of man with the Ground of his being. It rests upon, and derives from, awareness of the Unconditioned.

[1] *ST* II, pp. 80 ff.

within his system.[1] In the system, man is not saved on his own initiative, for he is saved by the power of being-itself in which he participates. Yet, if in the Unconditioned he meets *himself*, he is healed into unity with the Ground of his being because it is *his* Ground. He does not really receive anything which he does not already possess. He is healed by no power of healing which is not in him potentially before the healing-process begins.

This very aspect of the system is displayed by Tillich himself in an interesting passage where he argues that Regeneration can be thought of as preceding Justification, 'for Justification presupposes faith, the state of being grasped by the divine presence'.[2] In connection with the problem of self-salvation the question that immediately presents itself is, Whose faith? Calvin, who followed Luther in believing that Justification was the first article of the gospel of man's salvation, wrote unhesitatingly, 'We are justified by Christ's faith alone.'[3] But Tillich, while admitting that the traditional answer to the question of guilt and sin is given in terms of Christ, insists that Christ must be interpreted as meaning the New Being or the state of unity between God and man.[4] This undoubtedly means that it is impossible in the end to separate the self which is saved from the God who saves. Therefore to speak of Regeneration preceding Justification is to suggest that the real meaning of *justifying the sinner* is *accepting the (in principle) regenerate*.

In his day Luther protested vehemently against the 'pestilent and devilish gloss' of the Schoolmen which asserted that faith must be informed by love before Justification was possible. For Tillich it is the regenerating presence of *eros*-faith—which is faith equated with love—that makes Justification have any meaning. The difference between Tillich and the Schoolmen is that the scholastic theory laid down that God infuses love into sinful man by a special grace, while the system announces that man-as-such possesses this love because he is man. The similarity between the two views is that both deny that God can have any dealing with what is unlovely until it has been shown to be somehow lovable. So man is not justified as a sinner

---

[1] See above, pp. 104 ff.   [2] *Op. cit.*, p. 178.
[3] *Op. cit.*, p. 44.   [4] *Op. cit.*, p. 179.

and accepted because of the righteousness of Christ, but he is justified on account of being partly righteous.[1] Nevertheless, the views are utterly at variance in that scholasticism retains a 'supranaturalistic' and therefore a personal dimension. God *acts* toward man, and the mediation of Jesus Christ is altogether necessary to the process of salvation.

Justification by Faith Alone and Accepting Acceptance do not, and cannot, move on the same level. The former considers what God does for sinners which they cannot do for themselves. The latter looks at a cosmic process in which an eternal unity keeps itself from disruption because of the power inherent in itself. On the level of Justification there is communion between persons. On the level of Acceptance there is participation in the New Being, which means that parts play the rôle suited to parts—all accidental individuality left behind—in the divine self-manifestation:

'. . . by affirming our being we participate in the self-affirmation of being-itself. . . . If we know it we accept acceptance consciously. If we do not know it we nevertheless accept and participate in it.'[2]

It is good, says the system, to be part of the Whole. It is good to be at one with that eternal process which is (symbolically speaking) the life of the Deity—and it is better still to be aware of it! On the level of Accepting Acceptance, the union sought by *gnosis* is found. Yet this is a union which is found only by leaving behind the glad response of the justified sinner to a love, not his own, which comes from the faith of Jesus Christ, Saviour of men.

'The God Above God': the Certainty concerning the Whole as the Really Real

Standing as he does On the Boundary, Tillich is able to see that

[1] Tillich stresses the in-spite-of quality of the *agape*-love in the system ('*Agape* accepts the other in spite of resistance', *ST* I, p. 280). Yet is it just as much a because-of quality. This *agape*-love draws finite being to it in spite of estrangement—but only because of the ultimate unity of everything finite with the Ground of its being (*ibid.*, pp. 280–1).

[2] *The Courage To Be*, p. 172. In an excellent discussion of Accepting Acceptance Tavard points out that this concept makes our accepting irrelevant, 'at bottom it makes no difference' (*op. cit.*, p. 37). Biblical faith makes all the difference because it is selective, involving persons.

the truth is the whole. He is also able to see that the biblical and Protestant conception of trust in a forgiving God is included and transcended in the conception of the eternal unity of God and man. On the basis of this eternal unity as it is manifested in the New Being, Accepting Acceptance becomes a possibility for man-as-such. This possibility Tillich declares to be the possibility of experiencing 'absolute faith'; and absolute faith is faith in 'the God above God'.[1]

This last phrase is the third and final term in Tillich's vocabulary which I am investigating. It is not especially puzzling. If, as I have argued, Tillich's system produces its own revelation, then it is only natural that it should name its own God. Certainly, the system has from the first described the God whom it proclaims as being-itself and identified him with the structure of reality as a whole. (It is convenient to refer to a God as 'he', even when he is essentially non-personal.) It has even given him a descriptive name: the Unconditioned. But it has not named him in such a way as to distinguish him specifically from other gods. The term 'the God above God' supplies this want. The system, realizing the necessity for transcending theism, now demands that the God who is really God shall be recognized as being a God above the God of theism.[2] This God is really God, because he transcends all the symbols which the personalistic religions use and he likewise transcends the truth for which the mystical religions stand witness. The God of the system is better than the God of all religions put together, because the system explains all religions, correcting them from its higher knowledge. It, and it alone, can display the true God and identify him by name.

Since it argues from certainties, the system can claim no less.

Thus the term 'the God above God' fills in an obvious gap in the exposition of the system. It is required for several reasons, the most important one being the need to show that the system can substantiate its claim to be able to show that Christianity

---

[1] *Op. cit.*, p. 172. The whole discussion about absolute faith and the God above God is to be found in this work, pp. 163–80. (Compare also, *Theology of Culture*, pp. 27–9.)

[2] *Ibid.*, p. 176.

is final revelation. The system could not state confidently that Christianity was absolutely the highest of the religions unless it could actually locate the ceiling of the Universe. There might be a higher religion than Christianity somewhere, as yet unknown or else unborn, were it not for the system's knowledge of what lies beyond religious revelation. That it has this final and complete knowledge the system does not doubt. Is not its God the Unconditioned? There can be no God beyond him. He is ultimate reality. But, then, if the Unconditioned be God, why not worship him? If, through immediate awareness of the Unconditioned we meet with ourselves, why not worship ourselves in God? Why trouble ourselves over the symbols of the Christian message which points to being-itself when the Ground of our being presents itself directly? It is to such questions as these that the *Systematic Theology* provides an answer, for in it Tillich does not refer to the Unconditioned directly, emphasizing instead unconditional concern and the method of correlation. The *Systematic Theology* says that man, being immersed in existence, cannot dispense with symbols. Seeking the depths of the divine life in the depths of his own soul is possible only with the help that comes through human religions and their symbols. Man cannot escape his destiny as finite being, even though he can transcend his finite selfhood and discover it again in a new dimension. So much the system now asserts in general without naming its God, except as being-itself. So, in *The Courage To Be* where the system's God is given a name, it is not a proper name but a title based on his relation to the God of religious faith. The system's God has shown himself to be the God who cannot be worshipped as other gods are worshipped. In all the religions of the world, believers call upon the name of their God. But this is impossible in the case of the system's God, for he is the God above God. No believer can call upon his name directly. But the person who knows that there is but one true God can do this: he can call upon the name of the God who is named by religious faith, *knowing that his true devotion does not stop at the level of the God addressed but rises to the nameless ultimate.*

Against this background the system supports Christianity as

the highest revelation. It is highest, and so the man who wishes to choose the best possible religion will choose Christianity. He will make the symbols of the Christian message his ultimate concern. Yet he will do so, fully conscious that the content of the gospel preached about Jesus Christ is symbolic of a reality in which his full trust dwells. He will pray to the Christian God knowing that this God is the God of theism and that his prayers are not 'really' addressed to him. The meaning of Tillich's metaphor of the theological circle is at last fully clarified. The person who stands within the theological circle has taken the symbols of the Christian message as his ultimate concern, and yet he is not *a believer*. He cannot say—and Tillich apparently believes that no one at any time can say—that he is 'in the situation of faith'.[1] He is *a knower* and he knows that the ultimate reality lies beyond all religious faith and is not 'really' to be found where it seems to be, i.e. in the God proclaimed by the highest religion. From the heights of *gnosis* he can look down on mere *pistis*.

All this explains why Tillich expresses surprise over the way in which some readers of *The Courage To Be* have reacted to his statement there concerning the God above God, taking it (he says) to be 'a dogmatic statement of a pantheistic or mystical character'. He replies that this 'is not a dogmatic, but an apologetic statement', adding:

> 'But such an extreme point is not a space within which one can live. The dialectics of an extreme situation are a criterion of truth but not the basis on which a whole structure of truth can be built.'[2]

Tillich objects to the view that he wants to get rid of Christian faith in order to make room for a pantheistic or mystical faith. The objection is well founded in so far as Tillich's programme is not to set aside Christianity in favour of another *religious*

---

[1] *ST* I, p. 10. Later the theological circle is changed to an ellipse, with twin centres of existential questions and theological answers (*ST* II, pp. 14–15). The change shows that the stance Tillich is referring to is not standing on the ground of Christian faith but within the presuppositions of his system.

[2] *ST* II, p. 12.

faith. Religious faith is not the same as *absolute faith*, which is the faith required to find the God above God. Absolute faith is not a faith which will help us to worship. It is not an everyday faith, for everyday faith is, and must be, built upon the symbols of religion. And the symbols of religion can be ignored by no one, for they are the means by which man explores the world. This world is both the surface world and the world of depth—the world of time and space referred to in the literal meaning of the symbols and the transcendent world toward which the symbols point. Yet, although Tillich feels that those readers who have taken exception to his description of absolute faith and the God above God are guilty of misunderstanding him, perhaps the simplicity of these persons is wiser than his own discernment. For his answer overlooks the important point that a criterion of truth cannot simply hang in the air, but must be supported by a dogmatic proposition based upon a theory of what reality is like. It may be true that the extreme point of absolute faith is not a space within which one can live, but, unless it is no point at all, every space which is habitable will bear some definite relation to it. Also, an extreme situation must be relevant to every situation. Therefore, the fact that Tillich does not want people to start worshipping the God above God does not mean that he has avoided forcing them into a position where, if they agree with his analysis of reality, they cannot worship anything else.

Kierkegaard described the speculative view of the Universe which looked at everything *sub specie aeterni* as 'absent-minded', and it looks as though Tillich's exposition of the God above God given in absolute faith were a product of that same absent-mindedness. If Tillich, in an extreme situation, is aware that faith is ultimately faith in the God above God—that it is 'the accepting of the acceptance without somebody or something that accepts'[1]—, then this knowledge is universally valid for anyone who accepts the awareness as genuine knowledge. He has made a dogmatic statement when he affirms that what accepts without being anybody or anything is the power of being-itself. His affirmation is a confession of faith in a power the

[1] *The Courage To Be*, p. 176.

219

reality of which he is prepared to witness to in all situations, so that he will if necessary disbelieve in the reality of anything and everything else rather than deny this power and its effects. This no-thing in which he believes is

'. . . without the safety of words and concepts, it is without a name, a church, a cult, a theology. But it is moving in the depth of them all. It is the power of being, in which they participate and of which they are fragmentary expressions.'[1]

Surely, it can only be absent-minded to say that there is no dogmatic statement here, or that no structure of truth can be built on it. For the person who makes this affirmation can only make it when he has built his structure of truth on this founda-tion. On this foundation he will say dogmatically, when shown a church or a theology, 'Ah, yes! Here we have a fragmentary expression of the power of being.' He will argue, of course, that his dogmatic position is not arbitrary or unreasoned, and, if need be, will conduct those who disagree over the steps of his reasoning. But the steps will always lead back to the original awareness of the Unconditioned on which he stands; that is, the actual foundation of belief is the power of being-itself as the no-thing that supports absolute faith—the God above God, the really real which is the true deity of the system.

That theonomous metaphysics—or whatever name best describes the system—is a dogmatic faith is something which Tillich must do his best to deny unceasingly. Otherwise, not only does all the play over the basic unity and basic divergence of philosophy and theology stand out as mere contrivance, but the method of correlation evaporates entirely, leaving his theology plainly labelled '*gnosis*'. His defence of the God above God, as being not a rival to Christian faith but an illustration of the need for Christian symbols, is, in some ways, the crowning argument in his presentation of his case. Yet it is unmistakably an appeal to the system as the authoritative source of truth, the revelatory fount *par excellence*. Tillich does not argue straight from the 'extreme situation' (which is the modern consciousness

---

[1] *The Courage To Be*, p. 179.

of doubt and meaninglessness)[1] to acceptance of the God above God; he argues by way of the system. He teaches that the God above God is to be accepted as the object of absolute faith because the system tells us so. This is a faith. And, although the faith is rooted in an experience of immediate awareness, it at once develops its own symbolic language (since reality, according to true doctrine, appears by means of symbols in finite being). Thus, when the system speaks of being-itself taking finitude into itself, Tillich agrees that this is 'highly symbolic language'.[2] Most of the time therefore, the interpreting of Christian faith which the system engages in is translating the 'symbols' of the Gospel into the 'symbols' of the system. The statement that we affirm our being by participating in the self-affirmation of being-itself is not less symbolic than the statement that Jesus Christ came into the world to save sinners; it is only a symbol that points more clearly to the truth—and the truth is to be found in the system. In effect, the system turns to the religious believer, saying, 'You must accept my symbolic statements, believing that they are the best possible explanation of the symbolic statements made in your faith. In short, believe me!'

Thus, in spite of the absent-mindedness of the system in forgetting that to name the name of the true God (even if he be called the God above God) is to proclaim a faith to be believed, the true faith has been presented by the system and its form dogmatically and authoritatively outlined. But does the true faith make statements about its God which are 'pantheistic and mystical'? Tillich brings up the question in order to quash it. Yet, in his analysis of why the God above God transcends the religions of the world, he admits that the God above God is the object of all mystical longing.[3] Therefore, while the system rejects as inadequate the personal God of biblical symbolism, it finds that mysticism reaches out to the concept of absolute faith whose source is the God above God. Actually, what Tillich rejects is not mysticism as such, but the type of mysticism characteristic of the East.[4] And he rejects this type

[1] *Ibid.*, p. 164. (See also *ST* I, p. 49.) [2] *Ibid.*, p. 171.
[3] *Ibid.*, pp. 176-7.
[4] '. . . Eastern mysticism is not the solution of the problems of Western Existentialism, although many people attempt this solution' (*ibid.*, p. 177).

of mysticism only to the extent that it does not face the problem of meaninglessness because it never conceives that the concrete face of existence could hold any reality at all. In other words, Tillich seems to believe that mysticism seeks the true God but does not realize the full scope of his power. Mysticism's main error, when compared with the truth of the system, is that it seeks the God above God too exclusively *in the extreme situation* (for instance, through world-denying asceticism) and does not hope to find the truly divine in the concrete but only in the universal.[1]

As the mystical element in Tillich's description of the God above God is unmistakable, so is the pantheistic element which is twin to the mystical. The unity of faith, which Tillich holds to be the final goal for religion to seek, is for him to be found by the process of learning to distinguish 'ultimacy itself from that in which ultimacy expresses itself'.[2] This hope is clearly in line with the mystic view that all symbolic representations of the Ineffable are destined to fall away before true knowledge of the divine can be finally achieved. It is also in line with the pantheistic belief that Deity is 'the absolute substance which is present in everything' (Tillich's own description of the creed of pantheism).[3] Every God, in the last resort, corresponds exactly to the faith which he inspires, and absolute faith, faith having a concern identical with the desire to be united with the whole which is truth, is the faith inspired by the God above God. This is the same God which mystics and pantheists look to find as they search in the depths of the soul or contemplate the Ground of the structure of the Universe. This is the Absolute in which,

[1] For Tillich the mystical religions (Eastern) and the historical religions (Western) are two types of approach to the New Being. Tillich argues that the historical type can include the non-historical type—it includes more within the scope of the New Being—and therefore Christianity is the final manifestation of the New Being (*ST* II, pp. 86–90). Yet, since the non-historical type understands absolute faith and searches for the New Being apart from single historical manifestations, it knows—as Christianity does not—the truth that the New Being is not bound to any one form in which it appears. In that they reject supranaturalistic 'superstition' the mystical religions are (from the systematic view) purer religions than the historical. What they lose in breadth they gain in depth.

[2] *Dynamics of Faith*, p. 125.   [3] *ST* I, p. 233.

according to idealistic metaphysics, the concrete universal inheres.

Tillich's God above God is guaranteed by the certainties of his system. Yet this means that, while he is as strong as the strength of the arguments supporting the system, he is also as vulnerable as are their weaknesses. It is the central weakness of Tillich's system that it finds no place for the existence of God. So far as the system is concerned, 'the question of the existence of God can be neither asked nor answered,' for 'it is a question about that which by its very nature is above existence.'[1] What the non-existence of God means is that to participate in the power of the truly divine man must rise above existence. The New Being conquers existence only by drawing man out of the dimension of existence into that new dimension where finite being transcends itself, where concreteness remains (included in universality) but individuality does not.[2] The God above the God of theism is Lord over a wide domain, but it does not include a single existing individual.

This fact was always present to Kierkegaard, and it was his insight into the nature of the speculative system in this regard which lay at the base of his violent opposition to the System— not only to Hegel's philosophy but to every system claiming to be complete in itself and, because of that claim, revoking existence in the eternal. He wrote in his *Journals*:

'Immanently (in the fantastic medium of abstraction) God does not *exist*, he only is—God only exists for an existing man, i.e. he can only exist *in faith*. Providence, atonement, etc., only exist for an existing man. Faith is therefore the anticipation of the eternal which holds the factors together, the cleavages of existence.'[3]

System assumes that to discover one's self is to discover God, and *vice versa*, so that the fulfilment of man's being is to be in a

---

[1] *Ibid.*, p. 237.
[2] Therefore it is impossible to take at its face value the statement of Tillich's that God's grace 'gives unique participation to every individual being' (*ST* I, p. 285).
[3] *The Journals of Søren Kierkegaard*, edited and translated by Alexander Dru (London, Oxford, 1938), p. 173.

state of union with the Ground of Being. ('Faith is not an opinion but a state.')[1] Anti-system maintains that the individual cannot cast off his individuality like a cloak in order to discover Deity. Men remain existing beings, even when they engage in speculation, and so their actual fulfilment cannot be a state (conceived as eternal but hidden by the opacity of existence) but a relationship. Although God is the Eternal God and—as eternal—does not exist,[2] yet he exists for us in Jesus Christ, or else we could have no relation to him. This is the absolute paradox, which faith alone can grasp: 'Christianity has declared itself to be the eternal truth which has come into being in time.'[3] The Incarnation, which for the system is an offence against logical rationality, is for Christian believers the simple truth—*personal* truth. This is the truth which has to be taken literally or rejected outright. It is folly to the Greeks but God's saving presence to those existing individuals whom God calls into relationship to himself. On earth we can never anticipate the whole of reality and tie truth neatly into a unitary system. But we can anticipate eternity, for the Eternal has come to us in Christianity.

By way of the system the God above God can be known to be the one true God and the really real, who alone can help man in his extremest need. But he helps only man-as-such, in the hour when all symbols fall away and lose their power and the individual is aware of nothing except his essential being and the power of being-itself. He helps man on the boundary of the human situation, and in the depths of his being. This god does not help individuals in their individuality, as persons who have their personal hopes and fears and who do not ask only those questions which man-as-such asks concerning the totality of being. This is what Kierkegaard meant when he said that Christianity implied 'inwardness'. Inwardness is exactly the relationship of the individual to his God which the system denies and, for that reason, denies also that the Christian gospel can be taken literally. What Kierkegaard called inwardness was

[1] *The Courage To Be*, p. 164.
[2] *Concluding Unscientific Postscript*, p. 296.
[3] *Ibid.*, p. 191.

also what Calvin spoke about when he indicated that we never properly know God until that time

'. . . when we descend into ourselves and consider in what way the Lord manifests in us his life, wisdom, and power, and exercises toward us his justice, clemency, and goodness.'[1]

This is something which the system entirely overlooks. It believes that truth can never ultimately be personal, but that truth always drives beyond the relationship of trust and love to the 'really real' of eternal states. Tillich does not believe that Luther was rescued in his moods of despair by trust in the truth that God was God—the God who sent his Son and forgave each sinner. He explains that the statement that God is God 'reminded him of the unconditional element in human experience . . . this awareness saved him'.[2] He also explains that what Christ praised in Mary, when he said that she had chosen the better part, was that '*Mary was infinitely concerned. This is the one thing needed.*'[3] But, in each case, the lack of any place for *inwardness* makes these explanations inadequate and almost perverse. Mary was attentive to the one she called 'Lord', and not exhibiting a universal quality. Luther was not seeking an awareness of an eternal element in human experience; he was recalling himself to a remembrance that he was a justified sinner, and that the God who had forgiven him still ruled over all. If the 'symbols' of the Christian faith 'really' mean this message of eternity without inwardness, then Christianity cannot be a gospel, and the God who is God and Father of our Lord Jesus Christ must disappear so that the God above God may reign in his place.

Inwardness means risk, and it is the characteristic of Tillich's system that, even though it admits the risk inherent in existence, it will admit that this risk is superficial only. It is the risk of

---

[1] *Instruction in Faith*, p. 20 (compare *Institutes*, I, I, 2: p. 37). Note that 'manifests' here has nothing in common with Tillich's concept of manifestation (i.e. appearance). Calvin's word in the French original was *declare*: God acts and *personally demonstrates* his will for us.

[2] *The Courage To Be*, p. 162.

[3] *The New Being* (New York, Scribner's, 1955; London, SCM Press, 1956), p. 159.

choosing the wrong symbol for one's ultimate concern—for instance, identifying the picture of Jesus with the New Being. But real faith depends always on an eternal power about which no mistakes can be made, because it is something transcending existence. Faith 'is based on a foundation which is not risk: the awareness of the unconditional element in ourselves and our world'.[1] On this awareness the throne of the God above God is set eternal in the heavens. Christian believers, who have not this awareness but only faith held in inwardness, remain exposed to the risk of losing their faith without finding '*the God who appears when God has disappeared in the anxiety of doubt*'.[2] But they can say something which those who trust in awareness of the Unconditioned can never say. They can say, 'I know whom I have believed' (II Tim. 1.12).

[1] *Theology of Culture*, p. 28.
[2] *The Courage To Be*, p. 180—the last sentence in the book (italics in the original).

XI

THE CHALLENGE OF THE SYSTEM

To SEE Tillich's system as a whole is to see that it is incompatible with the Christian gospel. From the perspective of results the system is something the believer has to meet with a 'No!', since to accept it would be to put aside the *kerygma* in favour of a *logos* philosophy functioning as a self-contained and authoritative theology. But what about the perspective of intention? So far, my analysis has hardly glanced at this aspect of Tillich's work.

For what is most remarkable about Tillich's philosophical theology is not that it has failed to provide a firm apologetic basis for Christianity—it would have been almost miraculous had it succeeded—but that it attempted the task with such energy and such conviction. Only a very foolish or a very insensitive person could turn away from the *Systematic Theology*, remark, 'Well, that's that!' and forget about it. This is a theology that compels us to take note of it and to determine how we stand in relation to it. Because we have been confronted by it we are likely to look at all theological activity henceforward a little differently; and therefore we should bear in mind why, in the first place, Tillich thought it worth while attempting to construct his system. Here is his explanation:

'Since the breakdown of the great synthesis between Christianity and the modern mind as attempted by Schleiermacher, Hegel, and nineteenth-century liberalism, an attitude of weariness has grasped the minds of people who are unable to accept one or the other alternative [rejection of faith or of philosophy]. They are too disappointed to try another synthesis after so many have failed. But there is no choice for us. We must try again!'[1]

[1] *Biblical Religion and the Search for Ultimate Reality*, p. 57.

Now, no one who cares about the truth of Christianity can afford to pass over the intention thus stated. While every attempt to draw together faith and knowledge is dangerous, because it threatens to dissolve faith altogether, yet there is a double danger in the deliberate effort to keep them apart. There is the danger of a split mind in believers who cannot relate their faith to the rest of the world about them. And there is the danger of a progressive isolation of religion in society as a consequence of separating sacred and secular concepts and values. What Tillich has to say about theology becoming narrow and superstitious, and about culture requiring the 'thorn in the flesh' provided by an active and informed theology,[1] is true. Furthermore, in the past, theology has been at its most creative when it engaged without fear in an encounter with the thought-forms of its age. All efforts to forbid this encounter have the effect of fossilizing the expression of the truth of faith in the language of one bygone era. On that account, Tillich's dislike of static orthodoxies and his refusal merely to repeat accepted theological formulae[2] are alike well justified. His wish to bring faith into a living relationship with our total response to our environment and with our understanding of ourselves and our world is surely a sound one, by any standard. He has shouted a challenge which contemporary theology cannot pretend not to have heard.

Even if we judge his intention not to have been realized, we should accept the challenge. His system at least shows us what to avoid; and, when we are trying to find our way, a sign-board reading 'No Road' can be very useful and save a great deal of fruitless effort. Not only that, but a process of elimination may guide us positively toward a means of accepting faith without concurring in an irrationalism that endangers the unity of the human person. I believe such positive guidance is forthcoming. But, before looking so far, there are at least two lessons—one general and one quite specific—to be learnt from the system, negatively considered.

The first lesson (the general one) is that no apologetic theology can hope to stand when it seeks to reinterpret

---

[1] *ST* I, p. 7. [2] *Ibid.*, p. 305; *ST* II, Preface viii.

traditional doctrine by demanding that the latter conform to some pattern imposed on it from without. Here we meet again the question of authority which has arisen so often in these pages. While to remain complacently within the ecclesiastical definitions of the past is to be bound to a dead orthodoxy (and therefore to refuse the opportunity of growth both in understanding and in charity), yet to depart from the kerygmatic confession which is enshrined in traditional doctrines is theological apostacy. It is one thing to be dissatisfied with orthodoxy, and quite another thing to reject that which orthodoxy seeks (no doubt inadequately) to protect. And to contradict tradition at the call of a 'truth' set up independently and without reference to the faith cherished within the Christian community is to break decisively with Christian theology.

This is what George H. Tavard has in mind, I believe, when he says that if we look critically at Tillich's theology (or any other, for that matter) from the point of view of a believer 'this standpoint must remain dogmatic'[1]. Similarly, Tavard can say concerning Tillich's refusal to quote the Bible, the Church Fathers or the Reformers without first reinterpreting them:

'A Protestantism that has come to light only in the twentieth century can no more be Protestantism than a Christology discovered in the twentieth century can be the Christology of the Revelation.'[2]

There is a sense in which theology is free from tradition, because no thought-forms can ever wholly contain in their completeness the events witnessed to in the Old and New Testaments which are the charter of the Christian Church. But there is also a sense in which theology is bound by tradition, because the final authority in the Church is 'the faith which God entrusted to his people once and for all' (Jude 3); and the existence of that authority means that no single theologian can disrupt the continuity of dogmatic teaching in the tradition of the Christian Church to which he belongs. Therefore Tavard, examining Tillich's Christology, finds it wanting because it is a Christology incompatible with the dogma of Chalcedon, which Tavard

[1] *Op. cit.*, p. 114.   [2] *Ibid.*, p. 162.

rightly insists to be authoritative for orthodox Christians, whether Catholic or Protestant. At the same time, he believes that Tillich's desire to restate the Chalcedonian formula in other terms is wholly legitimate—*provided always that the formula is retained as a norm.* Why Tillich's own proposals are impossible is because they abandon this norm in favour of a 'philosophico-religious principle' denying the historical event (the coming of Christ in the flesh) with which Chalcedon was concerned.[1] In other words, there can be a post-Chalcedonian Christology employing twentieth-century categories; but there cannot be a non-Chalcedonian Christology fashioned to conform to the categories of an ontology recognizing eternal God-manhood but not Jesus the God-man. There can be a restatement of traditional doctrine; but there cannot be a sudden discovery of the 'real' meaning of doctrine. No external authority has the right to decide what the content of the Christian faith shall be. And this leads us into the second lesson which the example of the *Systematic Theology* teaches us—the specific lesson. Tillich admits the failure of the nineteenth-century effort at achieving a synthesis of faith and knowledge. Yet, with this example before him, he has set out to build his theological edifice on exactly the same foundation. He has not only chosen an authority other than traditional doctrine by means of which to develop an apologetic theology, but he has chosen as the touchstone of truth an idealism similar to that sponsored (each in his own way) by Schleiermacher and by Hegel. After their model, he produces Christianity as a particular manifestation of the time-less truth which we know through direct contact with ultimate reality.

Thus Tillich's system is the legitimate heir of nineteenth-century liberalism.[2] Probably the principal reason why this

[1] *Op. cit.*, p. 167. In order not to appear to be a spokesman for Roman Catholic theology alone, Tavard brings in as witnesses supporting his testimony Bultmann, Barth, Brunner, and Cullmann. He shows how these theologians, whatever their differences, do not depart from the Chalcedonian emphasis.

[2] Johnson has remarked that the 'close kinship' existing between the theological systems of Schleiermacher and Tillich is not widely recognized—see above, p. 134. This would seem to be the case, even though some connection is quite often noticed. Thus Tavard comments: 'Tillich in many

fact is frequently overlooked is the widespread impression that his thought is existentialist—and therefore must be new.[1] A supporting reason, nevertheless, may be found in the tendency today to identify liberalism with the anti-metaphysical Ritsch-lian development of the movement, a tendency which throws history out of focus by ignoring the roots of liberalism in idealism. We too often forget that the later liberal theology which wished to exalt the Jesus of History at the expense of the Christ of Faith grew out of the liberalism which took Jesus to be the outstanding proof of the reality of the 'essential Christ', or union of the human and the divine.[2] Although Tillich claims to stand between orthodoxy and liberalism, he actually criticizes both orthodoxy and the Jesus-of-History school from the standpoint of metaphysical liberalism. This means that he simply continues to voice liberalism's quarrel with orthodoxy, at the same time disowning that part of liberalism which, abandoning its idealistic heritage, has become naturalistically inclined.

The specific lesson which Tillich helps us to learn, then, is that the attempt to try once more the old liberal way of

ways belongs to the nineteenth century' (*op. cit.*, p. 4); and he also notes that the Tillichian understanding of the nature of faith was not current in Protestantism until Schleiermacher (*ibid.*, p. 51). Yet, while admitting a connection with Protestant liberalism and with Hegelian philosophy, Tavard does not try to place Tillich's 'ontologizing' (as he calls it) in its historical setting. Few other critics pay much attention to the link with Schleiermacher except to point out where Tillich has spoken of differences between them. Yet Tillich himself has indicated how close the link is. After saying that Schleiermacher's 'feeling of absolute dependence' referred to immediate awareness and not merely to a psychological reaction, Tillich writes: 'Schleiermacher's "feeling of absolute dependence" was rather near to what is called in the present system "ultimate concern about the ground and meaning of our being" ' (*ST* I, p. 42). In other words, Tillich is con-fessing that he and Schleiermacher adopt an almost identical criterion of theology.

On the side of philosophical idealism and the system, Tillich's indebted-ness to Hegel has been the subject of comment ever since his German years. Generally speaking, philosophers have seen where the system has its roots rather better than have theologians.

[1] See above, Postscript to Chapter II.

[2] This subject is considered in my article, 'Paul Tillich and the Idealistic Appraisal of Christianity', in the *Scottish Journal of Theology* XIII 1 (March 1960), pp. 33–44.

synthesis is not worth while. If it is impossible to develop a properly Christian apologetic theology by appealing to an authority other than that of traditional doctrine, it is most certainly impossible to appeal to *this* authority and hope to achieve any different results. Kierkegaard's accusations against the speculative system still hold good: by its very nature an ontology must claim to create the truth and, on its own authority, to judge how much and how little truth there is in the symbols of faith; and also, because of its claim to know universal truth, it cannot take seriously the individual and particular facts of history which are inseparable from the Christian message. The nineteenth-century liberal synthesis failed, alike in Schleiermacher and in Hegel, precisely because it could not grasp the particularity of Christianity but dissolved Jesus Christ into the Christ-idea. Tillich's surrender to the same vision has been documented throughout the present study, but one further example may be produced. In all that he writes about Protestantism, Tillich never once understands the word in its historical sense of a protestation or confession of the Gospel. Instead, he takes it abstractly as a concept signifying 'the attitude of protest against form'.[1] By means of such an interpretation—a drastic *re*interpretation, of course—he bends it to support his idealistic dogma that the eternal may appear in the temporal but can never be identified with anything found there. He expounds what he terms the *Protestant principle*, a principle asserting that the ultimate and the unconditional are not to be looked for in any historical forms of religion, except as 'a living, moving, restless power in them'.[2] This is a world away from the call to re-form the Church according to the Word of God which motivated the Protestant Reformation. As Tavard points out, a Protestantism which has come to light only in the twentieth century cannot be Protestantism; and his argument remains just as cogent if we substitute for 'twentieth century' the revised reading, 'nineteenth century and after'.

If the message of 'No Road This Way' is received because it

[1] *The Protestant Era*, p. 205.
[2] *Ibid.*, p. 239. The Protestant principle is constantly invoked in Chapters XI–XIV of this work.

is evident that Tillich has not succeeded better than did his predecessors in getting anywhere along this particular route, that in itself will be an immense gain. Some forty-odd years ago Emil Brunner, writing of the idealistic teaching 'stamped with the imprint of Hegel, Kant, Fries, Schleiermacher, or Schelling'. complained:

> '. . . it is not fully realized that it is impossible to combine the Christian Faith with this belief in a universal religion. . . . Thus here one faith confronts the other; the belief in "general" revelation, religion without a mediator, the faith of mysticism and Idealism, stands over again the religion with a Mediator, the faith of the Scriptures and of the Christian Church.'[1]

By forcing us to realize the impossibility of combining the content of traditional Christian theology with his 'idea' of theology, Tillich has given us conclusive proof of the opposition between any idealistic system and the Gospel. Yet such a negative purpose is far from being the only one served by the *Systematic Theology*. The system serves as a warning, but it serves too as a reminder that the apologetic task of Christian theology is always with us and cannot be set aside for no better reason than that we have not found, so far, any means of carrying it through successfully. So we are brought back again from Tillich's achievement to his intention and to his courage in seeking to stay with the problem right to the end.

As Tillich himself reminds us, theology 'must use the conceptual tools of its period'. It cannot simply repeat biblical passages, and therefore whenever it seeks to express the *kerygma* in terms intelligible to a contemporary audience it is committed to the work of interpretation.[2] No theologian can afford to ignore this reminder, even if he has no desire to become an apologetic theologian. At the very least, his theology will contain apologetic elements; and, the more strenuously he disavows an apologetic intention, the more pervasive these elements are likely to become and the deeper they will sink into the body of his work, influencing it from within. Thus Tillich is surely right in questioning, for example, Barth's attempt to

[1] *Op. cit.*, p. 71.   [2] *ST* I, p. 7.

evade the apologetic question—though to conclude that what Barth does must be self-deception is something which has no evident justification.

There is no short and easy solution to the problem of how apologetic theology should be related to kerygmatic theology, and clearly the details of the problem cannot be considered here. Nevertheless, some general conclusions about the matter seem to follow from the issues that have been raised during the course of my investigation into Tillich's theological method. The first is that, even though human language is the tool which theology must use and language mirrors the mental horizons of a particular generation, it does not follow that human language is the absolute limit conditioning the content as well as the form of revelation. The belief that we can only hear what is said to us by the divine-human reason in which we participate is a prejudice of idealism. If we adopt such a prejudice then we can conceive of faith only as *eros*-faith or the hidden power within ourselves. But, if we accept the perspective of traditional Christianity, we shall agree with Gore that in faith we receive the Word of God, a Word that speaks to us and not just in us. In that event, there is no insurmountable problem presented by the fact that the words used to convey the Word are always those current in the speech of a particular period and place. For the Word spoken in the Gospel concerns God's acts in relation to his world. It is a Word coming into history. Now, the study of history is not rendered void because historians use the language of their day and age. Historians do more than reproduce historical documents: they interpret them. Yet when we read history we expect to find more than the private opinions of historians and less than a complete panorama of historical truth, since we have come to know that the facts of history meet us both because of, and in spite of, individual historical interpretations. Just so, the *kerygma* meets us both because of, and in spite of, individual theological interpretations. Apologetic motifs in theological writings may help or hinder the hearing of the Word, yet they need not prevent the Word from addressing us. When they do, theology has ceased to be Christian theology.

This brings to the fore another conclusion concerning interpretation. The Bible, the creeds and confessional statements become dated in language, so that interpretation is not only possible but necessary. Yet they remain authoritative through all changes, because their authority lies not in themselves but in the events to which they bear witness. It is the reality of these events which any and every interpretation of tradition must respect. Therefore the apologetic elements in theology can never be allowed to become self-sufficient or to lay down their own terms in the matter of what interpretation is proper; for when that happens theology becomes, not an interpretation of the events in which Christians believe, but a reinterpretation of Christian words and phrases which may well be utterly at variance with Christian beliefs. We have seen this process at work in Tillich's system. The system considers itself competent to declare what the words used by Christians 'really' mean, because, in relating itself to the *kerygma*, it does not admit that there is any Word of God to be received. Instead, it proceeds to expound the meaning of 'the symbols used in the Christian message', on the assumption that it has to do with one further example of religious language expressing—like all the rest—the common spiritual awareness of humanity. Previously I have described this characteristic of the system by saying that it substitutes its own authority for the authority of the *kerygma*, or that it contradicts traditional Christian doctrine. But the same point could be made in another way by saying that the system has found a method of its own for achieving harmony with the Gospel: it accepts the words of the *kerygma* on condition that it is allowed to reinterpret them so as to deny the events to which those words witness.

Undeniably, apologetic theology which is to remain Christian theology must be the servant of kerygmatic theology and can never be its master. Without an authoritative *kerygma* there can be no interpretation of the content of the Christian faith which is not misinterpretation, and no explanation which does not mislead to a greater or to a lesser degree. For the introduction of a different authority teaching a different doctrine means a different Gospel, not just the Christian faith slanted in an unorthodox direction.[1] Here the mistaken starting-point which Tillich has taken over from nineteenth-century liberalism is altogether fatal; and, after Tillich, theologians will be without excuse if they try to build a synthesis of faith and knowledge on the same patently unsound basis—planning a palace to rise out of quick-sands. Yet, so long as the authority of the *kerygma* remains intact, there is no reason why new interpretations of the Christian message should not be central to theological endeavour. In rousing theologians from their dogmatic slumbers Tillich has done a good work, even though his failure to see the necessity for dogma, as such, has had such unfortunate results. It should not be impossible to keep the intellectual excitement which a theology such as Tillich's most certainly generates, while avoiding the metaphysical captivity of the Gospel—the subjugation of *pistis* to *gnosis*—which is that theology's undoing.

In any post-Tillichian theology, therefore, apologetics ought to be prevented from becoming self-sufficient, and at the same time it can be recognized as an omnipresent aspect of theology. If there is to be reinterpretation of the *kerygma* carried out within the kerygmatic perspective itself, then apologetics has work to do in bringing together the language of tradition and contemporary terms and categories. All notions of a pure faith uncontaminated by traffic with the relativities of worldly thinking lead inevitably to an absolutizing of the traditional sources of doctrine. The result is that we are told to believe exactly what the words of the Bible say (but who decides what they

[1] For this reason, it seems to me of small value to single out various heresies and to accuse Tillich of advocating these. At different times Tillich has been called a Docetist, a Sabellian, a Nestorian, a Pelagian, a Manichean, etc. Now, a person who accepts traditional dogmatic forms may well be labelled in this manner, for, if he deviates from orthodoxy, he will deviate from it in one particular direction. But someone who does not accept the traditional standpoint at all has nothing to deviate from, and he will appear to bring together heresies normally incompatible, with one another. (Tillich himself, commenting on Weigel's wish to call him a Nestorian, has remarked that this seems not to agree with the more common charge that he is a Docetist.) Johnson is surely right when he argues that the introduction of heresy labels in connection with Tillich merely confuses the issue. The important point is that, from the point of view of traditional Christianity, Tillich continually introduces *a shift in the question* (*op. cit.*, p. 122).

say?), or else we are told to believe exactly what the true Church preaches (but who decides where the true Church is to be found?). So, unless we are content to rest in fundamentalism or ecclesiastical authoritarianism, we cannot deny the place of apologetics in the proclamation of the Gospel. Yet, let apologetics be admitted—how then can it be prevented from asserting its authority over against that of the *kerygma*? This is the problem which Tillich admitted to be a serious one and one which his theological method was intended to solve. If he has tried and failed, is anyone else likely to succeed any better? I have suggested that we can give a negative answer, saying, '*Not* at least by the path of the nineteenth-century liberal synthesis!' But this brings us no nearer to a positive answer. We still cannot be sure that there is any other path to take. Every route may be a dead-end.

The most promising solution seems to be one of taking a stand on some philosophy which offers at least some points of contact with the kerygmatic outlook, and, using this to provide a general conceptual framework, advance toward a reconciliation between knowledge and faith. In adopting Thomism as its official philosophy the Roman Catholic Church has given approval to that solution. On the Protestant side, Rudolf Bultmann has taken the same path, with Heidegger as his philosophical guide. There is also the possibility of beginning *de novo* and, without help from any one philosophical school, working out the philosophical implications of the Gospel one by one.[1]

The great merit of such a solution, in all its forms, is that it faces the problem of authority. It does not start by assuming a synthesis but sees synthesis as a goal for which to strive. While believing that reason should not have its conclusions dictated to it by revelation, it nevertheless will not limit revelation to

[1] Cherbonnier suggests that this is the 'third alternative' to Tillich's ontological approach to Christianity and to the cosmological approach of St Thomas. His article on 'Biblical Metaphysic and Christian Philosophy' (already mentioned in connection with his rejection of Tillich's *eros*-faith) shows that Tillich's ontology is indeed a highly vulnerable Goliath; but it hardly proves that the David who is to overthrow Goliath can be none other than his 'third alternative'. The formulation of a 'biblical metaphysic' would probably engage philosophers in happy disagreement until the end of time.

any bounds set by the demands of speculation. (In this connection, the point is frequently made against Bultmann that he accepts Heidegger—or rather, his own version of Heidegger—far too uncritically. Quite otherwise, St Thomas drastically reinterpreted Aristotle when constructing his Christian philosophy.) Yet, attractive as is the 'both/and' solution to the problem of keeping apologetics in line with the *kerygma*, that too remains a hope rather than a reality. The path of synthesis-in-the-end is perhaps no less a dead-end than the path of synthesis-from-the-start, although it may appear to be much more inviting. If the rejection of Scholasticism at the Reformation was not a mere historical accident, Protestants should be wary of placing their trust in any kind of philosophy claiming for itself the adjective *Christian*. Luther's denunciations of Aristotle, in fact, link up with the warnings of a Barth or a Kraemer today against the belief that rational principles and concepts can be identified with the Word of God. The difficulty about every vision of a philosophy which shall support and not compete with the *kerygma* is the one pointed out by Tillich: namely, that there cannot be two ultimate concerns, but that the one will comprise the other. However pure the intentions of philosophers who wish to have their philosophy serve the interests of the Christian faith, experience suggests that they cannot avoid moulding the *kerygma* to make it fit into their favoured categories. This is the continuing Protestant objection even to the massive achievement of Thomism, a synthesis which towers over all later efforts to reconcile reason with revelation.

The conclusion that theologians can neither ignore apologetics nor construct any species of apologetic theology looks like a counsel of despair, and yet I believe that it is both a reasonable reading of the facts and also a pointer to a positive programme for theology. Tillich's stimulating intervention on the theological scene has proved that the apologetic concern cannot be denied, while his 'system-built' has demonstrated once again the incompatibility between the *kerygma* and all systems whatsoever. Thus we are brought back, in fact, to Kierkegaard's contention that we human beings—existing individuals—think before and after, but never *sub specie aeterni.*

The anticipation of the whole is not ours to command, and, to the extent that we imagine it to be within our grasp, we show ourselves to be less wise than comical. Therefore the true apologetic task is not to prove Christianity to be true. It is rather to reflect and discover how we can understand that the *kerygma* is something which reason can never grasp, except as an absolute paradox. It is also to recollect that, as individuals, we can relate ourselves to the *kerygma*. The Christian message speaks *to us*, so that a genuine hearing of the Word of God does not depend upon our correct formulation of the question to which we receive an answer in the Gospel. Thus our task is neither to build a complete apologetic theology which satisfies our rational aspirations nor yet to discover a pure kerygmatic theology free from every man-made misunderstanding of the eternal message. Our task is to think as clearly as we can in order not to be misled by sophistries, and then to learn, by waiting upon God, that 'hearing' of the Word of God which, in biblical language, is not separate from obedience.

Reason alone can recognize the limitations of reason. Faith alone can know what it means to have faith. Here both apologetic and kerygmatic theology find their charter. But in practice neither can be separated from the other. Tillich's system will have taught us much by its very failure to agree with the Gospel, if we see that it could not succeed because, wishing to make apologetic theology into a self-sufficient discipline, it tried to prove the Gospel to be true by alien standards. Yet in the end, perhaps, Tillich's tireless striving to make the Gospel relevant to contemporary man is what we need most to pay attention to and profit by. He has recognized that 'a fugitive and cloistered virtue, that never sallies out and sees her adversary' is no more praiseworthy in theology than in life. There is no future for a theology which does not gladly accept the apologetic task. Nevertheless, the most genuine apologetics is not that which seeks to commend the Gospel but that which shows the Gospel to be what it is, allowing it to speak for itself. Such an apologetic theology may yet find expression in our generation, inspired by Tillich's intention even while it takes a wholly different route and seeks quite other horizons.

APPENDIX

A review of Tillich's *Life and the Spirit: History and the Kingdom of God. Systematic Theology,* Volume III (Chicago: University of Chicago Press, 1963).

The appearance of the third and final volume of Paul Tillich's *Systematic Theology* is indeed an occasion. With it the long process of writing and revising which began (we are told) thirty-nine years ago at Marburg has come to an end. Now that we can see the whole, its ingenuity and orderliness stand out all the more clearly. There is even a symmetry about the sequence of the volumes (1951, 1957, 1963), reflecting something of Tillich's extreme competence. This competence we have come to expect as a matter of course—yet it is, somehow, always surprising.

Our surprise comes from the fact that we do not go in for systems much today, so that the ability to raise a complete, well-planned conceptual edifice is a rare one. T. S. Eliot provided an apt motto for our age when he wrote, at the end of *The Waste Land,* "These fragments I have shored against my ruins." "My friends and I sometimes feared that the system would remain a fragment," confesses Tillich. "This has not happened. . . ." Just so; *it has not happened.* But then, even a fragment written by him is no fragment in the modern sense. Like Arnold Toynbee (who is given a brief, approving nod in this volume), he brings a nineteenth-century confidence in comprehensive world-views to bear upon twentieth-century problems, aiming always at total explanations. Specifically, the first three parts of his system—"Reason and Revelation," "Being and God," and "Existence and the Christ"—outlined its shape fairly adequately, although there were gaps in the outline. Most readers, therefore, have already decided how they stand in relation to the system. And the publication of the two remaining parts—"Life and the Spirit" and "History and the Kingdom of God"—while filling in the gaps will serve chiefly to confirm previous judgments. Nevertheless, the achievement remains. On any estimate, it is impressive. And, since this volume is longer than its predecessors, Tillich's felicities of style, acute observations, and constructive ability show up to even better advantage than before.

If *Systematic Theology III* throws no new light upon the system as such, yet it may help to clarify the presuppositions of the system—which is perhaps more important than anything else. In *Paul Tillich and the Christian Message,* Father Tavard characterizes Tillich as a "philosopher of life," whose concern is the relationship of religion to existence, and who investigates what meaning the traditional Christian dogmas may or may not have in his system. As Part Four of the *Systematic Theology* discusses life, and contains material which Tillich says could be expanded into a complete philosophy of religion, the accuracy of Father Tavard's observation can be confirmed here. Interestingly enough, this part recapitulates some of the argument of Part One, "Reason and Revelation."

Tillich begins by defending once more against his critics (including the present reviewer) the systematic form he favors. His defense is that this form does not make "the unjustifiable attempt to derive theological statements from sources that are strange to relevatory experiences." He ignores the fact, however, that the chief objection to the system is that it demands a special *content,* one in which Christian beliefs "are stripped of their specifically Christian elements and made into universal philosophical concepts" (Tavard). His appeal to "revelatory experiences" is an appeal to one such concept. He finds the meaning of these experiences through an "essentialist" consideration of life which uncovers life's "multi-dimensional unity." Next, man is defined as "that organism in which the dimension of spirit is dominant." And, because life integrates itself in the dimension of spirit, man experiences spirit "as the unity of power and meaning in himself." In other words, he has revelatory experiences.

Such is the root of Tillich's philosophy of life. And such is the basis on which he proposes to raise his philosophy of religion. The difficulty of reconciling this starting point with Christian theology is immediately apparent. For not only is the revelation of God in Christ made into one revelatory experience amongst others, but also the nature of revelation itself is decided solely by reference to a theory of the essential nature of life. All depends upon Tillich's essentialism. He examines life from his chosen ontological outlook, observes certain features there which are applicable in terms of his outlook, and proceeds to state what Christian theology "must" mean by its doctrinal statements. Christianity, after all, is a religion; and religion is a special function of the spirit; and spirit is a dimension of life. If one knows what life means, everything in Christianity is known also.

In the previous volumes of the *Systematic Theology,* where the contrast between essence and existence was mostly at the center of the picture, religion (and so Christianity) was presented in terms of the possibility of overcoming existential estrangement. Here life becomes the main theme. Since life is seen as a "mixture" of essential and existential elements, religion is invoked in connection with the universal human "quest" for unambiguous life. The terms are the same as before; only the focus of attention has shifted slightly. We now learn that when Christians speak of the Holy Spirit they "must" mean the reality which is best described as Spiritual Presence. Man as man is conscious of being determined in his nature by spirit as a dimension of his life. Man, who is "the mirror in which the relation of everything finite to the infinite becomes conscious," is always the bearer of the spirit. And so man can become aware of Spiritual Presence as he engages in the quest of unambiguous life—he can be grasped by this Spiritual Presence, and this is the meaning of finding faith. In the midst of the ambiguities of life he has ever open to him the possibility of a self-integrated life, one "healthy" or "sound" in at least a fragmentary way. For life "is striving in the vertical direction toward ultimate and infinite being."

Here the completely immanentist character of the system becomes startlingly obvious. Classic Christian theology has always insisted that "the spirit is not from nature, but from regeneration" (Calvin). Only since the time of Schleiermacher have theologians spoken as though regeneration were a natural process of freeing man's true, spiritual nature from his lower, sensuous one. But the latter is Tillich's approach. Man's religions prove both the natural *eros* driving him to self-transcendence and also his existential involvement in the "profane" resistance to self-transcendence. In any one epoch, the existing religion, morality, and culture show the progress of the human quest for unambiguous life, and how far regeneration through the power of the Spiritual Presence is effective. Although Spiritual Presence cannot remove completely the ambiguities of life, yet it elevates all life from within. It created the Christ *within* Jesus, and it created and still maintains the Spiritual Community (the Christian church as a spiritual reality) *within* the actual churches. Once again we see Tillich's essentialism taking command and forcing Christian theology to accommodate itself to an ontological reading of life. For the reality of Spiritual Presence is deduced from the ontological concept of life as such. Tillich's appeal is to that which he finds immanent within life. Quite in keeping with his immanentist presuppositions, he admits the relevance of trinitarian doctrine on the grounds that life is the process of going out and returning to itself, and so involving the number "three." The Trinity is justified—in so far as it can be justified—by an appeal to the persuasiveness of Hegelian dialectic.

The Fifth Part of the system, as Tillich explains, is an extension of the Fourth Part. Just as Spiritual Presence means the conquest of the ambiguities of life under the dimension of the spirit, so the Kingdom of God and Eternal Life mean the conquest of these same ambiguities under the dimension of history and beyond history. Here, too, an essentialist philosophy controls the entire analysis. History "drives toward the universal, unambiguous fulfilment of the potentiality of being." So the Kingdom of God is manifest within history, but always ambiguously, as the meaning of historical existence. (Incidentally, Tillich's notion of the *kairos*-experience, or revelatory moment giving new understanding of the meaning of history, is very close to Schleiermacher's notion of revelation as *originality* breaking the historical chain.) Finally, the inner aim or *telos* of history is the end of history, or Eternal Life: the end of ambiguous life through *essentialization,* whereby the positive is freed from the negative with which it is mixed under the conditions of existence. All that has being is taken up into the Divine Life.

The conclusion of the system should give the death blow to the still prevalent opinion that Tillich can be termed an existentialist. His view of the end of history shows unmistakably that he belongs with those idealistic thinkers who believe that the Absolute takes up plurality into its perfect unity and *therefore* manifests itself in the phenomena of time. Tillich's explanation is that "the world process means something for God." He could hardly come to any other conclusion, since all that he says about God is drawn from the evidence he finds of his immanence within the world process. God *is* the ontological structure of being (Volume I), as that structure is set out by an essentialist philosopher. The process yields continual revelatory experiences.

243

Before *Systematic Theology* saw the light of day, Dietrich Bonhoeffer commented that Tillich set out to interpret the evolution of the world in a religious sense, and that in so doing he was sailing in the channel of liberal theology. And the liberal approach, said Bonhoeffer, meant abridging the gospel. This volume makes clear what was apparent before, namely, that the system has been constructed on the basis of nineteenth-century absolute idealism. The gospel has been trimmed so as to make it conform to the contours of a liberal religion of revelatory experiences, set in a mould of essentialist theory.

KENNETH HAMILTON

United College
Winnipeg, Canada

INDEX OF AUTHORS

INDEX OF SUBJECTS

246